# EXPLORATIONS
# IN THE
# HISTORY OF PSYCHOLOGY

*Persisting Themata and*
*Changing Paradigms*

# EXPLORATIONS
## IN THE
# HISTORY OF PSYCHOLOGY

*Persisting Themata and*
*Changing Paradigms*

Harry A. Van Belle

DORDT COLLEGE PRESS

Cover design by Rob Haan
Layout by Carla Goslinga

Dordt College Press                    www.dordt.edu/dordt_press
498 Fourth Avenue NE
Sioux Center, Iowa, 51250
United States of America

ISBN: 978-0-932914-99-6

*Printed in the United States of America*

The Library of congress Cataloguing-in-Publication Date is on files with the library of Congress, Washington D.C.

Library of Congress Control Number: 2014931194

*To all the history of psychology
students I have taught, who, I
am certain, will write their own
history in times to come.*

*All that [God] does is apt for its time; but though He has permitted human beings to consider time in its wholeness, they cannot comprehend the work of God from beginning to end.*
Ecclesiastes 3: 11 (Jerusalem Bible)

*This is the moment, and it belongs to God.*
Pablo Sosa

# TABLE OF CONTENTS

# Acknowledgements

This text is the product of many years of teaching the history of psychology to university students in North America and Africa. In discussion with them these students have taught me a great deal over the years. I compiled my lecture notes into a manuscript in 2005. That dates the book, since it lacks a description of the more recent discussion on the history of psychology. Even so, the unique perspective of this text offers a valuable contribution to the discussion of psychology's history.

In my opinion the value of this book is twofold: First, it participates in the debate, prevalent among historians of psychology, between the view that psychology's history is continuous and the view that it is discontinuous. It demonstrates the insight that both approaches are necessary in support of one another for the proper understanding of psychology's past. The history of psychology necessarily consists of both persisting themata and changing paradigms. The dynamic of history writing is to show how the two relate to one another.

Second, the book attempts to demonstrate the prescriptive principle, applicable to all kinds of research, but also to historical research, that the object of an investigation should define the method of an investigation. Method should arise from the material to be studied. The material determines which method is suitable to its investigation. If the material changes, or our understanding of it changes, so should the method. This investigative principle entails a methodological pluralism.

This principle furthermore implies that one should always hold pronouncements as to the results of one's research tentatively and be willing to change one's mind upon further study or in consultation with other investigators. Not only does the method change as a result of further insight, but so does what one considers psychological evidence. This prescription goes contrary to much of the history of psychology, in which the method of investigation, specifically the so-called *scientific method*, is deemed to define what may count as data in psychology.

The foregoing insights did not originate with me. In working with them I owe a huge debt to two scholars in particular who were my teachers. I first came in contact with these ideas many years ago in a class on Ancient Philosophy taught by the late Dr. H. Evan Runner (1916–2002), professor of philosophy at Calvin College in Grand Rapids, Michigan from 1951 to 1981. These ideas shaped my understanding of the history and culture of ancient Greece, ancient Rome, and of the Middle Ages in particular, times and places in which many of the concepts of modern psychology were first formulated.

The ideas Runner taught us form the components of the "problem-historical approach" to historical research. (A more detailed description of this method is found in 1.6 of this text.)

The problem-historical method was developed by Runner's teacher, Dr. D. H. Th. Vollenhoven (1892–1978), who was professor of philosophy at the Free University of Amsterdam from 1926–1963. Vollenhoven developed this method in his study of the history of philosophy to locate and catalogue the various philosophical conceptions found in the history of Western thought from ancient Greece to the present. I was privileged to attend some of his private lectures on this method during my stay at The Free University from 1967–1971.

For many of the insights into the history of psychology after the Middle Ages I am indebted to the late Dr. C. Sanders, who, during his lifetime and during my stay there, was professor of Theoretical Psychology at the Free University. His publications on the history of behaviorism were especially helpful to me.

I owe a major debt in writing chapter 13, "The Rise of Cognitive Psychology," to Drs. L.K.A. Eisenga and J.E.H. van Rappard, specifically for their publication, *Hoofdstromen en mensbeelden in de psychologie* (Boom: Meppel, Amsterdam, 1987).

No one had a greater influence on my overall understanding of psychology than the late Dr. H.R. Wijngaarden, who in his life was Professor of Conflictuality at the Free University, as well as my teacher, mentor, and friend.

In addition to my students I wish to express my thanks to the many colleagues and friends, among them Wayne Norman, Marinus van der Walt, Ray Klapwyk, and John Kok, who used, read, and/or responded to my manuscript. Their critical comments markedly improved the final version of the book.

How can I ever thank my wife Jenny enough for the many years she supported me as I taught and wrote about the history of psychology?

# PREFACE

## KNOWING AND NAMING:
### DISTINGUISHING HUMAN CHARACTERISTICS

We human beings are never satisfied with just existing. Without exception we all have a strong need to give an account of our existence. Talk to any man, woman, or child, and they will soon tell you who they are, where they came from, what their world is like, what they are doing, and where they are headed. Human beings are storytellers by nature; we have a persistent urge to describe ourselves and the world in which we live. This need to know and to name sets us apart from any other creature in this world. It is a uniquely human quality.

This quality of knowing and naming is given to every person by birth. It is part of our constitution, and it becomes manifest as soon as an infant starts to speak. It is, therefore, a *universal* human characteristic. Of course, knowing and naming are not all that human beings do. Descriptions of life always occur after the fact of living. Quite obviously, one has to have had an experience to be able to label it. Once we have had that experience, we have to think and speak about it. "Guess what happened to me the other day," we say to one another. The desire to reflect on and to label our experience is pervasive throughout the human race.

Some people make the task of knowing and naming their livelihood. Scholars, academics, artists, musicians, poets, writers, teachers, philosophers, and scientists all make a living doing this human task. It is their vocation to study and to interpret the human experience for the rest of us. They bear witness to human existence and presume to speak on our behalf. Their productions are testimonies to what they profess to know. These testimonies are customarily published, becoming publications in the sense that they are presented to us with the question: "What do you think? What do you say? Does this match your experience?" Books, papers, paintings, symphonies, plays, poems, lectures, treatises, and formulae are meant to be discussion starters. They are introductions to the dialogue about human experience that has been going on for millennia. By now we have an untold number of such publications for us to study and to respond to. Together these form the history of the human urge to know and to name the becoming of humankind in the world.

In studying these publications I find it interesting that the people who produce them are almost never satisfied with simply telling us about the structure of human life in the world. They want to do more than describe what, from their point of view, human life is like. Almost invariably they also want to tell us what human life *ought* to be like. People who produce these publications more often than not tend to be promoters of a certain way of living; they feel that they have something to say to us. They are "up to something," to use a phrase by Carl Rogers, or else they would keep their knowledge to themselves. They push us to live life in a certain direction. Their productions are prescriptive as well as descriptive. For this reason most publications about the human experience are a combination of factual descriptions and value judgments. Descriptions of human life are couched in perspectives on human life. Or, to put it in philosophical terms, ontologies and anthropologies most often tend to hide a system of rules for living.

At least, that is one of the theses of this book. This issue is of central importance to my understanding of the history of psychology, which is what this book is all about. In my view, the history of psychology does not deal with the history of the world, understood in the broadest sense as all the events that happened in the past. Nor does it deal with the history of culture, conceived of in the widest sense as all past events brought about by human beings. Rather, the history of psychology forms part of the history of how people have come to know and name the world. The history of psychology finds its field of investigation as part of what is sometimes called "the history of ideas," or also "intellectual history." This point is also crucial to my understanding of the history of psychology. To put it yet another way, I believe that the history of psychology is an aspect of the historical investigation of what we have come to call "socially or culturally constructed reality," not of reality itself.

## EXPOSITION AND DIALOGUE

This book consists of two parts: exposition and dialogue. The expository part is what one finds in most texts dealing with the history of psychology. In this part I attempt to give as faithful a rendition as I can of the actual history of ideas relevant to the construction of contemporary psychology. The fact is that, as a special science, psychology is entirely a product of Western Civilization. For this reason this survey deals only with the history of Western philosophical and scientific thought. Within this history I have further selected to write about only those ideas that to my mind were formative for the history of psychology. Thus, the book ignores many ideas that would be included in a book on the history of Western philosophy. Another limitation of the book is that it pays no attention to the cultural-historical context in which the ideas it writes about first arose. This book is not a *Zeitgeist* analysis, or a worldview analysis, even though I fully acknowledge that a description of the history of psychology could fruitfully be written from these points of view. The sole focus of the expository part of this book is to describe as clearly as possible the historical development of ideas relevant to psychology from ancient Greek philosophy to contemporary thought.

The dialogical part of this book is in essence that part of the text that is usually referred to as "critical thinking." In my experience most courses dealing with the history of psychology customarily ignore that part of the text. But for me this dialogical part forms a most important and integral part of a book on the history of psychology. It is not some sort of expendable afterthought tacked on to the back of each chapter. In the expository part of book I pretend that the only salient issue in writing a history of psychology text is the extent to which the book is true to the actual history of philosophical and psychological ideas. Implied in this view is the assumption that these ideas are objectively and infallibly available for all who are honest and skilled enough to write about them. Of course, nothing could be further from the truth.

No scholar has a corner on the truth, and therefore nothing he or she writes can be without error. But more importantly, it is impossible for anyone to research or write about a topic like this outside of a specific point of view or without a specific aim in mind. If people could indeed write error-free position-less texts on the history of psychology, one text would suffice. As it is, there are many such texts, each of which with an observably unique perspective.

Whether we write a text on the history of psychology or read that text to learn about that history, by this very act we, of necessity, enter into dialogue with others. Scholarship is essentially the dissemination or the assimilation of knowledge, and this is principally a perpetually ongoing process. The business of scholarship is not characterized by the pursuit of some end point at which we come to know the topic of research infallibly. Rather, scholarship is a social interaction process in which we mutually sharpen our insight into the object of our investigation through dialogue. Moreover, scholars do not engage in this process of dialogue with contemporaries only, but the dialogue occurs between the generations as well, in which case scholarship is usually referred to as education. The salient point in this is that for the generations to truly become educated, students must necessarily engage in critical dialogue with their teachers. I frequently have told my students over the years that nothing would please me more than that a decade or so from now they would be able to state and to demonstrate that I was wrong in what I taught them. Because then I would know that as a result of my teaching they have achieved a better insight into reality than I was able to obtain.

The foregoing discussion is relevant for the way I envision this book to be used. The reader will note that, at the end of each chapter in the book, I offer a list of (hopefully provocative) comments, questions, and observations, which I deem to be relevant for a dialogue on the topic of that chapter. Readers of this text may modify this list in any way they wish. But as they do this, and as they respond in their minds to the issues I raise, they thereby enter into a dialogue with me about the history of psychology. Insofar as this process takes place in a classroom, a teacher and other classmates are added to the community of dialogue.

If this book is used as the primary text in an introductory course on the history of psychology, I envision the following format for that course. Students would be expected to master the content of the book and to be tested on it, but classroom discussion would deal predominantly with the issues raised by me at the end of each chapter. Of course the issues I raise are only discussion *starters*. The teacher and the students should feel free to add their own issues. Too often students view a course on the history of psychology as boring because they are only asked to master the material of the text and nothing more. Hardly ever are they invited to interact personally with the course content. In my view a class text and the class lectures surrounding it should generate excitement and enthusiasm for the course content. In essence, when this book is used as a class text it should be viewed as a stimulant for class discussion. It is designed to engage students personally with the subject matter of the course. It is my hope that in that capacity this book may generate much good fruit.

# 1. History

## 1.1 *The importance of history for psychology*

The history of psychology studies the historical development of psychology. It seeks to know and describe how past conceptions of psychology have successively influenced our present understanding of the field of psychology. Does this history matter? Is it important to study the history of psychology? Many present-day psychologists do not think so. They are content to practice psychology without regard for how their discipline came into being. They believe that past conceptions of psychology are at best inferior formulations of how we view psychology today.

I think that is a mistake. Even a cursory review of the history of the discipline will reveal that present-day psychology struggles with issues that find their origin in times long before it became a separate discipline. Think of the mind-body problem, for instance, or the issue of nature versus nurture. In fact, it can be demonstrated that throughout history psychology has grappled with only a finite set of problems that are reformulated over time but that never seem to get resolved definitively. At the same time, the answers we give to these problems today are not the answers that others gave to them in times past. Furthermore, it is almost certain that our present view of the discipline will change in future times as well. A thorough knowledge of the history of psychology enables us to be properly critical of our present way of viewing the discipline. Thus, a study of history creates in us an awareness that we ourselves are also history makers. In that sense, it is the normal task of every psychologist, present or past, to constantly reformulate his or her own understanding of psychology.

Finally, the mindset that denies the relevance of history for psychology betrays a profound lack of respect for the efforts of psychologists who have preceded us. Many psychologists in the past, and before them philosophers, have spent their lifetime constructing conceptions of psychological phenomena that form the ingredients of present-day psychology. All we need to do to know that this is true is to ask why psychologists today study learning, sensation, perception, cognition, emotion, motivation, development, and personality while not considering some other set of phenomena. Present-day psychology is a historically constructed field of investigation.

## 1.2 *History written down*

Historians of psychology are not really historians at all, but rather writers of history. They study and describe past formulations of the field of psychology as these occurred in the course of history in order to show how present-day psychology came into being. Of course, these historians are not able to produce a completely unbiased, objective recording of the actual history of psychology. If this were possible then they would all produce history books that are identical in style and content. A quick look at the table of contents of only a handful of introductory texts to the history of psychology will convince anyone that there are considerable differences among them. The reason for these differences is that these texts are histories-written down. They contain the history of psychology looked at and written down from *a certain point of view.*

One case in point, among many, that illustrates the importance of making a distinction between history and history writing is E. G. Boring's book, *A History of Experimental Psychology* (1929). This book was for decades the standard introductory text for a course on the history of psychology at many colleges and universities. Boring was a student of Edward B. Titchener, who was the founder of the Structuralist school in psychology, and he dedicated his book to him. In his book Boring defended the thesis that, although psychology owes a huge debt to philosophy, it did not become a fruitful field of investigation until it became experimental. This thesis fundamentally shaped his treatment of the history of psychology of his time, in terms of what was included and excluded in his text, as well as what he deemed good and bad psychology. It was also responsible for his, and Titchener's, fundamental distortion of Wundt's psychology (Rieber, 1980, p. vii; O'Donnell, 1979).

The only way to do fruitful psychology, according to Boring, is to apply the experimental method to it. That this thesis was a belief on Boring's part and not a conclusion on the basis of a careful scrutiny of the evidence is clear from his book. Boring himself bemoaned the fact that since its inception as an experimental discipline until the time of writing his book, psychology had had little to show for itself in terms of insights. However, this fact did not lead him to discard experimentation in favor of another method. He merely expressed the fervent hope that further experimentation would rectify the problem of the poverty of data (Boring, 1929, pp. 653–661). Boring was an adherent of the Positivist notion that the only viable method for psychology is the experimental method. This belief had its origin in the nineteenth century, and it proved to be resilient over time. It is a widely held belief, even by contemporary psychologists. But the popularity of this belief does not absolve us from the task of carefully questioning its historical validity. Making a distinction between the history of psychology and the history of psychology-written-down is a first step in this critical process.

All historians of psychology, myself included, approach the study of the history of psychology with a certain method. This method extends beyond reading past formulations of psychology carefully, even though that is, of course, a primary requirement. Historical method also includes the selection and the description of what one considers the important factors in the historical development of the discipline.

For instance, some authors organize the material of their book by highlighting major changes in the history of psychology. They may make much of the change that occurred in the history of psychology from psychology as a sub-discipline of philosophy to psychology as an experimental science. They may also emphasize the change from a psychology of consciousness to one that only accepted behavior as its unit of analysis. These historians consider historical changes discontinuous; they tend to describe the history of psychology as a series of revolutionary paradigm shifts.

Other historians may also focus on changes in history, but they may consider them as more gradual. Therefore, they would describe these as a series of evolutionary changes. However, the central aim of both these historical methods is to demonstrate how much our present-day view of psychology differs from previous conceptions of the discipline. In addition, some of the historians who view history as a process of gradual change also believe that history is a process of progress or historical improvement. They write their books with the aim of showing that all previous conceptions of psychology were inferior to our current understanding of it. This form of history writing is called "Whig historiography," or also "presentism."

On the other hand, there are historians of psychology who do not focus on historical change at all. In fact, they do quite the opposite. They view the history of psychology as a number of persistent themes that keep reoccurring throughout every period of history. They write their books to demonstrate, for example, that the Greeks already wrestled with the problem of dualism and monism, or with the problem of the relation between the mental and the physical, problems with which psychologists still struggle today. The aim of their methodology seems to be to show that there is nothing new under the sun.

This is not the place to discuss the historical validity of these points of view. I merely want to reiterate that these different points of view profoundly influence the manner in which the history of psychology is recorded. In what follows I will discuss the views of a representative of each of the above-mentioned approaches.

### 1.3 *Thomas Kuhn: The history of scientific revolutions*

To my knowledge, Thomas Kuhn was the first historian to describe the history of science – more specifically the history of physics – as a series of revolutionary paradigm shifts. In his now famous book *The Structure of Scientific Revolutions* (1970), Kuhn outlines his view of the history of physics, based on a study of what physicists actually have done in the past. He found that what physicists studied (i.e., what they considered the object of science), how they studied (i.e., their methodology), and what they held to be true (i.e., what they considered facts) depended heavily on the *Weltanschauung*, or worldview that was dominant in the culture in which these physicists lived. Furthermore, he showed that their worldview in turn was heavily influenced by the *Zeitgeist*, or Spirit of the times, or the *mood* of the historical period in which they lived. These worldviews, Kuhn also showed, tended to change from one period to another. Moreover, often these changes in worldview were revolutionary; i.e., people appeared to discard an old view in favor of a new, totally opposite one. Owing to Kuhn's vision this is how scientists continue to operate even today.

Kuhn raised the question of how worldviews influence science. These worldviews, he wrote, accomplish this by giving scientists a way to do physics or biology, or psychology, by giving them a *paradigm*, i.e., a *disciplinary matrix* plus some *shared exemplars* by means of which to do their research. These paradigms, he held, are never scientifically investigated; they are the means by which scientists do their investigating. Like blueprints for builders, they facilitate science. They are the way to do science to which all agree for a while until a paradigm no longer works; then, there is a revolution.

### 1.4 *Critics of Kuhn: Toulmin, Lakatos, and Laudan*

To summarize, Thomas Kuhn views the history of science, and by implication the history of psychology, as a series of paradigm shifts. For a time, one paradigm is dominant and allows for a period of normal experimentation in a discipline. Then, for reasons stated above, the discipline shifts to a new paradigm, which is incommensurate with, or qualitatively different from the previous one. A revolution has occurred that ushers in a new period in the history of that discipline. These paradigm shifts are not the result of experimentation because paradigms precede experimentation in the sense of making experimentation possible. The implication is that other, non-experimental factors such as changes in cultural worldviews are responsible for these shifts. In the history of psychology such a qualitative paradigm shift would be the shift from behaviorism to cognitive psychology some half a century ago.

While not disputing Kuhn's original insight, later theorists, specifically Toulmin, Lakatos, and Laudan, have attempted to modify his theory to make it more compatible with what they view is the actual history of science. Stephen Toulmin, for example, sees science as an evolutionary process rather than a revolutionary process. Science evolves by natural selection. Concepts that gain acceptance are passed on to the next generation via textbooks or instruction. Those that fail to gain favor are discarded, those that become popular structure the way science is done for a while until they too are inevitably discarded. Note that this does not have to imply that science is an unbiased, rational process. It does not imply that what we hold for true today is any better than before. For all we know it may not be. But it does entail that the process is more gradual than Kuhn thought. There are no hiccups in the history of science (Toulmin, 1972).

Lakatos and Laudan point to the fact that paradigms do not only succeed one another in the history of a discipline. Contrary to Kuhn's view, multiple competing paradigms can exist simultaneously side-by-side within a given period of the history of a discipline. These paradigms influence each other mutually and are to some extent permeable to each other's experimental results. Thus, Lakatos and Laudan point out that paradigms do not exclusively define the periods in the history of a discipline. Also, paradigms are changed by incorporating parts of one another as well as by the evidence resulting from experimentation. In this way these later historiographers attempted to rescue the idea that there is a progression of insight in the history of science (Gholson & Barker, 1985).

### 1.5 *Persisting themata in the history of science and psychology*
At this point we may ask what accounts for the existence of these multiple competing paradigms side by side within a given period of the history of a discipline. Several historiographers have argued that there is a recognizable set of problems that persists from the time of antiquity to the present in the history of science as well as in the history of psychology

in particular. They point out that these problems reappear in some form or another in any given period of history and that the multiple competing paradigms are simply ways of attempting to solve these problems.

A number of students of the history of philosophy, of science, and of psychology have attempted to isolate a finite set of these persisting problems as well as their solutions. A.O. Lovejoy, in his book *The Great Chain of Being* (1964), talks about "unit-ideas." M.H. Marx and W.A. Hillix, in their introductory text, *Systems and Theories in Psychology* (1973), refer to "major philosophical solutions to the mind-body problem," F.F. Centore (1979) mentions "six possible theories." Finally, G. Holton (1973) calls the persistent components of the history of a science "themata."

Perhaps the greatest attempt at identifying abiding problems in the history of psychology is Robert I. Watson's *prescriptive theory* (1991). By studying contemporary systems of psychology Watson came up with thirty-six "prescriptions" (Watson, 1978, p. 10-14). Watson called them *pre*scriptions rather than *de*scriptions because "they tell us how the psychologist-scientist must or should behave" (1967, p. 437). They are attitudes that psychologists have about psychology rather than ideas (1980, p. 319). These attitudes are "frequently implicit," seem "self-evident" to those who hold them, are "held strongly," and remain "impervious to argument" (1980, p. 320). They have a "guidance function" (1978, p. 17). These prescriptions determine what one considers the proper research methodology for psychology as well as what one considers its nature as a field of investigation.

Watson arranged these prescriptions into 18 contrasting pairs to indicate more clearly what these were and what they were not. One other implication of this arrangement is that these prescriptions form centers of debate in psychology. Watson developed his prescriptive theory partially in confrontation with Kuhn's paradigm theory (1977, p. 131) to counteract Kuhn's extreme emphasis on change. As Watson studied the historical roots of these prescriptions found in contemporary psychology, he came to the conclusion that they had already been around for quite some time. Initially, he found their roots in the philosophies of such seventeenth century thinkers as Descartes, Locke, and Spinoza. As he continued his historical search, he eventually concluded that most of the thirty-six prescriptions were already evident in the thought life of ancient Greece (1980, p. 319).

## 1.6 *The problem-historical approach*

We seem to be left with two approaches or poles to history: Kuhn's approach that emphasizes historical change to the extreme and Watson's approach that stresses historical continuity to the extreme. Then, there are a number of modifiers in between, such as the views of Toulmin, Lakatos, and Laudan. Furthermore, as we have seen, there seems to be evidence for both continuity and discontinuity in the history of science in general, particularly in the history of psychology. There is clear evidence of paradigm shifts. But there is also evidence of typical problems that seem to reoccur in every period of history. What seems to be needed is a methodology that does justice to both.

I favor an adaptation of Vollenhoven's problem-historical approach because it appears to be able to account for both the continuities and the discontinuities in the history of psychology without placing these two in opposition to each other, as the other methods that I have surveyed seem to do. In fact, the problem-historical method holds that in the history of Western thought continuities and discontinuities actually complement one another.

The problem-historical method was developed by D. H .Th. Vollenhoven (1892–1978) who was professor of philosophy at the Free University of Amsterdam from 1926–1963. Vollenhoven developed this method in his study of the history of philosophy to locate and catalogue the various philosophical conceptions found in the history of Western thought from ancient Greece to the present. I intend to use an adaptation of this method in my account of the history of psychology.

The basis of this method is the view that historically important persons are influenced by their predecessors as well as by their contemporaries. They also exercise influence on their contemporaries and on the generations succeeding them. From this point of view, the history of philosophy, of science, and of psychology contains a series of successive conceptions about which we can distinguish two dimensions: periodicity and typicality.

Periodicity refers to the fact that a person's conception of reality is influenced by the period of history in which it occurs. In that sense the conceptions of persons living in the same historical period show a number of common characteristics that distinguish these conceptions from conceptions of persons living in another period of history. In other words, this view holds that there are such entities as historical periods and that therefore historical paradigm shifts are real. Typicality, on the other hand, refers to the fact that in any given period of history a number of qualitatively differing conceptions of reality can be found. Moreover, these conceptions often show a number of characteristics that are also found in conceptions present in previous periods of history. What is more, the things that unite these conceptions with the conceptions of their predecessors are the very things that distinguish them from conceptions of their contemporaries.

To put it more simply, historically important persons belong to a given historical period. Thus in analyzing the views of a particular scholar, we must identify the historical period in which his or her conception exists in addition to determining the persistent type of conception of reality to which he or she adheres. In opposition to Kuhn's view, I argue that types of conceptions have a certain historical continuity, paradigm shifts notwithstanding. But over against Watson I would argue that, if one wants to think historically, one cannot work only with a typology. It is true that types reoccur in succeeding periods, *but only in a transformed manner*. A historically typical conception of reality is always worked out in the language of a given historical period. In each historical period, typological diversity is evident; scholars living in the same period of history differ from one another because they stand in different intellectual traditions. But this diversity is always a transformation of the diversity of preceding periods. On the one hand, people always speak the language of their time, but when they speak they speak in a typologically diverse manner. Traditional types of conceptions are worked out in terms of the spirit of a given historical period, while historical periods come to concrete expression in the manner in which certain traditional types are worked out. It appears then, from this problem-historical viewpoint, that both approaches to the history of philosophy, science, and psychology have relative validity and need one another. Analyses in term of typicality and of periodicity, or in terms of continuity and of change, are complimentary.

The problem-historical method is based on the fact that all conceptions of reality have two dimensions: a *diachronic* (across time) and a *synchronic* (same time) dimension. Thus, by way of summary, as applied to the history of psychology we can say that *typology* refers to the abiding, recurring problems in the history of psychology. This is diachronic similarity. The answers to these typical problems can occur side by side in any period of history. This is synchronic diversity. We can also say that *periodicity* refers to the different answers given to recurring questions in the history of psychology from one historical period to another. This is diachronic diversity. These answers can capture the allegiance of an entire generation of psychologists. This is synchronic similarity.

The description of the problem-historical method I have given thus far is of necessity rather abstract. It was necessary to acquaint the reader with the basic tenets of the method first without using a large number of examples. However, the *ex-cathedra* character of my description may create the impression that I believe this method to be the ultimate in historical research, as if all we now have to do in this book is to squeeze historical data into this framework to obtain clarity about the history of psychology. Nothing could be further from the truth. Quite obviously I believe that this method has some merit or else I would not write about it. But for me, what I write in this chapter is only my current insight into the history of psychology. It is a discussion starter, and I fully expect my views to change as a result of my interaction with the actual documented history of psychology, as well as in interaction with those who hold to a different historical view. So, it is highly probable to me that upon further research my view of the proper historical method for psychology will change. In fact, I believe that R.I. Watson can be criticized for never changing his prescriptive theory once he had formulated it and for restricting himself thereafter to illustrating his method in the history of psychology.

I do not confess to the imperfection of my approach as an act of intellectual humility. Rather, it is a basic principle of the problem-historical method that one should always hold ones views about history tentatively. The problem-historical method is principally a method of trial and error. It is developed and revised in a continuous confrontation with historical data.

According to Vollenhoven, a method should:

> . . . arise from working with the matter itself. In fact, that matter remains recalcitrant so long as it is not examined in a manner fitted to its nature, whereas it opens itself easily to one who is completely prepared in his or her approach to respond to the contours native to the chosen field of research. (1961, p. 1)

To put it more succinctly, the object of an investigation should determine the method of investigation. This is the true meaning of objectivity in methodology. This viewpoint on methodology has several implications for the historical study of psychology. First, a method is nothing more than an aid to the object of an investigation. In this connection, Vollenhoven states that "the usefulness of a method can only be demonstrated by the results one books when using this method" (1950, p. 6). Thus, whether the problem-historical method is the preferred method can only be determined at the completion of this study, not at the beginning.

Second, and more importantly, in an investigation of the history of a discipline the conclusions one draws as the result of one's investigation may only be those that are warranted by the period of history one is studying, or else one reads into the material what is not there. One commits an anachronism. Anachronisms occur when historians describe past events in terms of present events. I will give several examples of this point.

For instance, almost all introductory texts to a course in the history of psychology in the first chapter of the text discuss the question whether and in what sense psychology is a science. Typically there is a discussion about "the" scientific method. Often the conclusion of this discussion is that psychology is scientific only insofar it has succeeded in separating itself from philosophy and has become experimental. However, historically speaking, the question in what sense psychology is a science can only be discussed in the description of that period of its history when it underwent the influence of Comte's positivism and later logical positivism. Both these movements in the philosophy of science held to the one-sided view that a discipline can only be called "scientific" when it is non-philosophical and experimental.

The problem with discussing this issue in the first chapter is that these (logical) positivistic criteria are thereby presented as scientific norms rather than as historical constructions. As a result, the history of a discipline is skewed in the direction of the achievement of these criteria. In essence the (logical) positivists hold that the scientific character of a discipline is determined by its research methodology. But that historical "insight" did not arise until the middle of the nineteenth century. To discuss this issue at the outset of ones survey of history prejudges the nature of scholarly development prior to this time.

The second example comes from certain tenets about writing history. One favored way of writing history is to interpret the meaning of past events in terms of the present. It describes all past events as leading up to the present. It attempts to understand a past way of looking at something as a variant of the way we look at it today. For instance, some authors may describe Plato's notion of the soul as prefiguring, or anticipating what we mean today by mind, or mental processes, or cognition. What is wrong with this approach is that it is backward history writing. It is saying that the present causes the past, whereas the mark of good historical research is that it shows how the past illumines the present.

Almost always this approach implies that we consider past formulations as inferior. It does not do justice to the actual history of the past. It also implies that we live in the best of all possible worlds or periods of history. It implies that the present cannot be wrong. This is an evolutionary bias in historical research. It is *Whig history* or *presentism*. This approach to history writing is another example of the fallacy of committing anachronisms.

A final example of committing an anachronism is one frequently committed by Christian history writers. This is the practice of evaluating past conceptions in terms of whether or not they are in agreement with a biblical view of reality. In my opinion, Vollenhoven, for all his insight into the history of philosophy has not entirely escaped this fallacy. An example of this fallacy is to describe Greek and Hellenistic views of reality as inadequate or incorrect because they lacked an understanding of the world as *created* reality. Such an approach is historically unacceptable. It ignores the fact that the Greek and Hellenistic philosophers could not include a biblical view of reality in their view of the world *because the Judeo-Christian view of reality was not introduced into the history of Western thought until after the Greco-Roman period.* Thus, the place to introduce a discussion of the influence of a biblical worldview on the history of Western thought is *after* a description of Greek and Hellenistic thought. At that point it is quite legitimate to review how these two worldviews differ from one another and to discuss how historically they were related to one another.

In my opinion the input of religious and ideological factors into the written histories of Western thought may only be evaluated on *structural grounds* and not on *directional grounds*. In other words, the value of a biblical view of reality, or for that matter of a positivistic view of reality, for researching the history of Western thought may only be determined by whether they illuminate or distort the actual history of philosophy, science, and psychology. Adherence to this rule allows us, for example, to distinguish between the absence of biblical motifs in the Greek mind and the modern mind. Its absence in the Greek mind was due to its *ignorance* of the Christian gospel, whereas its absence in the modern mind was due to its *rejection* of that gospel.

### 1.7 *Criteria for distinguishing periodicity and typicality*
The history of psychology gives evidence of both periodicity and typicality. This is not much in dispute among historians of psychology. Conceptions of psychological reality clearly have changed from ancient Greek times to the time when psychology became a discipline separate from philosophy. It is also clear that psychology has changed considerably from its inception as a special field of investigation to its present status.

Moreover, qualitatively differing periods are discernible in its history. The psychology of Wundt's voluntarism in the nineteenth century is not the same as the cognitive psychology of the twenty-first century. In short, there is evidence of periodicity in the history of psychology.

At the same time, within each period of psychology's history a wide diversity of competing conceptions, theories, and schools are evident. Furthermore, even though these conceptions, theories, or schools are never completely identical to the conceptions, theories, or schools of previous periods they nevertheless show a clear affinity to them. Synchronic diversity gives evidence of diachronic unity. In short, the fact that a finite number of intellectual puzzles keep on reoccurring in successive periods of history suggests that there is evidence of typicality in the history of psychology.

An important question to consider is how we are to distinguish typicality from periodicity. Is there anything in the history of psychology that allows us to distinguish between the paradigmatic changes that bring about periods of history and the abiding types of problems that give it continuity? R.I. Watson does not think so. According to him they both refer to the same intellectual phenomena insofar as they are both conceptions of psychology in the history of psychology. Furthermore, he calls them both "attitudes" rather than "ideas" to emphasize their prescriptive nature. About the only difference between them, as far as he is concerned, is in their duration. Types of problems, specifically the prescriptions he believes to have isolated, last longer than periodic paradigms. Periods come and go, while types endure (Watson, 1967, p. 438). What's more, he defines periodicity in terms of typicality. Periods arise when one type rather than others becomes the dominant prescription for a while (1967, p. 439). Laudan, with his concept of *research traditions*, the core of which can change over time, essentially also holds that the distinction is only valid as a difference in duration (Laudan, 1977).

As several types of conceptions can be present in any given period, I do not believe that the criterion for distinguishing a certain period is the dominance of one particular type. Rather, and in this I follow Vollenhoven, I believe that typicality and periodicity refer to two different sets of problematics in the history of philosophy and psychology. In the preface of this book, I suggested that the activity by important historical figures to know and to name the events of our world for us is twofold. They attempt to describe the way things *are* (or come into being) and the way things *ought to be* (or become). Philosophical and psychological conceptions are responses to both of these realities in our lives.

This formulation gives us the criteria for distinguishing between typicality and periodicity. Typicality, I suggest, deals with ontology (or in the case of human beings, with philosophical anthropology). Periodicity deals with normativity, or with the question what human beings are to do. Types of conceptions have a certain historical continuity. They typically contain a number of separate themata, which tend to form into clusters. Thus a type in the history of philosophy and of psychology is an ontological (or anthropological) basis structure – or a vision about the being and becoming of things – surrounded by a constellation of philosophical or psychological positions. Types exclude one another and are more or less persistent in the history of Western thought.

The implication of this suggested formula for types is that the history of philosophy and psychology in Western civilization deals with only a finite set of reoccurring problems. The further implication is that this set of problems distinguishes the Western tradition from other intellectual traditions in the world.

If one wants to think historically, one cannot only work with a typology. Types of conceptions do reoccur in succeeding periods of history but only in a transformed manner. Periodicity is as much a given as typicality in the history of Western philosophy and psychology. The central characteristic of a period is that it deals with questions of "ought" rather than questions of "is." It deals with normativity rather than factuality, with the ideal rather than the real in one's ontology or anthropology, with rules rather than statements, with prescription rather than description, and with the perspective and methodology of a discipline rather than its subject matter.

It is important to recognize that periodicity is primarily a matter of coming to terms with normativity. The succession of periods in the history of philosophy and of psychology often is brought on as a result of a debate about what is normative. One respected scholar or group of scholars gives an account of the nature of reality, of human life, or of psychology, *inclusive of* what is most basic, most important, or normative. For a time, this theory influences a whole generation of scholars. This conception dominates life or the study of philosophy or of psychology. In the history of psychology, this debate has generated *schools* of psychology: Structuralism, functionalism, behaviorism, or cognitive psychology. But sooner or later the next generation will question the validity of the theory. They will ask, "Is this how it is? Is this the way to do it?" They lose faith in the reigning conception and promote a new one, which gives a different answer to the questions raised that may capture the allegiance of a new generation of scholars. So also in the history of psychology, schools arise and fall in succession: Structuralism was replaced by functionalism which was, in turn, replaced by behaviorism, which in time made way for cognitive psychology. The motor of this historical change is *not primarily* a debate about what is, but a debate about what ought to be. If we miss this, we do not understand the *passions* involved in bringing about historical change.

At this point, it is important to remind ourselves that our focus of study is not on the history of the world, or on past events in general, but on *conceptions* of past events and of psychology as part of the history of Western science. Within this history, periods are discernible, and the notion of "periods" implies that there are methodological norms for science that change over time. These norms prescribe rules for doing "good" science. They are the basic prescriptions of scientific practice. It is these norms that change from one period to the next. Thus, every period has its own norms and forums for scholarship, which differentiates it from other periods in the history of psychology. As Laudan states:

> Since antiquity, philosophers and philosopher-scientists have sought to define sets of norms, or methodological rules, which are expected to govern the behavior of the scientist. . . . every historical epoch exhibits one or more of these dominant, normative images of science. . . . Every practicing scientist, past and present, adheres to certain views about how science should be performed, about what counts as an adequate explanation. . . . *These norms . . . have been perhaps the single major source for most of the controversies in the history of science.* (1977, p. 58, emphasis mine)

It is my suggestion for the history of philosophy, of science, and of psychology that when these norms change, a new period begins. To give but one example from philosophy, the period of idealism had a decidedly unique view of what constitutes methodological rules for scholarship. Following in the footsteps of Kant, it advised scholars to apply the a priori categories of their minds to the sensations that confronted them. This view of scholarship distinguished idealism from the views of the succeeding period of positivism, which emphasized the experimental method. Positivism promoted the approach to knowledge of letting the sensations determine one's thinking as the only valid methodology for scholarship.

It will be interesting to learn which types of ontological conceptions reappear time and again in the history of philosophy and psychology. It will also be interesting to discover what shape they assume in each period of this history. Finally, it will be good to describe what changes in rules for knowing and naming are responsible for these changes in typological conceptions.

With that, I will have completed the first chapter of this book. It is only the beginning or like a preface not even that, but rather something that must be said before we start describing the actual history of psychology.

## References

Boring, E.G. (1929). *A History of Experimental Psychology.* New York: Century.

Centore, F.F. (1979). *Persons: A Comparative Account of Six Possible Theories.* London: Greenwood Press.

Gholson, B. & P. Barker. (1985) Kuhn, Lakatos and Laudan. Applications in the history of physics and psychology. *American Psychologist* (July), 755–769.

Holton, G. (1975). On the role of themata in scientific thought, *Science,* 188, 328–334.

Kuhn, Th. S. (1970). *The Structure of Scientific Revolutions.* Chicago: Chicago U. Press.

Laudan, L. (1977). *Progress and its Problems.* Berkeley: U. of California Press.

Lovejoy, A.O. (1964). *The Great Chain of Being.* Cambridge, Massachusetts: Harvard U. Press.

Marx, M. H. & Hillix, W.A. (1963). *Systems and Theories in Psychology.* New York: McGraw-Hill Book Co.

O'Donnell, J.M. (1979). The Crisis of Experimentation in the 1920s: E.G. Boring and his uses of history, *American Psychologist,* 289–295.

Rieber, B. W. (1980). *Wilhelm Wundt and the Making of a Scientific Psychology.* N.Y: Plenum Press.

Toulmin, S. (1972). *Human Understanding.* Princeton, N.J: Princeton University Press.

Vollenhoven, D. H. Th. (1950). *Geschiedenis der Wijsbegeerte I: Inleiding en geschiedenis der Griekse wijsbegeerte voor Platoon en Aristoteles.* Franeker, Netherlands: Wever.

Vollenhoven, D. H. Th. (1961). De consequent probleem-historische methode, *Philosophia Reformata,* 26, 1–34. See: "The Consequential Problem-Historical Method." Translated by Robert Sweetman in: *The Problem-Historical Method and the History of Philosophy.* Edited by K.A. Bril, Amstelveen, NLD: De Zaak Haes, 2005.

Watson, R.I. (1967). Psychology: a prescriptive science, *American Psychologist.* 22, 435–443.

Watson, R.I. (1979). *Selected Papers on the History of Psychology.* Ed. by J. Brožek and R.B. Evans, Hanover, N.H: U. Press of New England.

Watson, R.I. (1978). *The Great Psychologists.* 4th ed. Philadelphia: Lippincott.

Watson, R.I. (1980). Socio-psychological approach: the study of personality. In: J. Brožek and C.J. Pongratz, eds. *Historiography of Modern Psychology.* Toronto: Hogrefe.

# Some Issues to Stimulate Class Dialogue

A study of the history of psychology is important, but it should never be dull. Below I have listed a number of issues that I deem to be relevant to the chapter you have just read. These comments presuppose that you are familiar with the contents of this chapter. You are expected to reflect on these issues and to write down some brief comments about them. These comments allow you to participate in the group or class discussion on this chapter, which I hope will be lively. In no way do I claim that my insight into these issues is infallible. But my aim is to be controversial. You are expected to respond to my formulations critically and with passion. Of course, you should also raise in your group or class your own comments and questions that may have arisen in you as a result of reading this chapter.

1. The idea that past conceptions of psychology are inferior to current formulations of the field is wide spread and, in my view, not always defensible because it implies that psychology is becoming progressively better. In what sense is this true and in what sense is it not? Compare 3.3.1, second to the last paragraph, where I contrast Augustine's description of memory (*Confessions*, 1993, p. 178 ff.) and Ebbinghaus's view of memory (Watson, 1979, p. 142–150).

2. Knowing the history of psychology safeguards one from naively accepting the current formulation of psychology as the only way to view and practice it. Fact is that in the past the data of psychology have been interpreted in many different ways. For example, during the time when I was a student, behaviorism reigned supreme. This paradigm arose in reaction to structuralism, which viewed the subject matter of psychology as "sensations" or "introspected bits of consciousness." Behaviorism banished all mental terms from the language of psychology and reformulated psychological data in terms of "observed behaviors." It in turn was replaced some fifty years ago by the currently popular cognitive psychology paradigm, which defines facts in psychology as "cognitions." What formulation of psychology will become popular, do you think, when members of your generation will be leaders in psychology?

3. Perspectives or paradigms in psychology have a way of either restricting one's vision or opening it up. Thus, we can compare the value of paradigms in terms of how fruitful they are in generating insights into the subject matter of psychology. In my view, Boring's adherence to positivism, which bases its pronouncements strictly on sense data, restricted his vision on psychology. Nevertheless, his book on the history of psychology was for decades the authoritative text at most universities in courses on the history of our discipline. Which paradigm do you find the most fruitful for psychology?

4. In my opinion, Kuhn essentially equates the history of science with the history of religion. This is ironic because ever since the modern period of philosophy, science with its inherent skepticism has been viewed as the fierce opponent of faith and religion. The history of religion shows a pattern in which someone develops a conviction about the nature of God, the universe, and mankind, or their relation to one another. He (usually "he") then teaches his ideas to others who become convinced about the rightness of his views and become his followers. Together they form a community that confesses this view (in Greek, the word for confession is *homologia*, which means "to say the same thing."). However, as time goes on, someone inevitably opposes the established view with a view of his own. He then is branded a heretic and is banished from the community of faith. This individual, in turn, propagates his views to others who become his followers; then, a new community of faith is born. Is this not how the history of religion often goes? Is there any difference between this process and Kuhn's "structure of scientific revolutions" with its "paradigm shifts" (Kuhn, 1970)?

5. It is fashionable today to say that all claims to knowledge are socially, culturally, and historically relative. There is no universal knowledge that holds for all times and places. True knowledge can only be "local" knowledge, i.e., knowledge that holds for the time being and serves the culture of a particular society at a particular time in history. Yet another way of saying this is that all knowledge is "immanent," i.e., that knowledge is embedded in cultural-historical perspectives. This view of knowledge generation is somewhat comforting to me since it emphasizes that knowledge must be concrete rather than abstract. Knowledge must be applicable and relevant to the situation in which it is generated. However, this cannot be the whole story related to knowledge claims. Whoever makes a claim to knowing something

implicitly appeals to an authority outside a given cultural-historical perspective. For example, in making the case that the history of science is embedded in changing cultural-historical worldviews and *Zeitgeister*, Kuhn paradoxically appeals to historical *evidence*, which per definition transcends the worldview of any one historical time and place. Do you agree or disagree with my analysis?

6. In my opinion, Kuhn's description of the actual history of science is one-sided. It demonstrates how the development of science is determined, or at least influenced, by changing cultural-historical worldviews. But without also showing how science has influenced changes in worldview, what is left unexplained is what causes these changes in worldview in the first place. Thus, to make the claim that his analysis is not one-sided, Kuhn would have to show that the history of science did not itself influence changes in cultural worldviews. In the absence of such an analysis, a more cautious conclusion on his part might have been that the relation between worldview changes and the history of science is interactive. What do you think?

7. A basic principle of the problem-historical method is that one should always hold one's views about history tentatively. Vollenhoven consistently presented his lectures on the history of philosophy as the presentation of "tentative thought results." This was often frustrating for his students because not infrequently he would make statements in one lecture that flatly contradicted statements he had made in a previous lecture. When this was brought to his attention he would say, "Yes, because of further study I see that differently now." What was not realized until later by his students was that his views about the tentative nature of knowledge claims was the result of his conviction that the material to be studied should determine the method of investigation and not vice versa. He argued that true objectivity is lost when method begins to dictate what one should study and what conclusions one should draw as a result of this study. Rather, method should be shaped by a constant interaction with the study material. So, for Vollenhoven the material was primary and method secondary. For him a good method generates insight into the material. In his mind, the merit of a method is entirely determined by the extent to which it opens up the material to be studied to understanding.

His conviction in this regard hid a seriousness about the empirical nature of scholarship that I find truly amazing. Throughout his scholarly life he was constantly testing his theories and methods against the nature of the material he studied; he would not hesitate to change his mind when he or his colleagues in the field could point to better formulations of the study results he had come to. Vollenhoven's field of study was the history of philosophy. His conviction about the empirical nature of scholarship dictated that he continually read and reread the writings of earlier philosophers and that he would refrain from drawing any conclusions about them until he felt in his bones, so to speak, that he understood them. Vollenhoven taught his students an attitude rather than a method or a theory. This attitude can be summed up succinctly as follows: keep studying, hold your views tentatively, and expect others to improve on your insights. For him, scholarship of any kind is an ongoing *dialogue*, which requires constant interaction with the material and with fellow scholars in the field. This kind of scholarship is hard work, but it does yield results. Scholarship is not about nothing. For this reason Vollenhoven encouraged his students to present their thought results with a conviction that comes as a result of this hard work. But he would add that when you do that, you can expect other scholars to oppose you. Furthermore, he would argue that we should consider our opponents as our friends, for they help us to sharpen our insight into the field of investigation.

To my mind, for historical studies the problem-historical method in essence represents an anti-anachronism. It recognizes that the material historians study dictates that we may not interpret prior events in terms of later events. Unfortunately, this rule is frequently broken by historians of psychology.

Here is something for readers to consider: I assume they are familiar with the so-called "scientific method" in psychology. It consists of formulating an hypothesis in quantitative terms, testing this hypothesis against reality by counting the number of instances that (dis)affirm the hypothesis and then, by means of the application of statistics, coming to some conclusion about the hypothesis. Which areas of psychology, if any, lend themselves to this method of research? Which areas do not?

8. According to Vollenhoven, the reason for periodicity in the history of Western thought is qualitatively different from the reason for typicality. My adapted version of this distinction in Chapter 1 states that periodicity is the result of changes in *pre*scription or normativity. By contrast typicality results from a continuity of *de*scription or ontology in the history of Western thought. Chapter 1 adopts this distinc-

tion as a hypothesis only; but for reasons of space and time I did not adequately work out the basis for this distinction. Perhaps someone more gifted with time and intellect than I should pursue this topic to see to what extent this distinction holds. If for the sake of dialogue I would give the reader my own understanding of the reasons for the distinction, I would say the following: We, people of the West in the twenty-first century, stand in a Western thought tradition that started with the Greeks. These ancient Greek philosophers asked only a finite number of questions about reality that keep on reoccurring in one form or another throughout the centuries and that are not asked in the same way in the far eastern thought tradition. To my mind these questions are the reason for typicality in the history of Western thought. Some examples of these questions are: What is the relation between the one and the many, between subject and object, between the individual and the universal, between body and soul, between mind and matter, between the infinite and the finite, between the definite and the indefinite, between order and chaos, and finally, between being and becoming? At the same time I think one can observe a recurring periodic skepticism about the answers given to these questions and an attempt to come up with new answers. This, I think, accounts for periodicity. In my view it is these times of doubt that usher in new periods in the history of Western thought. Typically, a given set of answers is considered as normal for a time, after which people lose faith in these answers and a new kind of normality is ushered in. I think we do an injustice to this historical phenomenon of periodicity if we define these periodic changes as a "change of mind" only. Rather these periodic doubts represent a loss of conviction, of nerve, a loss of certainty about what is real, what is worthwhile, or what one should live for. For the people of that time they are periods of emotional upheaval. I think we are currently in such a period of racking doubt.

# 2. The Classical Greek and Hellenistic World: Origins of philosophy, science, and psychology

### 2.1 *When does the history of psychology begin?*

We begin the history of psychology with the Greeks of ancient Greece. Why? Because psychology as we know it is a product of Western civilization, and because Western civilization started with the Greeks. We also begin there to demonstrate that many of the issues of psychology familiar to us today, such as monism or dualism, mind or body, elements or wholes, being or becoming, and many others, had their origin in Greek thought. But the Greeks had a past too. They were influenced by other cultures, the Egyptians, the Persians, the Chaldeans, and the Phoenicians. However, one has to start somewhere, and reviewing the effects of these cultures on the culture of ancient Greece is beyond the scope of this book.

I will divide the history of Greek and Hellenistic thought into a series of succeeding periods. What makes this part of our history move from one period to another is a series of what Kuhn calls "paradigm shifts" (1971), and what Cahil (1998) calls the "hinges" of history. These historical shifts or hinges are a series of responses by successively new worldviews to preceding older worldviews. Thus, in the search for something abiding, in search for something that one can count on, one influential Greek thinker might construct a worldview that captures the allegiance of a whole generation. But succeeding generations lose faith in that worldview and construct new ones.

At the same time, the *questions* that the old worldview raises do not go away. So, we see succeeding generations also struggle with them, but they give a different answer to them. Consequently, in the history covered in this chapter we can observe both historical discontinuity (the diachronicity of succeeding periods) and continuity (the presence of abiding questions). All this is to say that in my view the history of psychology shows evidence of both thought traditions (typicality) and historical periods (periodicity).

## 2.2 *Greek thought prior to 600 BC*

I start this survey with a review of the thought world of Greeks who lived prior to 600 BC. The thought world of these Greeks was the fundamental source of inspiration for the Greeks who lived after 600 BC, for the so-called pre-Socratic philosophers (Armstrong, 1983, p. 1). In one way or another, all of these pre-Socratic thinkers formed their own worldview *in response to* these prior mythical sources of inspiration. It is generally accepted that there are two fundamentally different pre-Socratic schools of thought. There is the Ionian school, which was located in Miletus in Asia Minor. This tradition finds its inspiration in the writings of a mythical figure we know as "Hesiod." Then there is the Italian school, also called the Pythagoreans and the Eleatics. This school was located in Southern Italy and found its inspiration in the equally mythical figure of Orpheus. This source of pre-Socratic inspiration is called the Orphic tradition. I will deal with the influence of the Orphic tradition when I discuss the Pythagoreans and begin with a discussion of the Ionian or Milesian side of pre-Socratic Greek thought. However, it is important to reiterate that these two sources of inspiration were fundamentally different from one another; they also existed alongside one another for a long time. Not until the time of Plato did these two traditions in Greek thought amalgamate into one worldview.

The essence of the myths that inspired pre-Socratics of the Ionian school are found in the two books written by Homer: the *Iliad* and the *Odyssey*. What specifically interests us here is the description Homer gives of the way the gods related to the world and to human beings.

Like so many other cultures of that time, the Greeks prior to 600 BC tried to make sense of the world they experienced and inhabited in terms of something outside of that world. The being and becoming of our world, they said, is the result of the actions of the gods outside our world. What the gods do directly governs how our world functions. Our world depends, they maintained, on the actions of these gods. These gods gave us *psyche*, our life breath, *thymos*, that is, our (e)motion, and our *nous*, or our ability to think. Our being, our feeling, and our thinking are totally determined by the actions of these gods.

Unfortunately, these gods were notoriously fickle, capricious, unpredictable, and totally untrustworthy. Human beings could not count on them. These gods could take your psyche away, disturb your emotions, or cloud your thinking for no good reason at all. That was because they were not in control of their own actions. They, and therefore we, said the Greeks, are governed by *ananke*, by blind fate. Thus they saw life as tragic. Ultimately, life made no sense at all to them.

Even though these gods were seen as fickle in their actions and not in control of themselves, it was believed that they were in touch with reality. They knew what was going on. The gods know everything, these Greeks held, that human beings don't. Divine thought is real knowledge; it can penetrate to the essence of life. Human thought, because it is clouded by the gods, produces no knowledge, only *doxa* – mere opinions – because our thought is dependent on appearances, tied to sense perceptions, or to what we can hear, see, touch, and smell. The gods know everything, these Greek thinkers said; human beings know nothing. Playthings of the gods and ignorant are we. The mood of that period was one of resignation (Kirk & Raven, 1963, p. 8 – 24; Runner, 1958).

### 2.3 *Mythology, cosmology, cosmogony*

Greek thinkers who came after 600 BC but before Socrates and Plato reacted strongly against this worldview. They lost faith in the gods; they no longer believed in their existence. All there is, they said, is the world we experience and inhabit, the cosmos. There are no gods; therefore, we must make sense of the world, of the cosmos in terms of itself.

The Greeks prior to 600 BC were mythologizing thinkers. They explained the being and becoming of the things of the world in terms of a myth, in terms of the actions of the gods outside the world. The pre-Socratic Greeks were cosmologists as well as cosmogonists. They tried to make sense of the being of the things in the cosmos in terms of the being of other things in the cosmos. Cosmogony is a variant of cosmology. Cosmogony explains the becoming of things in the cosmos as (re)combinations or transformations of other things in the cosmos.

#### 2.3.1 *Pre-Socratics and four substances: Water, air, dirt, fire*

These pre-Socratic cosmologists and cosmogonists ultimately arrived, with Empedocles, at a worldview that held that the world is made up of four "stuffs": fire, air, water, and dirt (or atoms). Everything we experience consists of a combination of these stuffs. The stuffs can also be explained in terms of each other via a process of rarefication and coagulation: water is rarified dirt, air is rarified water, and fire rarified air. Conversely, air is coagulated fire, etc.

These stuffs were seen as the *physis* or the *nature* of the things we experience; hence these cosmologists and cosmogonists were naturalists as opposed to super-naturalists. These stuffs were called "substances," i.e., things that "stand underneath," support, and are basic to other things.

Incidentally, the word "hypothesis" also means substance, or "that which is placed (thesis), underneath (hypo)." These substances were believed to be the "*prima causa*" (Latin) or the first causes of everything that exists. The Greek word for this is *arche* (ἀρχή). Knowledge of these *archai* (plural of *arche)* was deemed to be essential for making sense of the world. They are like the subway of a city, a simplified, essential version of the world we experience. Furthermore, unlike the gods, these substances were believed to be reliable, unchangeable solid stuffs that people could count on (Kok, 1998, p. 31–38).

Pre-Socratic Greeks did not come up with a worldview that contained these four basic substances all at once; it took a while to discover them. The process of discovery is, I think, more interesting for the history of psychology than the worldview that finally emerged.

In trying to understand the composition of things, as well as the way things come into being and decompose, the pre-Socratic Greeks had a model in the thoughts of Hesiod (Kirk & Raven, p. 24–36). The *Theogony* of Hesiod was particularly instructive. There Hesiod spoke about the generation of the heavens and the earth by the gods, but he went much farther than that. He also had much to say about the generation of the gods. That is in fact what *theogony* means. These gods of early Greek thought, whom Homer wrote about, with their petty jealousies and unreasonable, unpredictable bouts of anger, acted more like the worst of human beings than like gods. Thus the pre-Socratic Greeks, coming after Hesiod and Homer, had ample ground for rejecting this description of the divine on that account. But the most objectionable feature of this mythical view of divinity for the pre-Socratics was, I believe, that in it the gods *also* come into being. If the gods, who were seen as the *origin* of the cosmos, also come to be and ceased to be, then there is neither beginning nor end to anything. Via this mythical formulation one is driven to ask what it was that caused the gods to come into being; a cause that, in turn, must have had its origin in yet another cause. Thus this mythical formulation confronted early Greek thought with the problem of infinite regression. Furthermore, if these gods who were seen to be the origin of the knowable world could be replaced by other, quite different, gods, then the world could be anything, and nothing definitive could be said about it. Thus, Hesiod's theogony also confronted the Greeks with the potentially *indefinite* character of the world's origin and with the problem of how something definite, like the cosmos, could come out of something indefinite.

This is the reason, I believe, why pre-Socratic Greeks felt constrained to posit something eternally abiding and (more or less) definite as a starting point in their thinking about the world. They called this something the *arche*, the beginning, or the origin of everything. They viewed this *arche* cosmologically as the basic stuff of which the knowable cosmos was composed, or cosmogonically as the cause of the enfolding of the things in the cosmos. With this formulation a new, non-mythologizing, or even *anti*-mythologizing way of thinking about the world had emerged.

Thales is believed to have been the first of the pre-Socratics to think about the world in this way. Noting that everything that exists changes into something else, he said that everything is (composed of) water, because water is both definite and indefinite. It is both abiding stuff and it can change into air or ice, etc. Thus it was an ideal candidate for the *arche* of the world (Kirk & Raven, Ch. 2). But right away he presented the pre-Socratics with another problem: How can something (more or less) definite turn into something else that is also (more or less) definite? This is the problem that Anaximander tackled (Kirk & Raven, Ch. 3). For him, making water the *arche* was far too definite. So he asked: If everything *is* water, how can it change into something else? No, he said, the basic stuff is "*apeiron*," literally "void," or "indefinite," nothing. Nothing can turn into something that is anything.

But his formulation in turn raised a problem for Parmenides of Elea (Kirk & Raven, Ch. 10), who argued that anything that *is* cannot be *no* thing. So, he denied the existence of the void, or of nothingness and taught that only *that which is* (being) exists. Furthermore, he argued, since only being exists, change is an illusion, because if something *is*, it can only be what it is; it cannot become what it is *not*. He also stated that that which is, or "being," must necessarily be "One," that is, a seamless unity, since without change unity cannot possibly change into plurality. One final implication of his view was that if something can be thought, it must necessarily exist as something since it is impossible to think of nothing if nothing does not exist.

By now the reader might think that all this is pure intellectual sophistry and dismiss Parmenides' views out of hand. One might be justified in doing so, except for the fact that Parmenides raised issues that have preoccupied thinkers throughout the history of philosophy and psychology and that are with us to this day. In fact, these issues are for a large part the stuff that typicality is made up of. As I hope to show throughout this book, Parmenides initiated a number of thought traditions that are evident throughout the history of psychology; they form the theoretical core of several research traditions today. For example, when Parmenides asked the question, what is the relation between being and nonbeing or nothingness, he raised a problem that contemporary Existentialists like Heidegger and Sartre struggled to solve throughout their lives. Another example is the question about the relation between being and change. This question forms one of the central issues between, for instance, Titchener's structuralism and William James' functionalism. Answers to this question also differentiated European psychology from American psychology during the late nineteenth and early twentieth century. In addition, different answers given to the question first raised by Parmenides as to the relation between the one and the many, which deals with the problem of whether the origin of the universe is a unity or a plurality, distinguished thinkers from one another throughout the history of philosophy and psychology. Some, for example, unlikely bedfellows though they be as Carl Jung and the behaviorist Watson, stated that the origin of being is one. They are both *monists*. Others, like Descartes and Freud, argued that the origin of being is a plurality. They thought *dualistically.* Finally, Parmenides' assertion that thought equals being is clearly at the heart of the debate between realism and nominalism, which will be discussed in the next chapter.

This is not the place to elaborate on these issues. I merely mention them to demonstrate that many of the typical intellectual puzzles that face our discipline today find their origin in the thoughts of the pre-Socratics, and particularly in the views of Parmenides.

They also originated in the views of Heraclitus (Kirk & Raven, 1963, Ch. 6). In many ways Heraclitus was the antipode of Parmenides. He agreed with Parmenides that being is one, and was therefore a monist. But he disagreed with Parmenides' claim that change is an illusion. Heraclius was convinced that change was the central characteristic of being. In stressing the unchanging nature of being Parmenides was somewhat of an exception among the pre-Socratics. Most of them were cosmogonists rather than cosmologists. Noting that many of his contemporaries were trying to account for change – or how one thing becomes another – Heraclitus wondered whether we should not call change the basic stuff of the world. One thing, he felt, that we can count on is that everything is in the process of becoming, that nothing ever seems to stay the same. Becoming or change does not need an explanation, but being, or things-staying-the-same, does. Everything flows, he said (Greek: Πάντα ῥεῖ). Probably the best known of his quotations reads, "You can never step in the same river twice." Because Heraclitus saw change as basic to the world, he chose fire as a metaphor for the basic stuff, since change is most observable in fire.

Heraclitus is often said to be obscure. He is frequently misunderstood. But his worldview is extremely interesting and, like Parmenides, he has had a considerable influence on the history of philosophy and psychology. For these reasons I am going to give a more detailed description of his worldview. In essence Heraclitus taught that change is the law of all being. There is no rest in the universe. One of his quotations reads: "War is the father of everything." The world consists of a clashes of opposites, evil is opposed to good, hot is opposed to cold, wet is opposed to dry, etc. The only unity or harmony that exists is a harmony of conflict and contrast. The harmony of the world is a *contradictory* harmony. Everything that is exists in tension with its opposite. The image he used of this perpetual tension was the image of the bow and the lyre.

This notion of contradictory harmony also governed his worldview, specifically how the world comes into being ever anew. According to Heraclitus the primary *arche* of the world is fire. Fire *inverts,* or changes itself into sea (water), which as secondary *arche* then *diverts,* or separates into the heavens (air) on the one hand and the earth (dirt) on the other. However, simultaneously, as this cosmogonic process visible to our eyes is going on, an opposite invisible process also occurs: Sky and earth unite to become sea and sea converts itself to become fire.

The reason why Heraclitus might have come with such a complicated scheme needs some explanation at this point. The most common description of the pre-Socratics in the history texts is that they were the first philosophers to rid themselves of the vestiges of mythical religion in their explication of the world. They are painted as naturalists as opposed to supernaturalists. They are seen as the first to forge scientific explanations of the world, an activity with which we are all so familiar today. There is some validity to this picture of the pre-Socratics. However, this description of these ancient thinkers ignores the fact that in forging their own worldview they nevertheless had to come to terms with the mythical worldview of their forefathers and mothers.

Thus, we find Anaximander objecting to Thales that by calling the basic stuff water he made the origin of the world much too definite. This led Anaximander to assert that the world's origin was essentially *in*definite, *apeiron.* I see this as an attempt by Anaximander to honor the partial validity of the existing mythical worldview in which the gods as origin of the cosmos had indefiniteness as their essential characteristic. "OK," he might have said, "let's place the *arche* inside the cosmos rather than outside. But let's not change the *nature* of this *arche.*" Living at a time when mythical thinking was the tradition, he might have considered Thales' conception too revolutionary or too dangerous a departure from existing religion. In the same way, I see Heraclitus attempting to account for the notion of infinite regression inherent in the existing mythical worldview of that time by including it in his own world scheme, in which infinite *regression* and infinite *progression* are contradictorily both possible in the cosmos.

It would have been unsatisfactory for a deep thinker like Heraclitus to place these contradictory themes side by side in his worldview as a house divided against itself and to let it go at that. Certainly after Parmenides the question of the essential unity and harmony of the world had to be dealt with. Heraclitus was the first to posit a world Logos as the guarantee of that unity or harmony. The Greek word *logos* (λόγος) is hard to translate. It can mean reckoning, proportion of a mixture, relation, argument, reason, or even story. For Heraclitus, Logos was the universal proportion of the mixture of the world. He calls it the divine and ever-living Fire, which is the *arche* of the world. He saw this Logos as the cause of order, of proportion, and of rationality in a continually changing universe. This world Logos was said to provide the only harmony that is possible in a world full of change and strife between opposites. This harmony is the delicate balancing tension that exists between opposing world forces and directions.

We still need to deal with the views of Empedocles, Democritus, and Anaxagoras (Kirk & Raven, p. 319) to make the picture of the *Ionian* pre-Socratics complete. After that a description of the Italian pre-Socratics, specifically of the Pythagoreans, is in order to close off this period of Greek history.

As we saw already, Empedocles posited four substances as the origin of the cosmos (Kirk and Raven, Ch. 14). The things of the world we experience, he held, are composed of these four stuffs in differing proportions. Thus, by this time the Greeks had the following cosmology: water, air, dirt, and fire are substances, they lie underneath or behind the world we experience and they explain it. In the midst of all the changes we experience these are the things we can rely on because they have *being*, they remain the same.

## 2.3.2 *Connection between Empedocles and the theories of Hippocrates and Galen*

Next, I must first deal with the connection between Empedocles, Hippocrates, and Galen. This brief account is almost an aside to the main pre-Socratic story, but it is important for the history of psychology in general and for the history of personality theory in particular.

Hippocrates (460 BC) was a physician who came up with a scheme for the human body that was similar to Empedocles' worldview with its four substances. The body, said Hippocrates, contains four body fluids or *humors*: blood (Latin: *sanguis*), yellow bile (Greek: χόλος), phlegm (Greek: φλέγμα: puss: slime), and black bile (Greek: μέλᾶν χόλος). He claimed that sickness is due to an overabundance of one humor over the others. This is the idea, so prominent in Greek thought, that balance or proportion is the gateway to health.

Galen (AD 130), who lived 600 years later, like Hippocrates, was a physician. He lived during the time of Hellenistic philosophy. He turned the four humors theory of Hippocrates into a theory of four temperaments, thus, into something resembling what we would call a personality theory. Using the notion of these four humors, he came up with four personality types. These were: a) too much black bile: *melan cholic*: sad, depressed, and anxious; b) too much yellow bile: *choleric*: quick to act, angry, and assertive; c) too much blood: *sanguine*: warm hearted, volatile, optimistic, and easygoing; and d) too much phlegm: *phlegmatic*: slow to act, lethargic, and calm. This tradition of dividing people's personalities into four types has a long history. Today, for instance, it forms the theoretical centerpiece of Eysenck's four-dimensional theory of personality (Engler, 2003, pp. 326–328).

### 2.3.3 *Democritus, Leucippus, and Anaxagoras: The last of the Ionian pre-Socratics*

I now return to Empedocles. In addition to positing that the world consists of things that contain the four stuffs, he also taught that there are two opposing forces in the world, love and hate, that are responsible for composing and decomposing the things we experience. Love joins the four substances to one another to form things. Hate separates the stuffs from one another to take things apart. With the introduction of these forces a new *arche* is introduced into the pre-Socratic worldview. Not that the Greeks were unaware of the influence of some kind of moving or motivating forming principle that somehow gave the cosmos the shape and constitution that it had. There is repeated talk in early Greek literature about *Ananke, Moire, Dike,* and *Tyche* and their influence on the gods, on people, and on the cosmos. But these forces were usually considered divine and in any case existing *outside* the cosmos while influencing affairs inside the cosmos. What is new is that for the first time these forces are seen to belong to the cosmos itself.

At the same time, Empedocles' formulation did raise the question of whether the forces or the stuffs were to be taken as the origin of the world. So, the question became: Which is the *arche* of which? If the forces were to be taken as the primary *arche*, what then would be the status of the four substances? Would they for the first time become *the material* upon which the forces of Love and Hate could operate in order to form the things of the world and take them apart? It would seem that in Empedocles' scheme these substances were no longer seen as the origin of the cosmos but rather as the matter needed by the forces as *arche* to form the cosmos. Perhaps here we have the beginning of the later, more prominent motif of hylomorphism, or the form-matter motif in Greek philosophy.

The four substances that Empedocles designated as primary causes of things in the cosmos had also traditionally been seen as qualitatively different from one another, even though via a process of rarefication and coagulation they could be seen to turn into one another. In this regard the problem had always been how one definite stuff could metamorphose itself into another definite stuff or even how these stuffs could attach themselves to one another. The Greeks called this the problem of *metabasis eis allo genos*, i.e., of "going over into another kind." This is not an easy problem to solve. A modern equivalent of this problem, for instance, is how to convert mental phenomena into physical phenomena and vice versa. To solve this problem, Empedocles postulated the forces Love and Hate to join and to separate these substances from one another. He held that similar things join to one another through love, while opposites repel through hate (Kirk & Raven, 1963, Ch. 14).

However, all this resulted in an additional problem. The problem entailed in this formulation is that the *arche* necessarily includes a plurality of six components: the two forces and the four substances. This, after Parmenides, who stressed the unity of the *arche*, was also unacceptable to the pre-Socratics.

For Democritus (Kirk & Raven, Ch. 17) specifically, and his soul mate Leucippus, this was far too much complexity in explaining the being and becoming of the world. Thus, they tried to simplify things. They began by positing the void, or nothingness, as the *arche* of the world. This in itself was not revolutionary; it had been done before. But they also realized that nothing can come out of nothing. There has to be something (eternally abiding) for change to occur. Something had to exist *in* the void. Thus, they designated the basic stuff of the world as something-in-nothingness, which is why they are frequently called "elementarists" or "atomists." I will follow this practice, even though it is doubtful that they themselves used the term "atom." All they probably meant by elements or atoms was "entities that *are*, literally *beings*, or bits of beings." Everything that exists, they held, is a combination of these atoms, which themselves, because they are beings, always were and never change. This led them to conclude that, at bottom, the world does not change. The changes in things that we experience are merely re-combinations of the same old atoms.

Even so, Democritus and Leucippus still had to account for the fact that these atoms clustered together to form more complex things. They also had to explain why in some stuffs like air the connection between the atoms was more tenuous than for stuffs like dirt and rocks that appear to be more solid. In dirt, so to speak, there is less nothingness between beings than in air. Democritus and Leucippus were loath to posit a force outside the atoms to connect and to separate the atoms as Empedocles had done. The attracting and repelling somehow had to be done by the atoms themselves. To give the atoms this ability, they endowed them with motion. These atoms were said to be *in motion*, perpetually flying through nothingness at breakneck speed and to collide with other atoms to form the things of the world. To explain the difference between air and dirt, or as we might say gasses and solids, Democritus and Leucippus postulated a difference of shape between the atoms. Atoms that tended to form dirt when they collided were said to be irregular in shape. They also had hooks on them that made them stick together. Atoms that formed air had a smoother surface and were more spherical in shape, which made them less likely to cluster together with other atoms.

But before any of these atoms were able to form clusters of atoms, or things, they first had to come in contact with one another. Inevitably the question would have arisen among the pre-Socratics what now directed these atoms toward one another. To posit outside directing forces as Empedocles had done was unthinkable for Democritus and Leucippus. But they still had to answer the question. They rescued themselves from this dilemma by postulating the void as the *arche* of the world. Traditionally the void, or *apeiron*, not only denoted nothingness but also had as its essential characteristic indefiniteness, unpredictability, the absence of order, or we would say, *at randomness*. This characteristic of the void through which the atoms were said to fly suited Democritus and Leucippus just fine. There is no direction to the movements of the atoms, they said. Their motion is governed by chance. Which atom will collide with which other atom is completely unpredictable. It just happens.

Lastly, I need to say a few words about Anaxagoras (Kirk & Raven, Ch. 15). Even though he wrote mainly in reaction to Empedocles, he also in part provides us with an alternative to the atomism of Democritus and Leucippus. Essentially for the first time in Greek thought, Anaxagoras explicitly endowed the world with an active, creative, forming *intellect*. This world mind mostly has the characteristics of Empedocles' forces of love and hate, but has the advantage of being one forming principle rather than two. Moreover, over against the atomism of Democritus and Leucippus, Anaxagoras asserted that there is order in the being and becoming of the world. The world mind directs the material or stuff of this world to become the things of this world and it does this thinkingly, consciously, and intelligently. Here, perhaps for the first time in Greek thought, the distinction between mind and matter enters the worldview of the pre-Socratic Greeks, not just that human beings have a mind, but that the world has one too. The implication of this formulation is that the world mind and the human mind are made up of the same intellectual "stuff." Thus, it becomes understandable how the Pythagoreans could come to believe that via our thinking we have access to the order of the world. But this is running ahead of the story.

### 2.3.4 *The Pythagoreans*

Pythagoras (Kirk & Raven, Ch. 7; Kok, 1998, p. 32) was an early Greek thinker who lived not much later than Thales and certainly before Heraclitus. It is often difficult to distinguish what Pythagoras himself taught as opposed to his followers over the centuries. Thus it is better to speak of the Pythagoreans (Armstrong, 1983, p. 5–8). But a number of features of Pythagoreanism can be clearly stated. First of all they stood in the Orphic mythologizing tradition rather than in the tradition of Hesiod and Homer as is the case with the Ionian pre-Socratics.

From the outset Orphism focused on human beings rather than on the cosmos and held that people consist of two parts: a divine immortal soul and a mortal earthly body that was said to imprison the divine immortal soul during a person's lifetime. The Orphics also believed in the transmigration of the soul. That is, they taught that at death one's soul is reincarnated into another body, either that of an animal or of another human being. Thus, the divine soul was destined to an inevitable ongoing cycle of reincarnations or embodiments with no end in sight. The ideal of the Orphics was for the divine soul to escape embodiment of any kind and in that way to join the company of the immortal gods. The only possible way to accomplish this during one's lifetime was to submit to frequent purification rites and to live an ascetic life, in particular to abstain from eating meat. One might say that the Orphics were addicted to abstinence, that they favored the disembodiment of the soul, and that they were otherworldly in their conception of reality.

On all these points, the Pythagoreans followed them almost verbatim. They did, however, add something new that would prove to be very influential in later Greek thought. To the Orphic picture of the human soul as divine, they added that what made it divine was the human intellect, which they defined as the "ability to know eternal unchanging truth of being." What they considered divine and immortal, therefore, was the soul as mind. Furthermore, the "eternal, unchanging truth of being" referred to the *proportion* or the essential *harmony* of being. They found the model for this harmony in music. They had discovered that *musical* harmony is possible only because of the existence of fixed numerical proportions between the notes of the musical scale. Thus, ultimately they viewed this harmony of being as *mathematical* in nature.

The Pythagoreans believed that what these substances of the natural world – that the Ionian pre-Socratics talk about – have in common is that they can all be observed by our senses, via sense perception, however imperfectly we do that. But what is really *real* about these stuffs is that they can all be counted, computed, and (re)combined into (new) geometrical figures. So, underneath this world of sense perception lies another more substantial world, the world of numbers, of mathematics. And these mathematical processes cannot be accessed by sense perception. In mathematics there is nothing to see, nothing to touch; mathematics can only be accessed by intuitive reason. And this intuited world is the real, rational world; it is the world we can count on.

The Pythagoreans introduced a new form of knowing; not only knowing via sense perception but also knowing via intuitive reasoning. Furthermore, since there had to be something that does the knowing, they came up with a split within the psyche, the soul. In the tradition of Homer, everything has a psyche or soul, i.e., "breath of life," but only human beings have, said the Pythagoreans, a *nous/psyche*, i.e., a reasoning soul. And this *nous* is reliable because it has access to the real world. It is also immortal; it continues to exist when the breath of life is taken away from our bodies.

The Pythagoreans influenced Plato heavily with their distinction between the world of *physis*/nature and the world of *nous*/mathematical reason, and with their distinction between the immortal human soul and the mortal human body.

### 2.4 *The Sophists and Socrates*

The Sophists reacted against the cosmological and cosmogonic views of the world held by the Ionian and Pythagorean pre-Socratics. They viewed the search for universal substances and powers as futile. They either denied that these substances exist – or if they did exist – they held that human beings are unable to know them, since they lie under or behind the things we experience via sense perception.

The Sophists are known for the claim that "man is the measure of all things." What does this mean? Well, Democritus had said that because the substances, or atoms exist, we can have knowledge of them. Atoms out there produce *eidola* that imprint themselves on our minds so that we have a perfect copy of things out there. We can think them because they exist. The Sophists said, "No, we *believe* that these things exist because we think them." We come to rely on these substances on the basis of our knowledge. However, the Sophists continued, this presents a problem. All our knowledge comes from sense perception, and our sensory knowledge is imperfect because it is relative. It is *culturally* relative. What people in one culture see as the basic stuff differs from what people in another culture see. It is also *individually* relative. What one person sees differs from what another sees. Finally, our knowledge is also *perceptually* relative. Perception is always situated, from one place an object looks different than from another place.

So, the Sophists held that universal, unchanging substances do not exist, or if they do, we cannot access them. All we know is the ever-changing world of sense perception. That is the world we experience and live in. Since there is nothing abiding, nothing universal, i.e., nothing that is true for all times and all places, some of them argued, there are no values to live up to (relativism and cynicism). The only thing that made sense to them was to live in the here-and-now, to maximize pleasure, and to keep pain at a minimum (hedonism).

However, it would be a mistake, I think, to disqualify all Sophistic thought as relativistic. For one thing, not all Sophists were relativists or cynics. But, more importantly, a paradigm shift occurred between the pre-Socratics, and the Sophists that could be viewed as a positive shift. A new period began in the history of philosophy and psychology. The focus of the Sophists was not on the nature of the world but on the practice of human life in the Greek *polis* or city-state. In the same way, their interest was not in the generation of the world but in the generation of culture as the domain of human action. Coupled with that was the question of how individual human beings were to act given the fact that universal world principles were either nonexistent or unknowable via the human intellect. The focus of the Sophists was on culture *formation* with the aim of making individual human beings competent in forming culture by training them in the art of rhetoric.

Moreover, truth for them was not to be obtained by abstracting oneself from everyday life, as the Pythagoreans had taught. Rather, truth was to be found in the *practice* of everyday living. Truth, in the sense of knowledge necessary for one to be able to act, could be gotten not via thinking but by doing. Sophist philosophy is anti-intellectualistic. Hence the Sophists branded all attempts to construct cosmologies and cosmogonies via thinking as mere *speculation*. With this mindset came a much greater appreciation for nonintellectual ways of knowing as well. For example, they had a great deal of interest in the fine arts, in literature, and in the word play of rhetoric in particular. They were concerned with the most effective *way in which* truth was spoken. For them the medium of the message was at least as important as the intellectual message itself. Today we would recognize this approach to life as postmodernism and anti-foundationalism. However, to equate the two would deny that Sophism appeared much earlier in the history of philosophy and psychology. Thus, it would saddle Sophistic thought with a load of conceptual baggage it simply did not have.

With the Sophists we have entered the third period of Greek thought. The first is the period of mythologizing thought. The second is that of the pre-Socratic cosmologies and cosmogonies. What distinguishes these two periods from the third is that they were universalistic in character. They were preoccupied with the abiding structure of the being and becoming of the world. The third period focused on the place of individual human beings in that world. It should be noticed that this shift in emphasis was preceded by a loss of faith in the pre-Socratics' preoccupation with cosmologies and cosmogonies. New periods in history do not seem to come about unless there is a strong desire to do things differently or to view things differently.

This brings us to the views of Socrates. Even though he reacted against the Sophists he belonged to this period in the history of Greek thought in that he, like the Sophists, was concerned with the question of how individual human beings were to act in the world.

Socrates reacted strongly against what he perceived to be the relativistic, skeptic, nihilistic, and hedonistic worldview of the Sophists. He did it by positing another way of knowing next to sense perception, namely rational discourse or dialogue, which was a discussion that exercised the mind/*nous* of human beings to search for truth. In this he was not original of course. The Pythagoreans had essentially done the same. But Socrates placed this dialogue in the service of the practice of living in the *polis*. In this he proved himself to be a Sophist rather than an otherworldly-minded Pythagorean. This dialogical search for truth occupied the center of his thinking throughout his life. He left it to his pupil Plato to work out the cosmic implications of his approach to living and thinking. Plato did this by positing another, purely rational world, a world accessible by reason, next to, behind, or over the everyday natural world of sense perception.

Most pre-Socratics prior to Sophism believed in the primary existence of universals. They saw these universal stuffs or powers as the cause of all being and change. They either denied the existence of individuals or believed that their existence was secondarily dependent on universals. The Sophists reversed that trend. In essence the Sophists held that only individuals (whether human individuals or other creatures as concrete particulars) exist. Individuals have primary existence. Universals have secondary existence in the sense that they are the result of individuals. The *arche* of everything is individual; universals are formed by individuals. They are the product of individuals thinking, speaking, and doing things together. Universals reside only in concepts. This is conceptualism. When later on, William of Ockham added that universals are real in name only, we get nominalism. The Sophist equated universality with vagueness. Since everyone's worldview is individually relative, they held, no two individuals can ever think the same. Truth is individual and since there is no universal truth, i.e., truth that holds for all individuals, truth cannot really be communicated. Thus, when two or more individuals speak together, the product of their communication is at best a vague compromise of two or more individual truths.

Over against the Sophists, Socrates argued that by communicating with one another individual human beings can together come to discover one universal truth, and he proceeded to demonstrate how this was done by means of rational discourse or dialogue. Socratic dialogue was a question-and-answer process in which the discussion partners prodded each other constantly to define more clearly what they were saying by thinking about what they meant. The end result of this process proved to be that the discussion partners came to agree on one definition of the topic under discussion. In this way Socrates believed that knowledge of universal truth, or knowledge of one-truth-fits-all, could be obtained. It seems to me that the Sophists and Socrates here reenacted the dynamic of Greek thought throughout the centuries, i.e., the fluctuation between indefiniteness and definiteness, or between "apeiron" and "being," with the Sophists denying and Socrates affirming the primacy of being. It was most important for Socrates to reassert his belief in universal truth since he believed that knowledge of this truth was the indispensable prerequisite for personal piety. He and the Sophists agreed on one thing without reservation. Both believed that the most important duty of Greek citizens was to contribute to the welfare of the *polis* or city state in which they resided. The practice of this duty was what they referred to as "virtue" or "personal piety." So, in Socrates' mind there was an intimate connection between knowledge and virtue. In fact, Socrates equated knowledge of universal truth *with* piety. He believed that knowledge of the truth necessarily leads individuals to right action in the same way that ignorance of the truth leads them to commit wickedness. This is sometimes known as the "philosopher's virtue."

It should be noted in passing that, since Socrates never wrote anything, all we have is Plato's description of Socrates. Thus, the real Socrates may have been different from the Platonic Socrates. But of the latter it may be said that he placed a great deal of emphasis on the value of thinking for coming to know the truth. It is clear even from Plato's description of Socrates that by "knowledge" Socrates meant something holistic rather than abstract. Nevertheless, Socrates also clearly believed that individuals can only come to know the truth via a process of making ever finer logical distinctions, thus, via a process of abstract thinking. So, after the Sophists' rejection of intellectualization, and after their emphasis on the value of nonintellectual knowledge, Socrates reverts Greek thought back again to the Pythagorean conviction that intuitive reasoning is the royal route to knowledge of the truth. This overvaluation of abstract thinking or reason, or *nous,* was to characterize the history of philosophy and psychology for some time to come until the rise of irrationalism, perhaps as late as the nineteenth century (Armstrong, 1983, Ch. 3; Kok, 1998, pp. 38–43).

### 2.5 *Plato: Foreground and background worlds*

Socrates' most famous pupil was Plato. Plato was one of only two great systematizers of Greek thought; the other was Aristotle. I believe that the key to understanding Plato is that he attempted to harmonize the insights of Parmenides about the unity and unchanging character of "being" with the insights of Heraclitus that the cosmos is subject to unceasing change and strife. To understand Plato's view of the world, one must first realize what, historically speaking, he was up against. He had to account for the *ontological, universalistic* tradition of the Ionic and Pythagorean pre-Socratics with their grand cosmological schemes as well as for the *epistemological, individualistic* tradition of the Sophists and Socrates, with its emphasis on individual thought and praxis.

Reviewers of Plato's thought customarily begin with his view of human beings, that is, with his anthropology and with his theory of knowledge, or epistemology. Only then will they proceed to discuss his view of the world, or his cosmology as a derivation of his anthropology and his epistemology. I think we will get a better picture if we proceed in the reverse order. Accordingly, I will first attempt to describe Plato's cosmology, then his anthropology, and finally his epistemology.

Socrates had taught Plato that universal truth can be had via thinking about truth. But he never defined what this truth as the object of thinking consists of, nor what it contains. Plato proceeded to answer that question by asserting the existence of universal "Forms," or "Ideas" (Greek: εἶδος) such as the True, the Beautiful, and the Good as objects of thought and action. These forms in his view have the force that the substances had for the pre-Socratics in that they are the *arche* of the things we experience in the cosmos. But unlike the pre-Socratic stuffs these Forms in Plato's mature conception are said to reside not *in* the cosmos itself but *outside* the cosmos.

With respect to the place of the Forms, Plato's views about the world and human beings in it show a definite development throughout his life. Initially he adhered to objectivism, and believed, with Socrates, that the Forms are objects in the cosmos that determine the way human subjects are to think and live. But later in his life, he turned to realism in which the Forms as norms for living acquire their own way of being and belong to another world outside, beyond or behind, the world we experience. For the sake of brevity, I will restrict myself to describing Plato's realism.

On the surface it sounds as if realism is just another form of mythological thinking. But as we investigate further, we realize that Plato was trying to account for all that happened in Greek thought since the time of mythological thinking. As already mentioned, there are two worlds in Plato's cosmology: the world we daily experience, which I will call the "foreground world," and the world of the Forms, which I will call the "background world" because it lies behind the world we daily experience. In the background world reside the Forms, first of all. These Forms have a number of characteristics. Like the stuffs of the pre-Socratics, they are universal and paradigmatic in nature. They form the universal prototypes for the individual things we experience. They are, so to speak, the catness of the individual cats we experience. They are catness in perfection because they are immaterial. The background world is the world of being as contrasted with the foreground world, which is the world of change. The Forms in it form a unity. They are hierarchically ordered, with the Good being the highest Form. The Good is the *arche* of all the other forms. The Good is the most real, and the other Forms as well as the things in the world we experience are real only to the extent that they *participate* in the Good. This is Plato's response to Parmenides, who held that the world of being has unity, order, and harmony as its basic characteristic. In answer to Socrates' concern about the fact that human beings need to obtain knowledge of universal truth to become virtuous, Plato adds a number of other characteristics to the Forms. This relates to their paradigmatic, or normative nature. The Forms *hold for* human thought and action. Our thoughts must correspond to the Forms to be right thinking and our actions must conform to them to be virtuous. So, Plato's realism was not a repeat of earlier ways of thinking, nor was it a completely new conception, but it answered to the tradition in Greek thought.

Next to the Forms Plato's background world also contains a world soul or *nous*. Sensitive to the criticism that by positing a world of being and a world of change, he had inadvertently created a huge gap in his cosmology Plato constructed a world soul as a mediator between the two worlds. This conception is a composite of a number of thought traditions. It affirms Socrates' belief that the world we experience is directed by good, intelligent powers. It acknowledges the truth of the Pythagorean doctrine that the soul has a place in both the world of being and in the transitory world of becoming. And, finally, in this conception Plato sided with Anaxagoras who taught that the world mind is the cause of motion and of the becoming of the things we experience. All these are influences on Plato's doctrine about the place of the World Soul in the cosmos.

Thus, in *Phaedrus* Plato stated that the Soul is the immortal, ungenerated, self-moving cause of motion and change, or what Aristotle later was to call the *Unmoved Mover* of the world. Later, in his *Timaeus*, Plato added the notion that the Soul is an intelligent, directing power that rules and orders the material universe toward the Good. With this last formulation we have already hit upon the central characteristic in Plato's thought about the foreground world in relation to the World Soul. This is its character of being *material* or *matter*. The foreground world is material in the sense that the Soul needs it for its own ordering, forming, directing, and ruling activity. But it is also material in the sense that it provides *resistance* to the Soul by its opposition to the Soul's being as a resident of the background world.

If the background world is the world of being and eternal truths for Plato, the foreground world is the world of becoming, change, and transitoriness. If the background world is the world of purpose and reason, the foreground world is ruled by irrational brute physical necessity (*ananke*). It is the world of random motion. It is the world of disordered chaos. Apparently, themes from mythologizing Greek thought (Homer: *ananke*, Hesiod: *chaos*), as well as themes from early cosmologizing Greek thought (Anaximander: *apeiron*) die hard in later Greek thought. What we have here is another version of the struggle between the *indefinite* and the *definite* that was so prominent among the Ionian philosophers. What we also have is a devaluation of the foreground world (chaos, randomness, and transitoriness) and an overvaluation of the background world (order, direction, purpose, and immutability) that was so characteristic of Orphic and Pythagorean otherworldly cosmologies.

With these distinctions between the background and the foreground world Plato's view of the relation between good and evil is also given. Good resides at the pinnacle of the background world. Evil resides wholly in the foreground world. Good and evil are here identified by Plato as order versus disorder and as stability versus instability. Politically this marks Plato as a conservative who resisted constructive change.

Plato believed that ultimately order would triumph over disorder in the world because the World Soul as the principle of order in the foreground world was by nature oriented toward the Good in the background world. But he was not as naïve as Socrates who believed that since the World Reason was essentially good, all human beings had to do to have virtue triumph over wickedness was to think about this Reason. Plato realized that the task of establishing order was not accomplished without a struggle. Hence he had the World Soul, as mediator between the two worlds, also participate in the *disorder* and *instability* of the foreground world. He held that there is one part of the Soul, the *Nous* or Reason, that has to attempt to order the irrational part of itself by getting it to *participate* in the Good. Plato is in this manner reckoning with the contingent in the world. One upside to this is that in his anthropology Plato is less otherworldly than, for example, the Pythagoreans.

With the description of Plato's cosmology, a good deal of his anthropology is already given. This is so because, in his understanding of the relation between the universal and the individual, he subscribed to a macro-microcosm formula. For his anthropology, this meant that he saw human beings virtually as miniature copies of the cosmos. Thus, we can find many of the characteristics I described of the cosmos back in his description of human beings. For Plato, human beings too exist in a foreground world and in a background world. Human beings have a soul and a body. The body has all the characteristics of the foreground world and none of the background world. The body is subject to becoming and decay; it consists of matter. It comes into being when we are born and passes out of existence when we die.

According to Plato, human beings have a soul as well. His conception of the human soul is much more complicated than his view of the human body. Plato subscribes to a tripartite soul (Greek: *psyche*). The lowest part is the appetitive soul. As the seat of base human passions, it is closest to the body. Next there is an intermediate part, the emotional soul, in which the "higher" emotions of love, honor, fame, just anger, etc., reside. Lastly, the highest and most important part for Plato is the thinking soul (Greek: νοῦςψυχή). Plato likens his conception of the human soul to a chariot with two horses. The thinking soul is the charioteer that steers the two horses. One of these horses is the emotional soul. It is obedient to and supportive of the thinking soul. However, the other part of the soul, the appetitive soul is not at all in harmony with the thinking soul. It rebels constantly against its leadership. Thus, as with the World Soul, there is strife and conflict in the human soul.

The struggle that is hidden in this disharmony of the human soul is entirely due to the thinking soul's unfortunate connection with the material body. To put it succinctly, by birth the *nous,* which belongs wholly to the background world, is imprisoned by a material body, which belongs entirely to the foreground world. These two parts of human life are not just different from one another; they are *opposed* to one another. The one is not the other in the same way that being is not change, rational is not irrational, and immaterial is not material. Via this formulation Plato paints human life on earth from cradle to grave as a house divided against itself from which there is no redemption until we die.

To support this dualistic conception of human life, Plato adopted the Orphic and Pythagorean doctrine of the transmigration of the human soul (*nous*). According to this doctrine the human *nous,* or intellect, is eternally existent as part of the background world of Forms and is therefore intimately acquainted with these Forms. For whatever reason, this *nous* is implanted into some kind of material body (plant, animal, or human being) when that body is born and it leaves that body to be implanted in yet another body or to be reunited with the immaterial Forms in the background world when the body dies. The *nous* itself cannot die because it is part of the immortal background world of being. Thus, the nous *migrates* from one body to another until after a long series of incarnations it is blissfully (re)united with the Forms in the background world.

While on earth, however, as embodied in a material body, the *nous* has the task of re-calling, or re-thinking, the Forms of which it had perfect knowledge when it was part of the background world before it was born into a material body. Furthermore, how successful the *nous* is in doing this will determine whether it is reincarnated after death into another body or is reunited with the Forms in the background world.

With that we have come to a description of Plato's epistemology. The highest calling of human life after birth for Plato was to recall the knowledge of the Forms in the background world, which knowledge the *nous* had before birth. Being born into a material body clouds the *nous* so that it only has vague recollections of these Forms. But by deliberately focusing one's intellect on these Forms in the background world it is possible for human beings to regain access to these Forms. This process is similar to Socrates' approach to truth. Via a process of dialectical reasoning one *ascends* in one's thinking until one arrives at the highest Form, that of the Good. In this process one realizes that the things of this world as well as the other Forms *participate in* the Good. At the same time this process allows one to escape the limitations of the body and ultimately to return to the background world where one originated. Thus, this intellectual process is redemptive in nature.

Plato's motivation for constructing his epistemology was identical to that of his mentor Socrates. Both wanted to refute the perceived relativism of the Sophists. Plato attempted to refute the Sophists when he granted them the point that all sensory perception is relative to the state of the observer. Thus he had little good to say about sense perception and everyday experience as ways for coming to know the truth. He held that this approach to knowledge is much too much tied to the world of appearances and of change and can at best only give us opinions or beliefs (Greek: δόξᾰ) about reality. But, as we saw, Plato posited another world, a world of reason, a world of Forms, of Ideas – an eternal world of being – which was, for him, the real world, the substantial world (compare C.S. Lewis's book *The Great Divide* and also the second verse of the hymn *Abide with Me*). We access that background world when we *turn away* from sense perception and observation. As long as we are preoccupied with what we sense, with phenomena, appearances, observed things, or concrete here-and-now things, we cannot access that other world. We can only access it when we clear our mind/*nous* to contemplate or to think about that other world. This devaluation of observation and overvaluation of thinking or reasoning, this otherworldliness determines Plato's epistemology and his psychology, such as it was. Plato's view was a major influence on the thinking of the early Middle Ages, in the form of neo-platonism.

In summary, Plato was influenced by the Sophists (the relativity of sense perception), by Heraclitus (nature flows), and by the Pythagoreans (the pre-eminence of the immaterial, mathematical character of the background world, the "real" world).

Plato's notion of the soul is not the psyche of modern-day psychology. It is not the Christian notion of soul. For Plato a human being *is* (a) soul. The soul at its best, as "reason," is capable of contemplating, forming, containing, or contacting the Ideal Forms in the background world. The soul-as-reason, as *nous*, is eternal. It is (re)incarnated – Eastern religion influence – into a body, which "clouds" its intellect, its vision. The body is the individual counterpart of the foreground world or "nature."

Plato's view of the relation between soul and body, reason and nature, foreground and background world is ambivalent. On the one hand the body clouds or inhibits soul-as-reason. On the other hand the body is the "vehicle" of the soul. That is, through the sense perception of the body of concrete objects (as "shadows" of the real things) the soul is reminded of the Forms that it had perfect knowledge of before it was incarnated.

Plato clearly subscribed to a cosmological and anthropological dualism, in the sense that reason and nature, soul/mind and body, background and foreground world were defined as the other's opposite. Finally, Plato also clearly disqualified the latter in favor of the former (Armstrong, Ch. 4, 5 & 6; Kok, pp. 43–51).

## 2.6 *Aristotle: Form and matter*

The other great systematizer of Greek thought was Aristotle. Like all the Greeks before him, he too was preoccupied with the definite and the indefinite. His view of reality was essentially that *the indefinite is perpetually in the process of becoming definite.* There is some truth in saying that Aristotle was Plato's *opposing* follower. Initially Plato's pupil, he later came to a quite different worldview from that of his teacher. Where Plato was other-worldly, Aristotle was this-worldly. Where Plato devalued sensory perception, Aristotle celebrated it. For Plato the body was a tomb for the soul, for Aristotle it was not. Plato had a dichotomy in both his cosmology and in his anthropology. Aristotle had no dichotomy in his cosmology and the relation between mind and matter for him was one of hierarchical composition. Plato was a philosopher, Aristotle a philosopher-scientist. Plato idealized mathematics. Aristotle said mathematics was useless and favored observation and classification as a way to knowledge. These differences with Plato greatly influenced Aristotle's cosmology, anthropology, and epistemology. But for all that he shared with Plato the view that the greatest source of wellbeing for human beings is *theoria,* which is the intellectual contemplation of ultimate being, the Good, or what Aristotle called the *Unmoved Mover.*

Aristotle's greatest difficulty with Plato's worldview was his theory about the Forms. Forms that are cut off from the material world cannot, Aristotle argued, be the cause of the individual concrete things we perceive with our senses. Forms are immanent and not transcendent to the changeable world we perceive. Thus, we must not turn away from this world but look for the unchanging forms as objects of true knowledge *in* this world. In any case, for Aristotle the individual things we experience with our senses are the primary reality with which we must begin our search for forms.

Aristotle's influence on later thinkers, particularly on those engaged in scientific scholarship, has been huge. Throughout his long and fruitful career, he had many worthwhile things to say about almost any scholarly discipline, from physics to ethics and theology. Yet, for all the complexity of his thought he worked with only a handful of basic concepts, such as *substance and accidents, individual and species, form and matter,* and *actuality and potentiality.* With these few basic concepts he constructed his cosmology, his anthropology, his epistemology, and his ethics. In his writings these basic concepts function like the subway of a large city. To understand Aristotle's worldview, therefore, a description of these basic concepts is first of all in order.

Like all other Greeks, Aristotle regarded "substance" as the primary category presupposed in all other categories of being. For him, a substance is a real thing that actually exists. Substances are the definite things we daily experience with our senses. He further defined substances in terms of their *form* and their *matter.* The form of a substance is the intimate, inward structure of a thing. It is the "thingness" of a thing. It is the *species* of a thing, which at the same time guarantees the *individuality* of that thing. Form is what makes this cat a cat, this chair a chair, this tree a tree and not something else. Matter, by contrast is the potential of being this thing here or being any other thing anywhere, which potential is made actual for the time being by the reception of the particular form of this thing. In this manner Aristotle attempted to relate the changeability of our perceived world to the immutability of being. It was also his way of relating the indefinite (matter) to the definite (form). Matter, he stated, is the element of possibility, of changeableness in things. Form is the stable, permanent, knowable, logically definable element in things. In short, *every* thing is actually *some* thing that has the potential of becoming *other* things. Thus, a thing like a piece of wood can be one thing actually, that is, wood, but potentially it can be all sorts of other things like a chair, or part of the floor of a building, or heating fuel.

In his attempt to answer the question how a thing can be fully real and yet be capable of change Aristotle formulated his most important doctrine of *actual* and *potential* being. The theory of form and matter is really a special application of this doctrine, which has wide application in all of Aristotle's writings. This doctrine of actual and potential being stipulates that everything in the world has a tendency to *actualize* its potential. More abstractly, it is the "desire" of matter to become (in) form(ed). Aristotle has a *teleological* view of reality. Everything exists for a purpose or an end (Greek: τέλος). The purpose of a thing is to realize its form as perfectly as possible. This *telos* is immanent to a thing, it is the natural impulse of every being to be as good as one can be. Thus, it is the natural desire of a man to become a good man, of a tree to become a good tree, and of a horse to become the best horse it can be. Aristotle's teleological view of the world implies that there is a hierarchy of perfection and of actualization in the world. Thus, there are beings that are less formed and less actual, in which there is more matter than in other more actualized beings. In this way Aristotle constructs a view of the world in which the "kingdoms" (physical things, plants, animals, and human beings) find their place in relation to one another. This worldview later came to be called the *Scala Naturae,* or "The Great Chain of Being." In this hierarchical picture human beings are placed "higher" than animals because they are more formed, more actual, and have less need for change than plants, for example.

Following this line of reasoning, we come to a being that is perfection itself. Such a being is pure form, complete actuality, in which all potential is realized. This sort of being is pure being; it is an immutable, perfectly simple, indivisible substance that is complete in itself. This being is untouched by time, impassive and unalterable, the purpose of all purposes in the universe, and a perfect being at rest. This being is Aristotle's *Unmoved Mover.* This Unmoved Mover is the ultimate primary cause of all that exists because every thing in the universe is an expression of a desire for the perfection of this Unmoved Mover. By being the end point of all change and actualization in the universe, the Unmoved Mover draws all beings of lesser perfection to itself like a magnet. In this way it becomes clear how this Supreme Being teleologically becomes the *prima causa* of all that exists in Aristotle's worldview. In this connection another interesting aspect of Aristotle's worldview is his assertion that actuality always *precedes* potentiality. By this he means that the cause of a potential being coming into existence is always another being in which this potential has already been actualized. The prime example is that of a father begetting a son. In the same way, because it is a completely actual being, the Unmoved Mover begets all other potential being "below" itself.

With the above description of the basic concepts of Aristotle's thought, his rather complex view of causality is also given. The pre-Socratics had four substances out of which every concrete thing was made: fire, air, water and dirt. According to this worldview, to understand the concrete things of our experience, we only have to know what these things are made of, and in what proportions. These stuffs the pre-Socratics also called the first causes (*prima causa*) of things, i.e., they were what caused concrete things to be. The stuffs were said to give things their "being." For Aristotle this view of causality was far too simplistic. These stuffs, he argued, only explain the *material cause* of things, or what things are made up of. In addition there is also the *efficient cause*, that which makes things change, or move, like the cue moves the billiard ball, or more precisely, like a sculptor chisels a statue out of a block of marble. The efficient cause is an external cause. In addition there is the *formal cause*; this is the essence of things, that which makes one class of things different from another. Last, and by no means least, there is the *final cause*, or what the thing is *for*. This refers to the purpose, or *telos* of a thing. The final cause refers to what things are meant to be. It is an internal cause. According to Aristotle, to understand the being of a thing one must know all of these, not just its material cause.

We now come to what I believe is a characteristic peculiar to all Greek thought, namely that the primary principle of order in the universe is the *intellect*, not the human intellect but the World Intellect. We already met this notion with Heraclitus, who called the harmony of the world *Logos*. This adoration of the intellect is certainly a characteristic of Greek cosmology after Anaxagoras called the cause of order in the universe the *World Mind*. We subsequently find this idea back in views of Socrates and Plato. Not surprisingly, therefore, Aristotle defined the central feature of the Unmoved Mover as *thinking upon thinking*. Thinking stands in opposition to *matter*, which because of its potential nature is devoid of thought.

It follows from this view also that the ultimate *access* human beings can have to this World Order can only be through their intellect. For this reason Aristotle wrote extensively on the proper way for human beings to think. He is generally believed to be the first to formulate syllogistic *logic* as a separate discipline of study. The actual possession of intellect differentiates *human* beings from all other beings in the world. To get at what this means I must first discuss Aristotle's notion of *soul*.

For Aristotle all beings, more specifically all *living* beings, have soul. In stating this he was hardly original. *That* every living being has soul was held by all Greek thinkers, including the mythologizing Greeks. "Soul" or *psyche* was generally understood to be the *breath of life* of a creature. Thus, we are not surprised to hear Aristotle talk about the soul of plants and about the soul of animals in addition to the soul of human beings. But Aristotle gives his own twist to this notion of soul. For him the soul of a being is its form, or that which gives a being its unique characteristics, which allow us to distinguish it from other kinds of beings. Thus, plants have a *nutritive* soul, which is a minimum characteristic for a being that is alive. Animals, in addition have a *sensitive* soul, which gives them the power to desire and the ability to move in order to satisfy that desire. Finally, human beings have a *reasoning* soul, or *nous*. This soul includes the powers of plants to live and of animals to sense but in addition it allows human beings to actualize themselves to the highest form of being, that of pure intellect.

With that Aristotle's anthropology also comes in view, which for the most part is a theory of *mind*. He describes his view of mind extensively in a treatise called *De Anima*. Aristotle's view of a human being is that of an *ensouled* body or of an *embodied* soul. His view of the relation between soul and body is entirely governed by his *hylo-morphism* (Greek: ὑλο = matter, μορφή = form). The soul is the form of the body and the body is the matter of the soul. His view of the human mind hierarchically contains the following elements: the *senses, common sense, imagination and memory, passive mind,* and *active mind.*

Aristotle's view of mind implicitly contains his view of knowledge or his *epistemology.* By means of his view of the senses and of common sense he describes his theory of *sense perception.* Through sense perception we obtain knowledge of the other beings in the world. The Greeks before Aristotle had long debated the question whether we come to know the beings of the world because they are like us, or because they are *un*-like us. Aristotle held that both theories are true. Both are needed for a proper view of sense perception. Initially the senses are unlike the objects of sense perception but they have the potential of becoming like them. Our senses have the capacity to function as matter to the form of the objects in the world. Sense perception occurs when the objects of the world actualize the potential of the senses to become like them. In this manner Aristotle attempts to demonstrate how both the similarity and the dissimilarity of the senses vis-à-vis the perceived objects is essential for the occurrence of sense perception.

However, aware that each of the senses can only perceive one attribute of a perceived object (the eyes can only perceive sights, the ears only sounds, etc.) Aristotle added the faculty of *common sense* as a condition for sense perception to occur. In some rudimentary fashion common sense is able to grasp the object as a whole. This faculty is not so much a separate sense as the sum of all the senses. It refers to the fact that certain attributes can be perceived by more than one sense. For example, the size and the shape of a thing can be perceived by sight as well as touch.

Proceeding with Aristotle's description of the mind, the faculty of *imagination* actualizes the potential of sense perceptions to be *reproduced* and to be stored in our mind as *memories* and *dreams*. These mental pictures are less vivid than thoughts but they are necessary aspects of the knowing process in that they are the raw materials out of which our thoughts are formed. The job of actualizing images into thoughts is done by the *passive mind*. It essentially is the place where we receive the *form* of the remembered, imagined, and sensorily perceived objects in our world. Finally, it is the task of the *active mind* to actualize the forms of the passive mind into concepts with which we think about the beings of our world.

Hopefully it will be clear by now that Aristotle's cosmology, anthropology, psychology, and epistemology are entirely governed by the notion of potentiality and actuality, and by the notion of matter and form. This is no less true for his view of ethics. In discussing Aristotle's ethics several things must be kept in mind. First, for him individuals can only live the good life envisioned by his ethics in community with other individuals. The Greeks generally thought of people as members of a polis. Thus, his view of ethics is at the same time his view of politics. The good life of the individual must serve the good of the community and *vice versa*. Thus, as with the ethical views of Socrates and Plato, Aristotle's ethics is entirely geared to life in the Greek *polis*, even though the validity of his ethical and political prescriptions transcends their application to life in the *polis*. Second, ethics for Aristotle does not deal with how human beings actually live but with how they can and ought to live. This implies the possibility that human beings can also decide not to live according to certain ethical principles. Ethics for him always involves the making of choices, which in turn implies the pursuit of certain goals toward the good life. Thus ethics is inherently *teleological.*

To follow the path of virtue toward the good life human beings can take their cue from beings everywhere in the world. Recall that for Aristotle every thing has a built-in desire to become as good as it can be, or to actualize its full potential. An acorn, for example, strives to actualize its potential by becoming an oak tree. This characteristic of every being in the world Aristotle holds up as a model for human ethics. The path toward eudemonia (εὐδαιμονία, the good life) is for human beings to become the best they can be. Aristotle's notion of virtue, or *arête,* is "to be good at" something. It appears that he does not make a distinction between being *good* (in a moral sense) and being *good at* (in a technical facility sense). Thus, virtue and skill flow into one another in Aristotle's ethics. But being the best one can be (the good life) does not yet tell us what that good life consists of. Here Aristotle prescribes a life lived according to reason, which has at its end-in-view *theoria,* or the intellectual contemplation of the Unmoved Mover. For Aristotle the path toward the good life consists of intellectual virtue and moral virtue. By practicing intellectual virtue, which in essence is *theoria,* human beings can *formulate* rules of conduct for themselves that are according to reason. By practicing moral virtue, human beings can aim at the good life through building character, which one develops by *obeying* the rules of reason.

But what concretely is the shape of the life of virtue that ultimately emerges in Aristotle's ethics? It is that we should live our lives in accordance with the golden mean. Nothing in life should be lived in excess. All things should be enjoyed in moderation. This is essentially the ideal of *proportionality,* or of the right mix, which, as we have seen again and again, has been central to Greek thought from its inception. Apparently, for Aristotle too, old thought traditions die slowly (Armstrong, Ch. 7, 8, 9, and 10; Kok, pp. 51–59).

### 2.7 Hellenistic philosophy: In search of ataraxia

After Aristotle, a major shift occurred in Greek thought. Philosophy became Hellen*istic,* Greek*ish* rather than Greek. What does this mean, and why did it occur? Because of the conquests of Alexander the Great, Greek civilization – incubated and born in the *polis* – was spread all across the then known world. The world became a *cosmo*-polis. But at the same time non-Greek ideas and ways of living flooded *into* the *polis* and caused its Greek citizens to question the exclusivity and validity of their own system of thought. In short, the inhabitants of the *polis* became confused in their minds and troubled in their souls now that the self-evidency of *polis*-living was up for grabs. The main motive of Hellenistic thought, therefore, was the profound sense of rootlessness and a deep need for security, which characterized the inhabitants of the cosmopolitan world that Alexander the Great first, and the Romans later, had created. The overriding question of the Hellenistic period was not, "What is being?" Nor was it the question, "How can we know being?" Rather, the primary question on the minds of all Hellenistic thinkers was, "What must we do for us to regain a sense of security and peace of mind?" During the Hellenistic period ethics received priority over epistemology, and epistemology became more important than cosmology. Thus, the common thread running through all the forms of Hellenistic philosophy is that they are all striving for *ataraxia*, or a kind of resigned search for tranquility.

In the course of their search for *ataraxia*, the Hellenists initially began to question the old verities expounded so magnificently by Plato and Aristotle. The philosophic school of *skepticism*, led by Pyrrho of Elea, started the ball rolling. The Skeptics lost faith in the possibility of absolute knowledge, which had been a common article of faith for such giants of Greek thought as Socrates, Plato, and Aristotle. With all things being as unstable as they are, the Skeptics taught that the only path to attaining *ataraxia* is to suspend one's judgment about everything. Thus, their intent was to question the truthfulness of all philosophical positions and to refuse to commit to any one position so that, in that way, they might find some internal peace. We find this sentiment in the other Hellenistic schools of thought, the Epicureans and the Cynics, as well.

No school of thought has been misrepresented more than the Epicureans when they are described – as they often are – as advocating a hedonistic, wild pleasure-seeking lifestyle. The Epicureans were actually materialists rather than hedonists. In order to find a lifestyle aimed at *ataraxia* they reached back in time before Plato and Aristotle to the atomistic view of reality expounded by Democritus. Epicurus and his followers denied the existence of order in the universe beyond that of the random bumping into each other of atoms or bodies. According to them there are no Forms, no Unmoved Mover, no Mind, no Divine Providence, and no World Soul that orders our world and to which it is the duty of human beings to aspire. In the same way, there is no world beyond our world, no immortality of the soul, and no purpose or reason to the universe. Epicureans taught that all of these beliefs/illusions destroy our sense of *ataraxia* or inner peace because they make us chase after things that we cannot directly experience, make us afraid to die, and worry us about our existence after we die.

Epicurus sought to replace these notions with what he believed was a more rational theory of nature, one that aims at making people self-reliant and at peace with themselves. Such a theory begins with stating that we are nothing but material beings that are affected by other material beings in the world. This notion, which essentially is Democrates' notion of objects emanating *idolae*, gives us an immediate physical experience of the things of the world, which is all we need to live the life of *ataraxia*. So, the knowledge of the world that we need depends on how the things of our world *hit* us. Our experiences in the world either give us pleasure or cause us pain. From this it follows that human beings should live in such a way as to seek out actions and experiences that create pleasure and to minimize actions and experiences that cause pain. The good life for Epicurus, therefore, is not based on reason or thinking but on feeling and emotion.

Far from resulting in a life of wild abandon however, this philosophy led Epicureans to live modest, sober, and even ascetic lives, to eschew riches and fame, and to be satisfied with a diet of bread and water. Their hedonism was never more than a way to attain *ataraxia*. Their reason for the minimalist life they chose to live was simply that it was less disturbing to inner peace to live that way and that was, after all, the aim of their thoughts and actions. Even though their philosophy was definitely anti-intellectualistic, they were not opposed to order. In the end, their lifestyle was much more in line with Aristotle's golden mean, as well as with the much older Greek penchant for proportionality, than with a life of unrestrained pleasure seeking.

A similar emphasis on minimalist living is found in the Hellenistic school of *Cynicism*. Like all other Hellenistic schools of thought, cynicism was more a way of life than a philosophy. It preached the importance of a life "in accordance with nature" and held that all other ways of living were *tuphos*, a Greek term that can be translated by a combination of "wind," "fog," and "fart." In this lifestyle, which the Cynics practiced, the necessities of life are cut down to a bare minimum: bread, water, a roof over your head, and a place to sleep. Only this sort of life, they held, was able to protect people against the unrest of their age. Only it led to *ataraxia*, which for the Cynics was a state of imperturbable tranquility or detachment. What they had in mind was a kind indifference to the amenities of life, which Socrates, who was the chief source of inspiration for the Cynics, had practiced. For Socrates, however, this indifference was no more than an incidental side-effect of his pursuit of truth. For the

Cynics it became the centerpiece of their philosophy. They held that the goal of detachment was not easily attained. It required training (Greek: *ascesis*) and toil.

The Epicureans were quietists. They were quite satisfied to withdraw from conventional Greek life and to practice their minimalist lifestyle among themselves. The Cynics, on the other hand, believed that the ascetic life they aimed for required that they attack all forms of conventionality in their surroundings. Thus, they wandered around as beggars, dressed minimally in austere monk-like habits, preaching free speech and action, deliberately flouting conventions, and behaving like animals. Like dogs, for example, they would defecate in public. For this reason others called them "dog-men," which is what the Greek word *cynic* means. Like Socrates, they were practicing individualists, but then deliberately so, as protection against the unrest in their surroundings and in a much more extreme fashion.

Another school of thought during the Hellenistic period was the philosophy of Stoicism. This school was heavily influenced by Cynicism. The famous Athenian Cynic, Crates, for instance, was the mentor of Zeno, the founder of Stoicism. Unlike his master, however, Zeno was a more professional philosopher. Like the Cynics, he also prescribed a system of ethics for individuals aimed at achieving *ataraxia* and made it central to the Stoic philosophy. But unlike the Cynics he sought to found this system of ethics in a cosmology. Thus, I must first describe the Stoics' view of the world before I can outline their ethics.

In describing Stoicism I shall follow the summary of it given by Chrysippus, who was one of its later disciples, because his summary had the most influence on later schools of thought. The Stoics divided philosophy into three parts. The first was *logic*. This part included rhetoric, grammar, and also their theory of knowledge. The second part they called "*physics*," which also included their anthropology or psychology and their theology. Finally, there was the part they called "*ethics*," the centerpiece of their philosophy.

One cannot describe the Stoics' view of the world well apart from their view of human beings, their view of the mind, and their view of divinity. If the Stoics' view of reality seems rather esoteric to us we should remember that it was a rather eclectic attempt to formulate the best of past Greek thought into one system. And since that tradition was diverse, Stoic philosophy also was a bit of a hodgepodge of ideas. Here is a taste of it. According to the Stoics there exists a universal cosmic principle, which they identify in many different ways. Reminiscent of Heraclitus they call it *Logos*. This is the hot, fiery, intelligent breath of the universe or *pneuma*, also called *aether*, which permeates passive matter and makes it into living stuff. This Logos is constructive. It forms and orders things and turns matter into a living organic universe. They worshipped it as their god. Furthermore, they initially held to a doctrine of *universal conflagration*. They taught that the world is eternally destroyed and recreated in an endless series of cycles. In the path of generation, fire coagulates into air and air into water and water into dirt, after which the process reverses itself and the divine Fire reabsorbs all things into itself. Then for a while Logos is alone with its own thoughts, after which the process of generation and destruction begins again. The only way I can make sense of this Stoic world picture is to view it as their attempt to borrow rather indiscriminately, for their own purposes, elements of earlier philosophies such as parts of the writings of the Ionian pre-Socratics, of Heraclitus, of the Atomists, and of Plato and Aristotle.

Later on the Stoics abandoned this conflagration doctrine in favor of the view more common in Greek thought that the universe is eternal and static, but the principal elements of their cosmology remained the same. These are that there is a Being, immanent to the cosmos, that is responsible for the order we experience in the world. This Being can, furthermore, variously be called Logos, or World Mind, or World Reason, or Nature, or God, or Divine Providence. The key element is that this Logos wisely determines everything that happens in the universe, including the events of our lives. This Logos therefore deserves the passionate devotion and adoration usually reserved for a Divine being.

In their ethics the Stoics preached an absolute conformity with the Logos. This entailed the cynic way of life as the true vocation of human life. Assent to the rule of Logos entailed a complete indifference to the external things of this world. It also implied the capability of human beings to know the mind of this divine world Reason. Human beings have the ability to know the Logos, according to the Stoics, because at birth the Logos implants a little bit of itself into every individual human being. This *seminal logos*, or *logos spermatikos*, or "seed of Reason," or "right reason," allows human beings to know right from wrong in accordance with the dictates of the Logos, or with what the Stoics called "Natural Law."

Human beings are also subject to passions and emotions, which the Stoics called *perverted reason*, or *irrational reason*. These passions consist of wrong judgments about what is good or bad for us. They are the opposite of right reason and virtue and must therefore be *eradicated*. The ideal Stoic life is one of *a-pathy*, i.e., a life devoid of irrational affection. They were aware that this way of living is rarely completely achieved. So, they held that only sages are ever able to live consistently in accordance with the Law of Nature. This lifestyle must nevertheless remain a constant goal for all humanity. All human beings should live life in accordance with the dictates of Divine Providence, or so the Stoics taught (Armstrong, Ch. 11, 12; Kok, pp. 60–69).

### 2.8 *The beginning of the history of the theme of the* a priori

Following the Hellenistic period came a period in Greek thought that is frequently referred to as *Middle-* or *Mesoplatonism*, to distinguish it from classical Platonism on the one hand and from the Neoplatonism of Plotinus on the other. A mixture of Platonism, Aristotelianism, and Stoicism characterizes this period. During this period a change in tone occurred in Stoicism, which became less austere and more focused on the actual practice of everyday human life. Eventually the insight broke through that ordinary human beings could be *more or less* on the way to achieving the goal of complete indifference to the external things of this world. These later Stoics also adopted the notion of Plato's *tripartite* view of the human soul. This change in view made it possible to accept the emotions as a (good) part of the human soul and allowed for an understanding of human life in which the passions need not be eradicated, but only to be *controlled.*

In cosmology the view, anticipated as far back as Anaxagoras, became popular that the Supreme Being of the universe was a Mind, or a divine *thinking* substance. Under the influence of Neopythagoreans the issue to be debated became whether this Mind was a transcendent entity, completely self-existent and separate from the cosmos and thinking its own thought, or whether, as a productive thinking Principle, this Divine Being was in fact the prime origin of the visible world. With respect to the second option it became common to view God, or Being, as the cause of the First Mind, which in turn became the cause of a Second Mind, which was then viewed as the origin of the visible world in which we live (Armstrong, chapter 13).

In essence, this period saw the birth of the theme of the *a priori*, or the *a priorization of normativity*, in the history of Western thought (Brill, 1986, pp. 238–246; Hart, 1966, pp. 1–4). This development of thought is a process in which the norms for human conduct, which up to this point had for the Greeks always been located *outside* mind and thinking, now become viewed as a central *part of* the mind or thinking. I can do no better to describe this theme than to quote Vollenhoven, who has extensively traced the historical development of this theme:

> The **theme of apriority** is a method that arose in response to the critique of the Skeptics. It brought the law, which Greek philosophers had held to be external to us, into the mind of man; a law that continued to hold sway in a way, albeit now bastardized, as an apriori concept. This implied for the theory of knowledge of the conceptions thus affected that the law, *about* which Greek philosophy thought it could *gain* knowledge, now became part of what *was* known.
>
> The spectrum of diverging ways in which the theory of apriority developed has to do with the great divergence of opinions in Greek philosophy regarding the question of what was to hold as law. It is found first in early Hellenism. When Pyrrho questioned the knowability of the law to which Zeno of Elea still held, Timon, a disciple of Pyrrho, tried to address his mentor's skepticism by granting Pyrrho that the law did not exist where the neo-Eleatics had placed it, but then went on to claim that that law nonetheless exists, not beyond but within the human mind.
>
> Since that time the theory of the a priori has booked a long series of triumphs. In the Academy, e.g., first the Ideas, and then the numbers-themselves, were brought over from the extra-mental intelligibles to the knowing mind. The same thing happened with numbers among neopythagoreans, with logical necessity among the Stoics, and with the logical object in the late Middle Ages. The intellect equipped with such [innate] a priori was called "reason" (*ratio*) by Cicero already; such that one could say that the repeated embrace of the theory of the a priori made way for the rise of rationalism. (Vollenhoven, 1959)

I will resume the discussion of the historical development of this theme when I discuss the modern period in the history of Western thought (see 3.13, 3.14). At this point I will note that the theme of the a priori is immensely important for understanding the history of psychology. In a sense the beginning of its history marks the beginning of psychology as we understand it today. In particular, knowledge of this theme is crucial for our understanding of terms like *sensation, perception,* and *cognition*. In essence the theme of the a priori entails the view that thinking or cognition is productive of reality in the sense that it precedes and *constructs* reality. This notion that cognition is essentially revelatory and creative represents the heart of contemporary cognitive psychology.

### 2.9 *The neoplatonism of Plotinus*

The neoplatonism of Plotinus (204–270 AD) was the last major development in Greek philosophy before the influx of Christianity into the history of Western thought. Since it occurred at a time when the gospel was rapidly becoming a major influence in the Western world, it played the role of competitor to a Christian worldview. The history of Western thought was for some time to come characterized by the interaction between neoplatonism and Christianity.

Plotinus constructed a complex system that incorporated many strands of Greek philosophy, but Platonic and Aristotelian themes were predominant. His cosmology is essentially a hierarchy that stretches between a supreme god, or *Being*, and the lowest level of evil matter, or *non-being*. At the highest level of the hierarchy god exists in utter transcendence. This is the absolute *One*, a perfect unity, reminiscent of Parmenides' Being, about which nothing can be said. This One is *beyond* being and remains forever incomprehensible. This absolute "One," who is at the same time the "absolute Good," is for Plotinus an immovable, ineffable, otherworldly entity.

However, this One is also the primary origin of all that exists "below," including the visible world we inhabit. In order to harmonize the total transcendence of this One with its position of being the *prima causa* of the world, Plotinus put forth his doctrine of *emanation*. All levels of existence below the One emanate *from* the One in the sense that they "issue forth," or "proceed from" the One without in any way altering or diminishing the One. By way of illustration, Plotinus uses the image of the sun, which emanates rays of light and warmth without changing the sun into something else.

According to Plotinus, this emanation process occurs in stages. At the first level of emanation below the One, he locates the "Mind," or "Thought," the seat of Plato's Forms. This "Mind" is actually an amalgamation of Aristotle's Unmoved Mover and Plato's *demiurge*, which according to Plato, like a super craftsman, models the visible world in accordance with the Forms. This mixture of prior Greek conceptions is important to note. It honors Aristotle's thought in which the Unmoved Mover is the *endpoint* of the actualization process. In this idea the visible world, as it were, emanates from the Mind, whereas in Plato's view the demiurge, as Mind, emanates the world. This conception allows room for the new idea to break through that mind, or thinking, while it is the result of action, can at the same time also be *productive of* action.

This combination becomes evident in Plotinus's next level of emanation in which Mind or Thought emanates a double-sided World Soul. This level of emanation results in a higher, divine World Soul that contemplates, or looks up to the Forms, and a lower world soul, which looks down to the world below. From this lower World Soul during the next level of emanation proceed the numerous individual souls of human beings.

Farther down still and at an even greater distance from the One, we find the world of material things and of nature. Plotinus did not believe that the material world was in itself evil. But he did believe that the matter *contained in* the material world was inherently evil. He viewed matter as evil because of its remoteness from the One, whom he had characterized as perfect Being and perfect Goodness. Matter is evil because it is deprived of being and of goodness. Thus evil, according to Plotinus, is essentially *privation*. It is *non*-being, or the *absence* of good.

With that we have come to Plotinus's epistemology and anthropology. In Platonic fashion, Plotinus states that human beings are composed of a soul and a body, which for him means that they are a combination of being and non-being. In interaction with the body, the soul of human beings becomes contaminated with matter. It behooves human beings, therefore, to look upwards from whence the soul came to eliminate the evil effects of the body. The ultimate goal of human life should be to ascend upwards toward union with the One.

This ascension process is said to occur in four stages. First, one must gain complete control over one's body and purify oneself from all matter. This is the ideal of the ascetic life, common to the ethics of the Cynics and the Stoics alike. In the second stage, the soul must rise above sense perception in order to contemplate the origin of the visible world, which is the World Soul. Completion of this second stage clears the way for the soul to intellectually approach the universal Mind, which contains the eternal Forms. In this third stage a self-conscious union with the Mind becomes possible. In the fourth and final stage, a human being can literally lose his mind and can enjoy a mystical ecstatic union with the One. However, while we are in the body, this mystical union can only be achieved by a select few, and even for them only momentarily. Yet, for those who persevere in this practice there is the assurance that they will enjoy union with the One when they die, in the afterlife.

Thus far the neoplatonism of Plotinus. It will be clear that this system of thought reignited the intellectualistic flames of Plato's philosophy and, with that, the themes of a dichotomistic anthropology, coupled with a conviction about the inferiority of sense perception, a depreciation of the visible world we live in, and, finally, a belief in the unreality of evil. As we will see, these themes play a powerful role in the subsequent synthesis between Greek philosophy and Christian thought (Armstrong, Ch. 16, 17; Kok, pp. 69–73).

## References

Armstrong, A.H. (1983). *An Introduction to Ancient Philosophy*. Totawa, New Jersey: Rowan and Allenfield.

Bril, K.A. (1986). *Westerse Denkstructuren*. Amsterdam: VU Uitgeverij.

Cahil, T. (1998). *The Gift of the Jews*. New York: Nan A. Talese/Anchor Books.

Hart, H. (1966). *Communal Certainty and Authorized Truth: An examination of John Dewey's philosophy of verification*. Amsterdam: Swets en Zeitlinger.

Kirk, G.S. & Raven, J.E. (1963). *The Pre-Socratic Philosophers*. Cambridge: Cambridge U. Press.

Kok, J.H. (1998). *Patterns of the Western Mind, a Reformed Christian perspective*. Sioux Center, Iowa: Dordt College Press.

Kuhn, Th. S. (1970). *The Structure of Scientific Revolutions*. Chicago: Chicago U. Press.

Runner, H.E. (1958). *Syllabus for the History of Ancient Philosophy*, Grand Rapids, MI: Calvin College.

Vollenhoven, D. H. Th. (1959). Filosofische Artikelen. In: *Oosthoek's Encyclopedie*. Utrecht, The Netherlands: Oosthoek, 1–15.

# Some Issues to Stimulate Dialogue

1. To start an account of the history of psychology with the Greeks represents a choice. It underscores the difference between actual history and history-written-down. In some sense an account based on this choice violates the actual history of Greek thought because no period of history ever starts brand new. New ideas always occur in the context of a prior thought tradition and respond to that tradition. New ideas can be revolutionary and represent a complete departure from that tradition, or they may represent a more gradual change from what was thought before and in essence be only a re-formation of that tradition. But to *begin* an account of the history of psychology with the Greeks is to say that the Greeks themselves had no history. Of course, in actual fact Greek thought was also influenced by pre-existing ways of looking at reality derived from cultures from the Middle East. I will illustrate this by just two Greek notions: the Orphic/Pythagorean idea of the transmigration of the soul and the notion that human beings consist dualistically of two opposing principles, body and mind. These ideas were clearly evident in pre-existing Chaldean, Phoenician, and Persian cultures. Can you think of other Greek notions that originated in these and other Middle Eastern cultures?

2. As I mention in this chapter in connection with the *Theogony* of Hesiod, one *has* to start somewhere in order to avoid the problem of infinite regression. The problem is that, as soon as I show where the Greeks came from, the question arises where these cultures originated and so on. A neat simple illustration of infinite regression is found in a tin I own that contains powder to make chocolate milk. Painted on this tin is a lady who holds a tray on which there is a tin. This painted tin in turn also has a lady on it who holds a tray on which there is a tin with a lady on it who holds a tray, etc.

3. Vollenhoven's assertion that history contains factors related to typicality and factors that show periodicity is intended as a hypothesis that needs to be verified by the data. Identify areas in this chapter that show or fail to show evidence of typicality and periodicity and discuss these in your group or class. Repeat this exercise for every succeeding chapter. By doing this, you become properly critical of the method of investigation

used in this text.

4. Auguste Comte, who lived in the nineteenth century, constructed a theory in which he argued that the history of Western thought went through three stages (see 4.6 for a more detailed description). According to Comte, our civilization first went through a *theological* stage. This stage is roughly equivalent to the mythological thinking of Hesiod, Homer, and Orphism. The second stage is the *metaphysical* stage. It more or less corresponds to period that runs from the pre-Socratics to the Renaissance. Finally, the third stage is the one we live in now. Comte dubs it the *positive* stage. This stage is the stage of scientific thinking. The implication of his view is that the Western world has by now discarded both religious and metaphysical thinking in favor of pronouncements that are exclusively based on scientific evidence. I think that Comte's description of the development of Western thought is incorrect, at least in its application to the history of psychology. Think of Jung's fascination with the occult. Consider Freud's emphasis on the unconscious. Add to these the many theories of personality that make frequent reference to some unobservable entity as the explanatory construct for what is observable. Finally, think of movements like transpersonal psychology as well as the renewed emphasis on spirituality in contemporary psychology. All these theories and movements demonstrate that mythological and metaphysical thinking is by no means dead in the psychology of today. So, unless one is willing to eliminate these vast domains of thinking and research from the history of psychology one would have to conclude that Comte was wrong. In short, my contention is that the endurance of mythical and metaphysical themes represents evidence of typicality in the history of Western thought. A fruitful exercise might be to investigate my thesis.

5. The problem of "going over into another kind" (*metabasis eis allo genos*) is that, for a causal relationship to exist between two entities, they have to be of the same kind. We are most familiar with this problem when we say that something mental cannot cause something physical. We all agree that we cannot landscape the garden or change the furniture arrangement in the room merely by thinking about it or wishing it were so. The thought or the wish has to be converted into physical action first. Only after that has occurred can something mental have a powerful effect on something physical. Is this not the essence of the mind-body problem we hear so much about in psychology?

6. In this chapter I argue that the main theme of Greek philosophy is

the problem of the relation between the definite and the indefinite. In fact, throughout this survey I keep pointing out how this problem is a recurring theme that reappears time and again as a typological item in the history of psychology. To confine myself to Greek thought, the two poles in the relationship seem to take turns. The mythological thinkers stressed the indefinite pole of the relationship, the pre-Socratics the definite, the Sophists emphasized the indefinite, Plato and Aristotle's focus was on the definite again, and, finally, Hellenistic thought became characterized by the indefinite. Other terms for this relationship in the history of Western thought are order and chaos, form and matter, science and freedom, determinism and indeterminism, or cognition and affect. With Nietzsche, the relation became defined by the wonderful description of Apollo vs. Dionysus. From the Greeks on it seems that, when faced with the disorder of life, people made attempts to order the chaos, usually by means of mind or reason, into some kind of logical system. But when people attempted to live in accordance with the order they had constructed, they found it too confining and rebelled against it.

7. The overriding opinion about the Sophists in the literature is that by questioning the existence and/or the knowability of truth (as defined by the pre-Socratics) they promoted a moral relativism that Socrates, and later Plato and Aristotle, tried to combat by their method of dialogue. However, in my view, the Sophists were very much concerned with ethical issues and the promotion of virtue, provided that one understands their ethical concerns to be about how the individual Greek should contribute to the life of the *polis*. In fact, for every Greek at that time the *polis* was a religious community similar to what we today would call a church or a mosque. Every individual Greek had the sacred duty to contribute to the life of the *polis* (see Fustel de Coulanges' *La Cité Antique*). That was how they were required to practice their virtue. The Sophists with their emphasis on rhetoric rather than reason viewed their philosophical contribution as making this virtuous life of individuals more effective in the *polis* community. Their philosophy of life was mainly practicalism and an anti-intellectualism. Thus they focused the attention of the Greeks on the value of the non-logical aspects of life, such as the arts and crafts, poetry and literature. By contrast, Socrates and later Plato made intellectual contemplation of the eternal verities once again the supreme value for Greek life. But this preoccupation with *theoria* frequently occurred at the expense of the other aspects of living.

8. Plato can be forgiven for making thinking the supreme value of Greek life. For, by the time he came on to the scene, the answer to all the major questions of life had been put in doubt. Given this skeptical tradition he had to find an answer to these questions. In response to the question about the structure of reality he constructed his two-world ontology. In answer to the question what human beings were like, he formulated his anthropology with its dichotomy of soul and body. He formulated his epistemology of reminiscence to answer the question of how we come to know. Lastly, given all that, there was the question of how then people were supposed to live. To that question Plato responded by saying that the highest calling of mankind was *theoria*, or the contemplation of the Good. Many of the notions we hold as common sense today were first formulated by Plato. Can you think of some?

9. I have given an extensive description of Aristotle's view of mind, or of his answer to the question of how we come to know. The fact that Aristotle's description of concept formation does not seem completely farfetched to us shows how much he has influenced the history of psychology to this day. However, modern epistemologies are not totally identical to his. Since his time a good deal of historical water has gone under the bridge. A good exercise would be to compare his version of knowledge acquisition with the modeling theory of Bandura, and with the information processing view of cognitive psychology.

10. Socrates believed that a person who *knew* what is ethical would always *do* what is ethical. This is called the "philosopher's virtue." Aristotle equated skill and virtue and taught that to be *good at* something (*arête*) is the path toward being *ethically* good (*eudemonia*). What do you think? Also compare these two views of ethics with Kohlberg's theory of moral reasoning.

11. How does the Hellenistic period of Greek thought compare to our times? Today the world has become a global village (a *cosmopolis*) because of the influx of free trade, globalization, television, and the internet. What are the similarities and differences?

12. The notion that the path toward holiness requires an ascetic, minimalist lifestyle and a life of contemplating otherworldly/spiritual realities is often viewed as a Christian doctrine. Given my description of Plotinus's neoplatonism, is this view tenable? It seems to me that this religious doctrine actually has its origin in Greek pythagorean, platonic, and neoplatonic thought.

# 3. MIDDLE AGES, RENAISSANCE, AND MODERN PERIOD

### 3.1 *From Christianity to Synthesis*

The main characteristic of the Hellenistic world after Aristotle was disillusionment with the bankruptcy of the grand Greek cosmological thought experiment. Many people doubted that they could ever come to know the nature of things. It was a time of skepticism, cynicism, resignation, and escapism. The world at large was in an uproar. Wars were everywhere. It was a time of danger, sickness, confusion, and uncertainty. It was a time not unlike our time.

During this time a new religion and a new worldview were introduced into the Greco-Roman world – the Christian gospel. It brought with it a Judeo-Christian mindset, totally different from the Greco-Roman way of thinking, and the impact of its introduction into the world of that day was nothing short of revolutionary.

At this point in our survey of the history of psychology, it is imperative that we highlight the difference between the Greek mind and the Christian gospel, for without this distinction the further history of psychology is unintelligible. The Christian gospel as described in the Bible differs fundamentally from the Greek mind. I will give only a few examples of this difference, but more could be given.

The biblical picture of God is not one of a universal Force or Form, but of a real concrete Person, with whom one can have an ongoing conversation as with a friend. The God of the Bible is a God who walks with human beings, with Adam and Eve for example. He is not immutable. He not only speaks to human beings but also listens to them and changes his mind for their sake in response to their prayers. Such a God would have been unthinkable for the Greeks (Armstrong, 1983, p. 166).

This biblical God is not part of this world but is its creator. The notion of creation as well as that of the linear history of creation from a beginning to a final end is foreign to the Greek mind (see for this difference, Cahil, 1998: *The Gift of the Jews*). For the Greeks the world is eternal and history goes in a circle. At best the Greeks viewed God as a craftsman, a *demiurge*, who takes eternally existing matter or substance and perpetually (re)shapes or (re)combines these into the things of this world.

Probably the most offensive biblical teaching to the Greek mind is the teaching of God's incarnation. What for Christians is the central source of salvation, i.e., that God should be born into the world as a human being and take on a *body*, that God in effect should become *matter*, was for the Greeks tantamount to the destruction of the world order. From their perspective, if the Divine *Being* becomes *nonbeing*, and if the source of all Goodness becomes *evil*, then all is lost. The notion of the incarnation totally upset the Greeks' conception of the meaning of human life. The whole of Greek thought was geared toward helping human beings to *escape* the body and to *ascend* to God, via a laborious process of intellectual contemplation unencumbered by the input of the senses. It is a process characterized by world denial, by self-denial, and by abstinence from pleasure. In short, the Greek view of the religious life is one characterized by an ascetic lifestyle. According to the Greeks, ascending to God is difficult and can only be accomplished by performing a complicated set of rituals. To the Greeks, God was a distant, far away Being; only a few wise sages, or holy men could reach him. The biblical teaching of the incarnation professes that God came down to people and lived in their neighborhood, so to speak. That notion made no sense at all to the Greeks. It fundamentally questioned their system of values (Armstrong, p. 166).

The God of the Bible makes a contract, a deal or a *covenant*, with people. He makes promises to them and keeps his word. For the early Greeks, who believed that the gods were fickle and untrustworthy, this picture of God was unbelievable. Later on, when the Greeks began to conceive of the divine as the height of all goodness and perfection in the world, they turned God into the Unmoved Mover of the world. Their god, they believed, is unaffected by the affairs of the world. He is unemotional, distant, unchangeable, and as cold as an iceberg. The description of God in the Bible is one where God is said to love human beings and who cries and becomes angry when they go astray. The biblical God is a God who argues with people and who gives human beings a second chance. He is a passionate, compassionate, emotional God. Such a God was an affront to the Greek mind. The Greeks could only see the biblical view of God as an undignified caricature of the Divine.

Thus it was when the Christian gospel was introduced into the Western world the people of that time were faced with two radically different, and in many ways opposed, views of God and of the world: Greek philosophy and biblical Christianity. The one was old and bankrupt, the other new and untried. They had to choose. They could convert to Christianity and reject the Greek worldview. That would have been a revolutionary choice, one that the people of that day seldom made, though some tried (e.g., Tertullian). They could also look for similarities between the two and forge a synthesis between them.

Most scholars of that time chose synthesis. They found the points of connection they were looking for between Christianity and Greek thought especially in the neoplatonism of Plotinus. But synthesizing Christian thought and Greek thought had its consequences. Medieval Christianity was not biblical Christianity pure and simple, but at first it was neoplatonic Christianity (Augustine and Bonaventure) and later neo-aristotelian Christianity (Aquinas).

### 3.2 Philo of Alexandria and the Church Fathers: Allegorical interpretations of the Bible

To understand why the medieval Christians so readily – and perhaps so uncritically – embraced a synthesis between the Christian gospel and Greek philosophy, we must first of all discuss the views of Philo of Alexandria, who lived in Egypt around the time of Christ's life on earth. Philo was a devout Jew, who based his belief system on the Old Testament part of the Bible. But he was also greatly attracted to Greek philosophy. So, he had a problem of how to harmonize these two systems of thought.

To accomplish this, he developed an allegorical method of interpretation. An allegory is a story that aims to teach a lesson, and the lesson is usually intended to point to a hidden, deeper truth lying behind the story. According to Philo, the stories of the Old Testament about God's dealing with Adam, Abraham, Jacob, Moses, and others that the Bible clearly identifies as historical events are actually myths. They were to be read as allegories that point to deeper truths than what the surface story would lead us to believe. These deeper truths in Philo's allegorical interpretation of the Bible turned out to be (Pythagorean and Platonic) themes of Greek philosophy.

Thus, his allegorical method was in reality an *eisegesis-exegesis* approach to interpretation. That is, this approach made it possible for Philo to read into (*eisegesis*) the Old Testament themes from Greek philosophy that are foreign to it and then to read these themes out of (*exegesis*) the Bible, thereby baptizing them with the aura of divine revelation (Armstrong, pp. 159–164; Copleston, 1972, pp. 21, 126; Kok, 1998, pp. 78, 79).

Many of the church fathers who became leaders of the church after the apostles had died adopted this form of interpretation in their struggle to harmonize the Christian gospel with themes from Greek philosophy. By the time that Augustine came on the scene, allegorical Bible interpretation and preaching had become a well-established practice among medieval Christian biblical scholars.

### 3.3 Neoplatonic Christianity

The overall effect of this way of reading the Bible was that it turned medieval Christianity into a neoplatonic Christianity. I will briefly describe the negative consequences of this turn of events for the lifestyle of medieval Christians.

Two of the central tenets of biblical Christianity are the notion of "revelation," and a notion with which we are more familiar today, that of "evidence." Biblical Christianity holds that revelation is the condition for knowledge. This means that human beings can only come to know what God chooses to reveal to them in the Bible and in creation. This notion is designed to cut off speculation. It means that the things that matter in this world are not hidden but are revealed, and are therefore evident. They are there for all to see. They can be known by all who are willing to open their minds, to read and to observe by means of their senses.

By accepting that Christianity is close to platonism, the neoplatonic Christians of the early Middle Ages exchanged "revelation" for "*illumination*," an eminently platonic notion. Illumination means that an impersonal World Reason or *Nous*, which was called divine by the Stoics, reveals itself to human beings in the reason, or mind, or soul of individual people. World Reason, according to this Stoic doctrine, puts a little of itself into our soul when we are born, and reason is therefore innate, *a priori*; it precedes experience. The Stoics called it the *logos spermatikos*, or the "seed" of Reason (*Encyclopædia Britannica*, 1911, pp. 919–921).

The focus of knowledge in this conception is on coming to know what this World Reason reveals about itself to us *in our soul*. This kind of information is unobservable; it is hidden from sense perception, i.e., it is not evident. It can only be gotten at via contemplation, or introspection, and that can only be accomplished if we shut off our sense perception and turn away from the everyday, natural world we experience.

Neoplatonism thus turned medieval Christianity into a world-avoiding religion, in which the most important activity of life was to come to know that hidden God *in our minds*. The observable, evident things of this world were said to obstruct this process; *the idea of* God became the most important thing in life. Everything else had to fall into place around it (Copleston, 1972, pp. 17–49).

### 3.3.1 *Augustine*

The life of Augustine (354–430) is a case in point of the influence of neoplatonism on medieval Christianity. Augustine has been called the last great Greek philosopher and the first great medieval Christian philosopher. All he wanted to know, by his own admission, was "God and the soul" (*Soliloquia*). In this desire he was a typical medieval thinker. He did not want to understand the mind or the soul for its own sake but as a clue to the invisible reality of God in heaven. In this desire he also betrayed the influence of neoplatonism. He believed that the soul has access to God because it reflects the image of God. He believed that, to worship God, one has to turn away from world of sensory experience and use reason to access God in the background world, or heaven. Augustine's type of Christianity, at least initially after his conversion, advocated contemplation of God *away from* everyday life, rather than obedience *in* concrete everyday life. The essence of this kind of Christianity promotes a life of otherworldly spiritualism that has little to offer short of abstinence for the practice of every-day living. No wonder that this world-and-life view later led to the reintroduction of Aristotle by Aquinas, then to the humanism of the Renaissance, and finally to the empiricistic rationalism of the modern period (Armstrong, 1983, p. 215).

A brief biography of Augustine's life is in order. Augustine was a well-educated Greek scholar and an accomplished teacher of rhetoric. For most of his earlier years, he was a pagan and an adherent to Manichaeism. This pagan religion taught that there are two forces in the world: good and evil. These two forces were said to be constituent parts of world and that they rule the world from all eternity to all eternity. Life in this pagan religion is a perpetual, inevitable struggle between good and evil. The Manicheans believed that good would eventually triumph in the lives of human beings but only if they lived a life of strict abstinence.

Sometime during his middle forties, Augustine was converted to Christianity, ironically as a result of listening to the allegorical preaching of St. Ambrose. Ambrose was the bishop of Milan and belonged to the generation of church leaders that came after the period of the church fathers. Augustine spoke highly of him and considered him his mentor. Sometime after his conversion Augustine himself became the bishop of Carthage in North Africa, his birthplace. During the rest of his life, he wrote many books that were very influential for the further history of Christianity. Many of his books are still worth reading today, also for psychologists. Initially his writings showed a heavy influence of the neoplatonism of Plotinus. Later in his life biblical insights became more and more evident (Augustine, *Confessions*, 1942, pp. ix–xxx).

His conversion to Christianity was undoubtedly genuine, but his life after his conversion also continued to show the heavy influence of neoplatonism. I will briefly relate two examples taken from his *Confessions*.

Augustine was a deep thinker who devoted his entire life to a search for truth. But, by his own admission, he also was a passionate man and had a virulent lust for life. He frequently was subjected to intensely felt desires for the pleasures of living. Throughout his life he had difficulty harmonizing these two sides of his nature. His need for food and his need for sex were especially troublesome for him. During his youth he often engaged in drunken parties and sexual escapades. For a long time thereafter he kept a mistress and even fathered a son by her.

When he was converted to Christianity he did not marry his mistress, who loved him dearly, but summarily sent her away, unmoved by the tears of the woman who not only lost the love of her life but also her child, since Augustine was unwilling to part with his son. After his conversion Augustine lived a life of celibacy. Thus, his conversion was not only one from paganism to Christianity but also one from a life of pleasure seeking to a life of abstinence, or "continence" as he called it. Even so, he continued to struggle with deeply felt desires throughout his life, but he attributed them to the sinful nature of his body (*Confessions*, p. 144).

In line with his neoplatonism, Augustine had little good to say about his body or anything in his life related to it. He particularly had a low view of human emotions, which carried over into his view of women, since in contrast to men he considered women to be beset by emotions. This neoplatonic influence on his life is evident in his description of the death of his mother Monica. Augustine had an exceptionally close relationship with his mother. He was also deeply devoted to her. Her death represented a major loss in his life and also in the life of his son. However, when she died Augustine reprimanded his son for wailing at the loss of his beloved grandmother. He considered such a display of emotions unseemly. But then he himself became unable to control his grief and privately cried bitterly. One would think that he had enough reason to cry, but Augustine prayed God for forgiveness for letting his sinful body get the better of him (*Confessions*, p. 167).

Even though Augustine was influenced by the neoplatonism of Plotinus, it would be wrong historically speaking to dismiss Augustine's world-and-life view as just another form of neoplatonism. In spite of his deep admiration for this Greek system of thought, he was a Bible-believing Christian who was quite aware that on some crucial points neoplatonism was incompatible with the gospel. A case in point for him was the story of the incarnation, which quite arguably forms the heart of the Christian gospel. He wrote about the inconsistency between neoplatonism and Christianity in his *Confessions*. After pointing to the fact that in what he calls the "books of the Platonists" he found a number of themes that were also found in the Bible, he states that these books do not make any reference to the incarnation, or to the fact that God humbled himself to be born as a flesh-and-blood human being in order to save sinners. For such a doctrine would be an affront (and here Augustine minces no words) to "those who wear the high boots of their sublimer doctrine" (*Confessions*, p. 117).

Quite apart from his sometimes penetrating critique of neoplatonism, Augustine also offered us many powerful descriptions of Christian insights. I will mention only a few taken from his *Confessions*. For instance, in his lifelong search to know God he hit upon the insight that, contrary to Greek philosophy, the world is not divine, but that God is the creator of the world. In his characteristic style of writing Augustine then went to the earth, to the sea, the sun, the moon, the stars, and even to himself with the question, "Tell me of my God." They all gave him a singular answer: "We are not God." But that answer would not do for Augustine. He pleaded with them, and there was urgency in his voice: "Tell me of my God, since you are not He. Tell me *something* of Him." And they all cried out in a great voice: "He made us" (*Confessions*, pp. 176–177).

The other insight, which I believe is the result of his conversion to Christianity, is his wonderfully insightful description of memory (*Confessions*, pp. 178–191). What to my mind makes Augustine's description of memory so wonderful is that it is an invitation to the dance of dialogue. Reading his description makes one wonder what more can be said about this gift of human life. I find his description of memory unsurpassed in the history of psychology. By way of contrast, the writings about memory of Ebbinghaus, who is generally considered the father of memory research, seem sterile to me (Watson, pp. 142–151).

But what made these two important figures in the history of psychology write so differently about the same topic? For Augustine knowing the ins and outs of memory (as part of the soul) was extremely important because he believed that memory was the place where one could find God. After all, the search for God was – for him and for most of the medieval thinkers after him – the supreme preoccupation of human life. This was not a concern for Ebbinghaus, who lived in a period in the history of psychology when it was most important to know *by what experimental method* one could best study the faculties of the mind, such as memory. Thus, Ebbinghaus's description is necessarily more abstract than that of Augustine.

Contemporary psychologists ought to be thankful to Augustine for his writings, especially for his *Confessions*. This work is an excellent illustration of the use of self-analysis, or introspection, that was to play such an important role later on in the history of psychology. Furthermore, we can hardly overestimate the importance of introspection for psychology as a whole. Without it, psychologists are unable to make use of such well-known psychological tools as surveys, opinion polls, psychological tests, and psychotherapy. All of these require some form of self-analysis, or introspection, that is, the act of looking inside oneself for the answers (Copleston, p. 43).

### 3.3.2 *Medieval thought after Augustine*

The influence of Greek thought on medieval scholarship continued to be evident during the Middle Ages after Augustine. It manifested itself in three trends prevalent during the early Middle Ages: in mysticism, hierarchy thinking, and in the desire to logically prove the existence of God.

### 3.3.2.1 *Mysticism*

Mysticism is the purest form of neoplatonism. It is contemplation or introspection in search of what is hidden. It is an attempt to point to, to describe, or to speak about the ineffable, in an effort to penetrate the mysterious. This form of intellectualizing the mysterious in life pervaded the thinking of medieval scholars in one way or another. Nor has it disappeared from contemporary ways of thinking. We find it back in present day transpersonal psychology, with its "levels of consciousness." We also meet with it in some forms of faith healing when it is asserted that the healing that takes place is only the work of God when it is medically inexplicable. In this mysticistic world of thought the things of everyday reality are only symbols, icons, or faint copies of the much more real, mysterious, but hidden things revealed in our souls. However, as I pointed out earlier, this emphasis is not altogether a dead loss for the history of psychology. Because of it we know more about introspection today (Kok, 1998, pp. 78–79; Bril, 1986, pp. 157–160).

### 3.3.2.2 *Hierarchy thinking*

The second trend evident during the early Middle Ages was hierarchy thinking. This is thinking about everything in the world in terms of its distance from God. The closer a being is to God, the more value or status it has. This is really a platonized form of aristotelianism. Remember that in Aristotle's worldview, in the "Great Chain of Being," everything has its place in terms of potentiality to actuality, from matter to God. This idea greatly influenced the way people thought during the Middle Ages. People thought of everything in terms of this scheme. The world, the church, society, and the human soul were all viewed as hierarchical:

| **World** | **Church** | **Soul** | |
|-----------|-----------|----------|---|
| God | Pope | Active mind | What is Platonic about this scheme is not that things were arranged in a certain order, but that what is lower is *devalued* in favor of what is higher. |
| angels | archbishop | passive mind | |
| humans | bishop | common sense | |
| animals | priest | special senses | |
| matter | laity | body | |

Note that in present day cognitive psychology we also tend to think of psychological functions in this way, and that we implicitly favor cognition over perception, perception over sensation, and sensation over emotion (Lovejoy, 1964).

### 3.3.2.3 *The attempt to logically prove the existence of God*

Other characteristics of medieval thought were the various attempts to logically demonstrate the existence of God, notably by Anselm and later by Aquinas. In essence these medieval scholars used Greek logic and Greek categories of thought to prove the existence of the Christian God. Anselm, for example, logically tried to demonstrate that God must exist by defining him as "a Being than which nothing greater can be thought or conceived." This type of reasoning based itself on the Greek conviction that infinite regression cannot be imagined. One's thinking has to start somewhere. There has to be a beginning, or an *arche,* from which thought proceeds. The Greek thinker Archimedes called this starting point his *pou sto,* or his place-to-stand. However, to define God as the beginning of thought says little or nothing about the nature of the God of the Bible (Copleston, 1972).

At best these arguments for the existence of God succeeded in showing that the Greek God as the "Unmoved Mover," or "World Mind," or "One" was in fact the *arche* or *creator* of the visible world. But with all that, medieval scholars lost sight of the God of the incarnation in Jesus Christ, which doctrine is, after all, the heart of the Christian gospel.

To read these attempts to prove God's existence is rather boring. One may legitimately wonder why these medieval thinkers were so obsessed with hairsplitting arguments about God's existence. To understand this obsession we should realize that, for the medieval, the issue about God's existence was a burning existential question. Had not Augustine taught that the meaning of life was to know God? These medieval thinkers believed that if God did not exist then there would be no God to be known; thus, life would be meaningless.

By way of contrast, for the people of the Renaissance who lived at the end of the medieval period, the question about God's existence was irrelevant to their lives. They wanted to know *Man*. They were not interested in the nature of God, but in the nature of human beings. Again, by way of contrast, to the people living in the modern period of Western civilization the question about God's being also was not important. They were far more concerned with knowing the physical nature of the world.

Undoubtedly the question about God's existence was a serious question for the medievals. And yet, the way they answered the question makes us feel uneasy. For to make the being of God dependent on logical argumentation somehow seems to be an affront to the majesty of God. What's more, the question about God's existence fundamentally is not an intellectual puzzle but a question born out of despair. It is a question about the meaning of our existence. As an existential question this question is familiar to every Christian. In the depth of their despair Christians often cry out, "God, where are you?" We meet with this question in grieving people, especially when the death of a loved one seems senseless. Grieving Christians especially feel this despair when someone they love dies an untimely death as, for example, when a mother of young children dies of cancer. Psychotherapists are also frequently faced with this question about God's existence when they are trying to treat Christians suffering from depression. A typical complaint by depressed Christians is their experience that "God is so far away." As an existential question the issue of the reality of God is not whether he exists but, as a character in Fyodor Dostoyevsky's novel, *The Brothers Karamazov* (1880) so aptly put it, *whether he cares!* To give an intellectual answer to this existential question shows an insensitivity to the despair that lurks behind questions about the existence of God.

### 3.4 *The voluntarism of Duns Scotus*

There are also some negative consequences to the attempts to logically prove the existence of God. For if we logically prove that God is such and such, then he must necessarily be that way and not otherwise. Logical necessity is inexorable. Two plus two can only be four. The problem with the attempt to prove the existence of God via logical argumentation is that it makes God subject to logical necessity. He must obey the laws of logic if he is going to exist. This issue is illustrated by such logically unsolvable problems debated by the medievals as to whether God can create a stone so large that he himself can't lift it. In short, scholars began to realize that by making the existence of God dependent on logical arguments, logic, and reason would restrict the freedom of God to do as he pleases.

Enter Duns Scotus's *voluntarism*. Like William of Ockham (about whom later) Scotus wrote in reaction to the Nature-Grace synthesis position of Thomas Aquinas. For organizational reasons I deal with Scotus before discussing the position of Aquinas because Scotus's critique is equally relevant to the medievals who were preoccupied with the question of the existence of God as outlined above.

Scotus (1266–1308) wanted to rescue the theological notion of God from the trap that earlier medieval thinkers had gotten themselves into by concluding that God must be subject to logical necessity. He did this by emphasizing the (free) will of God over reason, and, by implication, the (free) will of human beings over their capacity to reason. God and human beings, he argued, have a will; this will is free, and it is superior to reason. Scotus gave the will primacy over reason because he believed that the primary relationship that God has to the cosmos and to human beings in it is not one of reason but one of love. In this he hails back to Augustine who said much the same thing much earlier.

Love implies the making of a choice. Love is an act of free will. If it is coerced, it is not love. One cannot love on command. Love also implies otherness, or individual uniqueness. This is clear from romantic love (see 3.8.1). We are often attracted to others because they are different from us. Finally, love is frequently impulsive, non-analytical, and non-deliberate. By emphasizing will over reason, Scotus highlighted an attribute of God and human beings that is in many ways the antipode of reason.

It is generally believed that this emphasis on will is Hebrew rather than Greek in origin, although there is also something to be said for viewing the relation of reason to will as yet another example of the age-old problem of Greek philosophy regarding the relation between the definite and the indefinite. In any case, problem of the relation of reason to will – which soon became re-baptized as the relation between *reason and faith* – was picked up time and again, by scholars in the further history of philosophy and psychology. In this light we have to interpret Pascal's famous statement, "The heart has reasons, of which reason knows nothing." Will is also the key element in the reaction of both romanticism and idealism to the scientific rationalism of the Enlightenment. Finally, Wilhelm Wundt, who is said to be the father of empirical psychology, was an outspoken Voluntarist. Thus, it is apparent that this emphasis on will as more central to the nature of both God and human beings was to become very important for the history of psychology (Copleston, 1972, pp. 225–229).

### 3.5 *Reintroduction of Aristotle*

At this point we will pick up our chronological account of the history of psychology with a description of the re-introduction of the writings of Aristotle into Western thought. It is customary in accounts of the history of the Western world to distinguish between the early and the later Middle Ages. As we saw, Christian thought during the early Middle Ages was characterized by a synthesis between neoplatonism and Christianity. By way of contrast, the dynamic of Christian thought during the later Middle Ages was essentially a synthesis between Platonized Christianity and Aristotle's philosophy. The shift from the early to the later Middle Ages was brought about by a battle between (neo-)platonism and aristotelianism with the latter eventually triumphing over the former. Christian scholars waged the war but it was not a Christian battle. It too was the result of a synthesis between Christianity and Greek thought. The generals in this intellectual battle were Bonaventure and Aquinas, though, of course, they were not fighting alone. Many medieval scholars were engaged in the struggle and the actual paradigm shift was a longtime in coming. It is, however, in the views of Bonaventure and Aquinas that we most clearly see the difference between the old and the new synthesis.

The *occasion* for this shift in thinking was the reintroduction of the writings of Aristotle into the thought world of the West. To understand the radical nature of this historical shift we must first highlight what happened to the synthesis between Greek thought and the gospel during the early part of the Middle Ages. After that we must note the importance of the fact that Aristotle was reintroduced to the West by Arabian, Islamic scholars.

At some point during the early Middle Ages the synthesis between neoplatonism and Christianity, promoted by such luminaries as St. Augustine, ceased to be seen as just one way of looking at the world among many, i.e., as a philosophy. Instead it came to be viewed as the divinely revealed description of the way things are. In short, it became dogma or infallible church doctrine. The church demanded strict adherence to this view from its members, on pain of being branded a heretic if one failed to do so. Moreover, since the church was the most powerful public institution of the Middle Ages, it could insist that the rest of the world would also fall in line. Hence everything that was written was tested for its truth-value or heresy in terms of whether or not it agreed with this neoplatonic-Christian synthesis. As far as the powers that be were concerned, this was the only way to look at the world. Plato and Jesus reigned supreme.

Then the writings of Aristotle, which had been lost previously, were reintroduced to the West via Arabian and Islamic scholars. Copies of Aristotle's writings initially found their way to the East. There they were translated from Greek into Arabic by Islamic scholars such as Avicenna and Averroes; there, they stimulated a great deal of cultural and scientific activity, notably in the field of medicine. These writings in this form eventually found their way back to the West where they were translated from the Arabic into the vernacular of the West.

I think it is historically significant that Aristotle's works were reintroduced in the West as *Arabic* translations by *Islamic* scholars. This Arabic and Islamic influence gave the writings of Aristotle an overly deterministic and absolutistic flavor. In short they were presented to the West *not* as yet another view of reality, but as a religious worldview on par with and in competition with the biblical worldview. Here were writings that were not Platonic. Moreover, they were produced before the coming of Christianity to the West and therefore outside of the authority of the church. The question became what to do with this Arabic-Islamic Aristotle.

Probably the most offensive thing about Aristotle's views to the medieval scholars was that they were empiricistic rather than rationalistic. They were this-worldly rather than other-worldly. Aristotle's knowledge was obtained by observation, via sense perception, not via introspection of the soul. And this was contrary to the doctrine of the church at that time. According to church dogma, that kind of approach gave only "*natural*" knowledge, knowledge of the external world, not internal, real, divinely illuminated knowledge.

At the same time, the medievals could not deny that the knowledge of Aristotle had real status. Had they not used his philosophy of the Great Chain of Being to come up with their hierarchical view of the world? So, these medieval scholars were faced with a dilemma (Copleston, 1972, pp. 154–159).

### 3.6 Bonaventure: Neoplatonic otherworldly spiritualism

The conservative voice in the struggle about what to do with Aristotle was the voice of Bonaventure (1221–1274). Bonaventure was an Augustinian neoplatonist monk who resisted the introduction of Aristotle into Christian thinking. He was a dualist, who sharply separated soul and body as two independent substances. According to his view the immortal soul merely uses the mortal body during our earthly existence. The essence of a person is the soul, which is capable of two kinds of knowledge.

a)  *Knowledge of the external world*: In this Bonaventure follows Aristotle to the letter. Knowledge of the external world is empirical knowledge, which is not based on innate pre-existing knowledge of the Forms or the Ideas. Empirical knowledge builds up universal knowledge via abstraction from concrete individual objects. However, this knowledge must be joined to "divine illumination from God in the soul" to become "true" knowledge.

b)  *Knowledge of the spiritual world, including God*: This knowledge, according to Bonaventure, can only be obtained via introspection. Introspection discovers the image of God, illuminated in the soul without the need for sensory perception. The Idea of God is not gained via sense perception and is, therefore, innate (Copleston, 1972, pp. 160–170).

### 3.7 Aquinas and synthesis: Christianity and Aristotle's naturalistic empiricism

The progressive voice in the struggle about Aristotle's views was that of Thomas Aquinas (1225–1274). Aquinas solved the dilemma facing medieval thought by forging yet another synthesis. He said that both kinds of knowledge, knowledge via introspection of divine illumination and knowledge via sensory observation and syllogistic reasoning, were equally valuable and, what was more, they complemented each other. He designated Aristotle's knowledge as knowledge for the realm of "nature." This knowledge he called *philosophy*. In addition, he designated neoplatonic-Christian knowledge, i.e., the knowledge due to the introspection of the illumination of the soul, which by that time had become the doctrine of the church, as knowledge for the realm of grace. This knowledge he called *theology* (following Augustine, Aquinas called the study of the mind "theology" rather than psychology, because the medievals only wanted to know what was in the mind or the soul for the sake of coming to know God).

According to Aquinas, philosophy, i.e., knowledge of the realm of *nature*, can be obtained by anyone who opens his or her eyes and applies his or her reason, be they Christian or not. It is real knowledge; it must not be despised. But it must remain the *ancilla*, i.e., the *handmaiden* of theology, or of knowledge in the realm of *grace*. To obtain *this* kind of theological knowledge observation and reason are not enough. Knowledge of the realm of grace, or theology, requires a *donum superadditum*, i.e., something added, namely *faith,* or the adherence to church doctrine. So, Aquinas had a platonic-Christian-Aristotelian picture of the world, which emphasized introspection *and* observation, faith *and* reason as two equally valid sources of knowledge, with harmony between them. Talk about a synthesis! He had it both ways (Gilson, 1956).

In time Aquinas's nature-grace scheme replaced the old Neoplatonic-Christian synthesis as the official doctrine of the church. He scuttled neoplatonism and gave Aristotle's empiricism independent status as a way toward truth, *next to* church doctrine. But by doing this he also opened the lid to a Pandora's box called "the Renaissance," and later to "Mechanistic Scientism." These two movements soon became rivals of the church in the struggle for cultural leadership.

### 3.8 *Transition from the medieval to the modern period*

At this point we have arrived on the threshold of another major paradigm shift in the history of Western thought. The medieval mind is moving toward the modern mind. There are various ways of describing this dramatic shift in thinking. We can say that it started when Aquinas's grand synthesis between nature and grace fell apart and the culture of the Western world began to orient itself increasingly to the nature pole of this synthesis. We can say that this shift represented a change from an emphasis on universals to an emphasis on particulars. These changes began in earnest with William of Ockham. We can also say that the shift had to do with a shift in focus on humankind rather than on God and with a change in emphasis on the human individual rather than on social systems. In this case we make the Renaissance responsible for the shift.

Finally, we can highlight the fact that for many people of that time the Bible rather than church doctrine became their rule for faith and life. If we say that, we stress the rather short-lived influence of the Reformation on the thought life of the Western world. All of these influences were important. I will describe each of these influences in more detail, beginning with the influence of the Protestant Reformation.

### 3.9 *The limited effect of the Protestant Reformation on the transition to the modern period*

The Protestant Reformation occurred toward the end of the Middle Ages. It was important to the history of Western thought because it broke the near exclusive domination of the church over everyday life, and it thus contributed further to a paradigm shift from medieval to modern thinking. Like the contemporary movement of the Renaissance and the materialistic scientism movement of the later modern period, the Protestant Reformation was essentially *anti-synthetic*. That is, it broke with the medieval synthesis between Greek philosophy and the Christian gospel. However, the adherents to the Renaissance and to materialistic scientism were against this synthesis because they wanted to ban the influence of the Christian religion from the thought life of the Western world and root themselves exclusively in Greek philosophy. By contrast the adherents to the Protestant Reformation were against the medieval synthesis because they wanted to ban the influence of Greek philosophy from the Christian religion and root themselves exclusively in the biblical gospel. The Reformation was an attempt to make the Bible the primary criterion for determining the truth of church doctrine as well as of non-ecclesiastical views and practices. Its intention was to create a biblically-based worldview and lifestyle.

Thus, this movement had the potential of developing a truly Christian Mind (Blamires, 1963), which would find its inspiration in the biblical gospel. However, while the Reformation was instrumental in returning many people to the Christian religion and while it kept many believers from becoming seduced by the increasingly anti-religious tenor of the times, in my judgment it failed to formulate a genuine Christian mind. That is, it failed to develop a biblically-based cosmology, anthropology, and epistemology on a par in quality with Greek philosophy.

The reasons for this failure are probably many. One significant reason, I think, is that second generation Reformers, notably Melanchthon among them, reverted to using scholastic (i.e., Greek-Aristotelian) logic to systematize biblical doctrine (McGiffert, 1961, pp. 70–80). Their goal was in some sense laudable. It was to expound biblically-based Christian doctrine as clearly as possible. However, in the process of doing this they ran into problems that were eerily similar to the problems the medieval scholars encountered when they sought to logically prove the existence of God.

For one thing, when one lets logic decide the infallibility or trustworthiness of the biblical account, then one reduces the question of whether the Bible is a trustworthy "rule for life and faith" to whether or not one ought to believe that the events described in the Bible are factually accurate. This practice initially led many Protestant denominations into interminable inerrancy debates and later to an outright rejection of biblical truth by proponents of higher criticism because the accounts in the Bible of miraculous events allegedly did not square with the dictates of modern science. In the meantime, the Bible itself is devoid of any such debates about scientific accuracy. It simply and quite naively assumes that the creation occurred in seven days, that Jonah spent three days in the belly of a fish, or that Jesus walked on water. Thus, the concern for the inerrancy – the factual accuracy of the biblical descriptions of events – represents a case of *eisegesis-exegesis*. It reads into the Bible problematics that are not there; with the result that the Bible *itself* became a problem and a source of argument rather than a source of inspiration for Christians. Over time it has had the effect that Protestant denominations tend to split over arguments about the turn of a phrase.

Second, the application of Greek-Aristotelian logic to the Bible reduced the Bible to a series of discrete syllogisms, or propositions, or discrete Bible "texts." This practice has in the past lead to the misuse of the Bible to legitimate all kinds of un-Christian views and styles of living from slavery to patriarchy. For example, under this scenario one can uncritically combine any group of Bible texts in defense of one's prejudice. Or one can give priority to some texts over others and turn them into proof texts for a certain position or practice one holds dear. Finally, one can take certain Bible texts or biblical doctrines, say ten or so, and pronounce these to be the fundamentals of the Christian religion. The rich literary variety and storied character of the Bible is thereby reduced to a number of "truths," which, like the United States' Declaration of Independence, one then holds to be self-evident. This practice of using logic to distil these truths from the biblical narrative sounds suspiciously like the allegorical method of interpretation practiced centuries earlier by Philo and the Church Fathers.

Finally, the application of scholastic logic to the systematization of biblical truths had the unfortunate effect that the resulting "theology" was esoteric, sterile, and boring to read. Thus, it had the same effect as the earlier attempts by the medieval scholars to logically prove the existence of God. The exciting, life-inspiring message of the biblical gospel became a matter of hairsplitting arguments.

I have gone on at length to show that, though the intent of the Reformation was to be anti-synthetic, in the long run it failed to sufficiently exorcise Greek thought patterns from its understanding of the Bible. Like the medieval church, it failed to realize that the Greek mind was also rooted in a religion, namely in the Ionian and Orphic religious traditions. Furthermore, it failed to realize that these traditions were inimical to the Christian religion. Consequently, by uncritically applying Greek-scholastic logic to biblical interpretation, the Bible lost its character as the source of inspiration for Protestant Christians and became a source of contention among them instead. Where there is contention in a faith community, the formation of a unifying mind becomes impossible. Thus, the Protestant Reformation failed to become an effective voice in the further intellectual history of Western civilization. A consequence of this is that, other than contributing to the paradigm shift from medieval to modern times, the Reformation had little influence on the history of psychology (Dillenberger & Welch, 1954, pp. 78–85).

### 3.10 Ockham's nominalism and renewed empiricism

Ockham's nominalism was another factor that brought about the paradigm shift. Like Duns Scotus, the British monk William of Ockham (1287–1347) became alarmed at the danger that Aquinas's two-realm theory posed to the Christian religion. The synthesis of Aquinas between grace and nature was a danger to Christianity they felt, because in it there were two independent sources of truth, church doctrine and Aristotle's philosophy. These two sources were said to be in tenuous harmony with one another by Aquinas. Both Scotus and Ockham, who came after Aquinas, soon realized that two captains on one ship in the long run does not work. Once you give the philosophy of Aristotle equal status with the theology of Jesus, Christian theology will soon be replaced by Greek philosophy. Thus, in order to safeguard the doctrine of the church from the onslaught of natural philosophy à la Aristotle, Scotus and Ockham tried to drive a wedge in the synthesis of Aquinas between "faith" and "reason," where faith was equated with will and love, and reason with thinking, logic, and scientific observation. Scotus and Ockham sharply separated the realm of nature from the realm of grace, as well as the two kinds of knowing attached to them. In their view the two had nothing to do with each other in the sense that what one could know by faith could not be known by reason and vice versa. This was not a new doctrine. It had much earlier been asserted by the Church Father Tertullian, who claimed that faith had nothing to do with reason, nor reason with faith.

Ockham tried to safeguard Christianity further by diminishing the authority of Aristotelian reason in the realm of nature. He denied that via empirical observation and syllogistic reasoning we can come to know the universal essences of things "out there." He argued that all we can have via naturalistic observation and syllogistic reasoning is knowledge of particulars. In this manner Ockham tried to limit the status and scope of Aristotelian reason.

Until he came along it was commonly accepted by all the parties of the debate that knowledge, whether obtained by introspection or by observation, was ultimately knowledge of universals, of classes, species, or essences of things. True, according to Aristotle you started with the observation of concrete particulars, this-chair-here. But then via syllogistic reasoning you could come to knowledge of the real object of knowledge, the universal species, *the* chair, or chair*ness*.

Ockham denied this. He stated that the object of observational reason (i.e., Aristotle's reason) can only be knowledge about particulars, i.e., knowledge about this concrete chair here, this concrete person here. We cannot observe chairness, or personhood via naturalistic reason. We cannot have knowledge of abstract universals, he argued contra Aristotle, simply because universals do not exist out there. The only things that do exist, that can be apprehended by naturalistic or observational reason, are concrete things, incomparably unique things.

What we call universals, Ockham went on to say, are constructions of our own mind. They are names with which we label things. We have a mental habit of grouping unique things in our head together. Universals exist only in our minds, not out in the real world. They cannot be seen. This view of knowing is called nominalism. Universals are a matter of psychology rather than ontology, i.e., they are the product of a *mental* habit and only reside "in our head."

If there are universals at all, said Ockham, they cannot be known by observation and reasoning. They can only be apprehended by faith. We *believe* that there are abiding universally applicable truths and norms. But this can never be proven via observation or by reason. Neither, for that matter, can they be *dis*proven. Hence, church doctrine, which was believed to be infallibly true, had nothing to fear from empirical reason or philosophy. These two ways of knowing via faith and via reason, according to Ockham, are totally different; they are incomparable, incommensurable. Therefore it makes no sense to ask which one is better.

Like the Sophists, Ockham doubted the observable existence of universals (the substances), but unlike the Sophists he doubted their existence in order to safeguard universals from the attack of particulars. For, if I assert that all swans are white (universal), and you can show me a black swan (particular), then you disprove the universality of my assertion.

It should be noted, however, that when Ockham proposed that the existence of universals is dependent on faith rather than reason, he, perhaps unwittingly, used a Greek notion rather than a Christian notion of "faith." The Christian notion of faith is one of a "sure knowledge" based either on the Bible as the Word of God or based on God's illumination of the soul. In both cases what is meant by "faith" is "absolute certainty." The Greek notion of faith, or *doxa*, is best translated as mere opinion, or bias, or hypothesis, as in "I believe so, I hope this is true." Faith as *doxa*, or opinion, is a matter of only relative certainty. Thus, with his theory Ockham opened the door for a later idea that (especially scientific) knowledge is *probabilistic*. By way of illustration, for Ockham "I see a white swan" is intuitively absolutely true, but "all swans are white" is only probably true.

In this connection we can also better understand why Ockham formulated his *economic principle* for the logic of explanation, better known as *Ockham's razor*, which reads: *do not multiply entities needlessly.* For, if, as Ockham argued, universals or generalizations are a matter of naming only, then good thinking requires that one should only formulate those generalizations that cover the greatest number of particulars. Thus, for example, when faced with two generalizations, such as "human beings and animals learn in the same way" and "human learning is distinctly different from animal learning," the former generalization is to be preferred because it covers both human and animal learning. It should be noted, however, that Ockham's razor is one-sided in that it is inherently reductionistic. A counter-assertion, by Leibniz, I believe, is the doctrine that has come to be known as the *law of sufficient reason.* This rule essentially states that one must do justice to the actual diversity in the object of one's study. These two rules tend to balance each other in the logic of explanation.

As we saw at the beginning of this section, Scotus and Ockham formulated their theories in order to defend the Christian religion from naturalistic empiricism. Ironically, their views had the opposite effect. By separating nature from grace, reason from faith, and science from religion, people began to focus more and more on nature, reason, and science, and less and less on grace, faith, and religion (Copleston, 1972, p. 372).

### 3.11 *The Renaissance: Individualism and humanism*

The Renaissance movement was also instrumental in ending the period of the Middle Ages. As such, and like the Reformation, it proved to be a transition movement in the history of Western thought. During the time that the Renaissance gave cultural leadership to the Western world a shift in focus occurred in the West. Unlike before, the emphasis in Renaissance thought was on concrete individual human beings (individualism) rather than on the universal of society. Renaissance thought was also characterized by a focus on human beings (humanism) rather than on God.

### 3.11.1 *The Renaissance and individualism*

In the late Middle Ages, and more clearly during the Renaissance period, a renewed emphasis on the unique individuality of human beings occurred in medieval culture. "Renewed," because the Sophists had more or less made the same point in the pre-Socratic era of Greek thought. Since it was an emphasis on the particularity of individual human beings, this emphasis on unique individuality also had some affinity with what Ockham had taught.

The movement to a focus on individuals arose in popular culture, i.e., in the vernacular writings of the day, rather than in high culture, i.e., in the Latin writings of scholars. One might say that it was a grassroots movement that reacted to the prevailing emphasis on viewing a person in terms of his or her "station" in life or status in society, hierarchically conceived.

In the hierarchical view of society, it will be recalled, the most important factor in human life was to know one's place in the scheme of things.

As an aside, a good example of this traditional neoplatonic hierarchical view of human life was *misogyny*. Women were considered lower than men because they were more emotional. Men were more rational, and rational meant that one was closer to God. Women were more emotional, and emotional meant that one was closer to the animals. Women were considered more susceptible to erotic or sexual passion and therefore more influenced by the devil, unless they abstained from sex, and remained virgins, in which case they could be seen as more holy than men. Hence, the veneration of the Virgin Mary. The point was that, because of their capacity for feeling, ordinary women had to know their place, and that place was below men.

The notion of individuality arose in the popular writings on romantic or courtly love. The traditional view of love and marriage was that you marry in accordance with your station in life. Farmer married farmer, poor people married poor people, and wealthy people married rich people. The trick was to marry above your station, rather than below, in order to improve your status. Whether two people loved each other as persons was of less importance. By contrast, in romantic love people are attracted to and marry each other because of their uniqueness, their difference in personality. They love one another because of how they feel about one another. Their status in society matters much less.

Thus the notion of the uniqueness of people's personality, their individuality, and individual difference from one another – all notions that are commonplace in present-day psychology – found their origin in the Renaissance. Moreover, what we call "human rights" today were inconceivable prior to the Renaissance, except perhaps in early Christian circles because the notion of human rights implies a respect for individual persons quite apart from their status.

### 3.11.2 The Renaissance and humanism

The Renaissance also involved a shift in emphasis from God to human beings. We call this humanism. Remember that, during medieval times, everything centered on knowing God. God was the center of human life. Note further that this God was not the concrete personal God of the Bible who revealed Himself to us in the flesh and blood person of Jesus Christ, but an abstract, hidden, mysterious neoplatonic God, more an idea than a person.

The people of the Renaissance gave up on this idea and, inspired especially by the Greek classics, became fascinated with the creative potential of concrete, bodily, individual human beings. They were impatient with the emphasis on universal systems and eternal verities because in this emphasis concrete individual human beings had gotten lost in the shuffle. They were also like the Greek Sophists, except that the people of the Renaissance were far more optimistic about the potential of human beings than were the Sophists, at least initially (E. Cassirer et al., 1948).

### 3.11.3 The Renaissance and science

The influential people of the Renaissance period were mostly artists, not scientists. Their difference from the artists of the Middle Ages was most evident in the way they painted the human body. The bodies in these paintings were robust and solid, made of muscle and bone. They were real.

Though they themselves were not scientists, the optimism of these humanists about human beings aided a renewed emphasis on science. It fostered a climate of opinion, which held that with the help of science human beings could perhaps create their own world order based on empirical observation rather than on faith or intellectual speculation. Such a climate allowed Francis Bacon to posit the primacy of experience over faith and dogma. This sentiment sounds strangely familiar to me; we find it back in the writings of Carl Rogers (see Van Belle, 1980, p. 174). This faith in the primacy of individual human experience is also why Rogers is called a *humanistic* psychologist.

In any case, this emphasis on experience and scientific observation led many people to believe that they could rid themselves once for all of traditional medieval neoplatonism or platonized aristotelianism. The scientific method alone would create a new world order, one based on experience and observation rather than on faith. By means of this method, one could create a scientific world, or so they thought.

Paradoxically, it was the *loss* of faith in humankind at the end of the Renaissance period that also contributed to the rise of science in the modern period. When human beings are studied as intently as the Renaissance scholars did, then sooner or later the dark side of humanity also comes in view. Eventually the realization broke through that human beings are not just wonderfully creative beings but that they are also capable of atrocious behavior. The development of this loss of faith is especially evident when one compares two of Shakespeare's sonnets. A verse from *Hamlet*, II, ii, 300–303 describes the glory of humankind: "Man," it says, "is like a god." Another verse by Shakespeare's *Macbeth*, V, v, 17–28 refers to the accomplishments of human history as a "tale told by an idiot." This latter verse poignantly expresses the later Renaissance's disillusionment with the accomplishments of human beings. It was especially the Renaissance writer Michel de Montaigne who articulated the limits of human creativity. As an object of admiration and study, mankind had lost some of its glamour. Thus, the trend became to look for salvation elsewhere. Perhaps in the study of the physical world (Kristeller, 1961)?

### 3.12 *The modern period: Newton and the scientific revolution*
At the end of the Middle Ages, a profound skepticism arose about the medieval conception of reality. *In reaction to* this medieval worldview, there arose a new epistemology, a new ontology, and eventually also a

new system of ethics, all of which can be called "*(natural) scientific.*" This reaction is usually called "*the scientific revolution.*" The impact of this revolution represents a paradigm shift in the history of Western thought that was as profound as the impact of the introduction of Christianity into the Greco-Roman world earlier. I will first give a description of this revolution to let the reader feel what it was like. Then I will deal with Descartes, who, more than any one, ushered in this new era.

This scientific revolution created a new epistemology, ontology, and system of ethics. In epistemology it moved from a view of knowledge based on faith in God and the authority of the church to a view of knowledge based on the free speculation and experimentation of human beings. In ontology it moved from an Aristotelian worldview to a (natural) scientific worldview. In ethics it moved from a synthesized Christian-spiritualistic understanding of what people ought to do to a secular, naturalistic, materialistic, and hedonistic understanding of normativity.

This new way of thinking, feeling, and doing took about one hundred years to prepare (1600–1700). The revolutionary character of this new way of life is best illustrated by looking at the changes that occurred in ontology, or in the modern view of the world.

The medieval world and that of the Renaissance was essentially Aristotle's Great Chain of Being. In this worldview the place and character of everything is determined by what it aims for, by what it serves (teleology). What is "lower" in the Chain aims for, serves, and is included in what is "higher." The Chain moves "up" from matter, to plants, to animals, to humankind, to angels, and finally to God. It moves from matter to spirit, or from potential to actual. What is potential is material, what is actual is spiritual. Spiritual is more real than material. Prayer and devotion to God are required to understand this world. Everything "*is*" a symbol of God and points to God. The world is in essence spiritual. The medieval and Renaissance world is a world of qualitative differences, a world of colors, textures, smells, tastes, sounds, feelings, and passions. It is the world as we naively experience it, and, especially for the people of the Renaissance, it is an eminently human world.

The new, modern worldview was a natural scientific, mathematical, material, and a mechanical world. What does this mean?

That the world is natural scientific means that life in this world can be improved via speculative reason and experimentation.

The moderns also viewed the world as mathematical. This mathematization of the world was perhaps the most profound change. Newton held that the differences that exist in the world are all either quantitative rather than qualitative, or can be reduced to quantitative differences. Everything that exists, with the exception of the mind, exists in a certain quantity. All existing things can be described via a mathematical formula. Moreover, what can be described via mathematical formulae is more real than what cannot be described in this way. This viewpoint can best be illustrated by the distinction between primary and secondary qualities. This viewpoint held that our experience of the world occurs by means of two kinds of qualities or sensory perceptions that we have of it.

| PRIMARY | SECONDARY | |
| --- | --- | --- |
| weight | color | Of these two sets of qualities, primary qualities are more reliable and more in contact with the real world, because the real world is in essence quantitative. Secondary qualities are merely our interpretations of what is real. |
| size | texture | |
| shape | smell | |
| motion | taste | |
| waves | sound | |
| measurable | not measurable | |
| objective | subjective | |
| quantitative | qualitative | |

The Moderns viewed the world as quantitative. They also viewed the world as material. Matter here is not viewed as potential (for the spiritual), but as itself actual, a "thing in itself." It has its own being and essence. Rather than matter serving humankind and God, humankind must adjust itself to it. Matter determines mind or spirit (note the reversal of Aristotle here; in effect we have a kind of downward teleology: matter is now actual, spiritual is potential). "Material" also means that the world is made of atoms in space that can be counted, and (re)combined. These atoms randomly influence each other in time and space, and this action can be described with mathematical formulae. Note that the moderns reached back before Aristotle and Plato to the pre-Socratics, to Democritus's atomism in particular and to the Pythagorean belief that the harmony of the world is mathematical. According to the people of the modern times this is what the real, physical world we live in is like.

Not only is the world viewed as quantitative and material. It is also viewed as mechanical. This means that the things of the world are not understood in terms of what they are *for* – we would say "their function" (teleology) – but in terms of how they work, what they are in themselves, what they do and how they are composed. The things of this world are neither dependent on a creator God nor are they dependent on our knowing them. Mechanisms per definition are self-sufficient things in themselves. They are, however, amenable to mathematical description. They consist of parts (atoms), which move (in space), and a whole, which is the sum of its parts. Thus, the best model of a mechanism is a mathematical formula.

The upshot of the natural scientific worldview proposed by Newton and other physical scientists and of the scientific revolution was that they left us with two world pictures that can best be illustrated by the ambiguity in our understanding of the word "nature." We first of all have a picture of nature as that world of plants and trees, mountains and streams, that we go to for recreation, to enjoy. And, second, we have a picture of nature as the world of physics, chemistry, and biology, the world of the mathematical sciences. The one world is concrete, the other is abstract. The difference is captured by a difference between the metaphor of a plant and of a clock. The one picture is the world of art, the other the world of science. It is the latter scientific worldview that dominated the modern period. The scientistic bias of this modern view of the world is still very much with us today, also in psychology. This is the bias that the abstract "physical," mathematical world is determinative of the concrete subjective world we experience. This view holds that we can explain and understand our concrete everyday world by reducing it to a natural scientific model (Copleston, 1960, pp. 147–156; Hazard, 1963, pp. 304–319).

### 3.13 *The origin of the scientific revolution: The logos speculation or theme of the* a priori

Where did this shift in thinking come from? More than any other factor, the impetus for the change was provided by the philosophy of Rene Descartes. To understand Descartes we must first deal with the *logos speculation*. Earlier (see 2.8) I referred to this historical phenomenon as "the history of the theme of the *a priori*." At that time I promised to pick up the history of this theme later when the modern period became the topic of discussion, as it is now. The history of the theme of the a priori is one of the interiorization of Plato's Forms (the True, the Good, the Beautiful, and the mathematical Ideas) from something extra-mental to something intra-mental. At first, these Forms or Ideas were said to reside in the mind of God but later they came to be viewed as part of the mind of individual human beings. This was a process that developed from Plato to Descartes. We cannot understand Descartes and the influence he had on the modern world without understanding this development.

The reader will recall that for Plato the Forms did not reside in the mind of God or in the mind of human beings, but in the background world. However, Plato taught that human beings do have access to these forms via their reason, i.e., their intellect or thinking. The Forms are intellig*ible* to reason. Plato stated his position in reaction to the Sophists who said that these Forms or Ideas were only the products of our minds. We create them. Plato said, No, they are real. They exist outside of us. It is not so that these forms become real to us only when we think them. It is rather that we *can* think them because they are real. They can and must be discovered, or (re)cognized by our reason; but they are not constructed by us. Aristotle held the same. Furthermore, both Plato and Aristotle held that we must pay attention to these Forms or Ideas, because these Ideas are also the ideals, the norms, and the determinants for our existence. They are, to use a phrase common during the Middle Ages, "*eternal verities.*" This view describes the position of realism.

After Plato people began to doubt the existence of the Forms and of the background world. This doubt about the external existence of the Forms implied that, since people were always talking about these Forms, they must, therefore, be the *product* of some mind. Somebody must be thinking up these Forms or Ideas.

This initially led to the view that they exist in the mind of some deity. Plotinus held that they exist in the Mind of the highest, the One. Augustine, following the Stoics, held that they reside in the Mind of God, who then illuminates our mind with them.

We should note that in this formulation the Ideas become mental. We move from thinking as giving us knowledge *about* ideas and norms to thinking as norm *giving*, or to knowledge *as* norms. Thought now *creates* the forms and the ideas, or the ideals, the norms for living, and thinking now dictates how we should live and what the world is like. In this viewpoint thinking is properly called *Reason*. In this world picture Reason *creates* reality. This was the position of the Stoics. They held that there is a World Logos, or World Reason. This reason is divine. It produces a rational order for the universe, a *natural law* that makes everything the way it is. So, according to the Stoics, this World Logos thinks up the forms/ideas that determine the order of the things of this world. Augustine accepted this Stoic view and applied it to the creative activity of the God of the Bible.

Initially with Augustine it was God's thinking that creates norms and reality. And he viewed it as the task of human beings to think God's thoughts after Him. We have to look within to find God's thoughts illumined in our minds.

But under the influence of the secularization process promoted by such people as the Renaissance thinkers, these ideas came to be viewed as the *equipment* of the individual human mind. Roger Bacon, for example, reinterpreted the illumination theory of Augustine as the light being internal to the human mind. We have that light put there by God by virtue of being born, he said. The ideas of Plato are inborn, *innate* ideas, and they are *a priori* to any experiences we might have. They have the character of lighting up our world. They are not the product of God's revelation to us. They are themselves revelatory; they are *faculties* of our minds. In saying this Bacon was not original. The Stoics had already asserted the same idea with their doctrine of the *logos spermatikos.* This doctrine stated that the World Logos endows each human being at birth with little bits of itself, or with certain *germs of truth*, also later called by Descartes *innate*, or *a priori* ideas by means of which we can get infallible knowledge of the world (*Encyclopædia Britannica*, 1911, pp. 919–921).

### 3.14 *Descartes*

René Descartes (1596–1650) lived at a time when there was a profound skepticism. Doubt was rampant not only regarding the Renaissance faith in humankind (Montaigne), which made people look to the physical world outside of human beings for guidance on how to live. But people also doubted the possibility of obtaining absolute truth at all via reason, even if that reason was supported by faith in the infallible doctrine of the church. This doubt was, in no small measure, the result of Ockham's nominalism. There was also a radical doubt about the efforts of the ancient Greeks to come to universal truths. Neither Plato nor Aristotle was considered reliable any more. Reason needs a new basis, a foundation other than faith, or the classics; or else we can never know anything for sure, so said the Spirit of the times, the *Zeitgeist.*

In order to counteract the skepticism of his time, Descartes – very much like Plato – sought to provide the people of the Western world with a new foundation for reason via a new formulation of reason. This earned him a place in history as the father of rationalism.

Descartes essentially beat the doubting skeptics of his time at their own game. In effect he said, if we cannot obtain absolute truth on the basis of faith, let's see if we can obtain it on the basis of doubt. So, let us begin by doubting everything until we come to something that cannot be doubted, and that then must be absolutely, necessarily true. This is a sort of minimalist philosophy, in which doubting has become the essence of thinking.

By following this method Descartes came to the conclusion that, when doubting, he could not doubt that he was doubting. This was intuitively, self-evidently true. And he built his entire worldview on the basis of this one clear and distinct fact. If he could not doubt doubting (or thinking), then he must exist, since someone had to do the thinking. He expressed his conclusion in the phrase for which he has become famous, *cogito ergo sum*. I think, therefore I am. And since thinking cannot be about nothing, he argued, there must be a world, and God also. Hence, he concluded that the one thing he could not doubt was that he was a thinker and that God and the world exist as *thought about* entities.

Descartes explained the possibility of coming to absolute truth in this way with an appeal to the logos speculation. God, he held, has implanted in us certain germs of truth or *a priori* ideas that are so self-evident to us that they cannot be doubted. They must therefore be innate. They are not the result of experience. We think *with* them. We make sense out of everything we experience *in terms of* these ideas (later Kant was to take up this theme).

These innate ideas, Descartes went on to argue, are like mathematical proofs. When we solve a mathematical problem, its solution is immediately self-evident to us. It is necessarily true, for all times and places. This is why Descartes held that the preferred way of thinking about the world was mathematical thinking, and his goal was to think about the things of the world exclusively in quantitative terms.

The practical consequence of Descartes' rationalistic philosophy was that it reinforced the mathematical, mechanistic conception of the world of the modern period. It also reduced the mind to something very small, containing only a consciousness of oneself as a thinking being. As a result, he held that the mental functions of sensation, motivation, perception, memory, etc., which the ancient and the medieval thinkers all held to be faculties of the soul, are attributes (mechanisms, not powers) of the body understood as a physical entity in space. They were seen as spatial-temporal processes, which may be investigated and described, just like any other physical process in the world, in terms of attraction, motion, force, and contiguity, in other words, as measurable processes located in the body and the brain.

In short, Descartes started the quantification of psychological processes. Because of Descartes, a good deal of present day psychology consists of statistically measuring these psychological processes. It is also the reason why so many consider psychology to be a natural science (Copleston, 1965).

## References

Armstrong, A.H. (1983). *An Introduction to Ancient Philosophy*. Totawa, New Jersey: Rowan and Allenfield.

Augustine. (1993). *Confessions,* Transl. by F.J. Sheed, Cambridge: Hackett Publishing Co.

Blamires, H. (1963). *The Christian Mind*. London: S.P.C.K.

Bril, K.A. (1986). *Westerse Denkstructuren*. Amsterdam: VU Uitgeverij.

Cahil, T. (1998). *The Gift of the Jews*. New York: Nan A. Talese/Anchor Books.

Cassirer, E., Kristeller, P.O. & Randall, J.H., eds. (1948). *Renaissance Philosophy of Man*. Chicago: U. of Chicago Press, 1948.

Copleston, F.C. (1972). *A History of Medieval Philosophy*. Notre Dame: U. of Notre Dame Press.

Dillenberger, J. and Welch, C. (1954). *Protestant Christianity*. New York: Scribner and Son, 78–85.

Dostoyevsky, F. (1971). *The Brothers Karamazov*. Baltimore, Maryland: Penguin Books.

*Encyclopædia Britannica*. (1911). 11th ed. Vol. XV, 919–921, New York.

Gilson, E. (1956). *The Christian Philosophy of Thomas Aquinas*. New York.

Hazard, P. (1964). *The European Mind, 1680–1715*. New York: Meridian Books.

Kok, J.H. (1998). *Patterns of the Western Mind: a Reformed Christian perspective*. Sioux Center, Iowa: Dordt College Press.

Kristeller, P. (1961). *Renaissance Thought*. New York: Harper and Row, 1961.

Lovejoy, A.O. (1964). *The Great Chain of Being*. Cambridge, Massachusetts: Harvard U. Press.

McGiffert, A.C. (1961). *Protestant Thought before Kant*. New York: Harper Torch Books.

Watson, R.I. (1979). *Basic Writings in the History of Psychology*. New York: Oxford U. Press, 142–151.

# SOME ISSUES TO STIMULATE DIALOGUE

1. The most radical point of difference between the Greek mind and the Christian gospel concerned the notion of *ascension* (Greek) vs. *incarnation* (Christian). Greek thought saw religion as a way to escape ordinary life and to reach upward to the Divine. Doing so required effort, self-denial, and an ascetic lifestyle. In the Christian religion God comes down to us into ordinary life, to live among us. Contact with the Divine is a free gift. It takes no effort. All we need to do is make room for God in our lives. It was not until the Reformation and Luther and Calvin that the Church began to recognize this difference. What do you suppose are the effects of synthesizing two totally opposed religions on the way people live their lives?

2. There are many different methods of interpreting the Bible, or for that matter books in general: allegorical, scholastic, biblicistic . . . hermeneutics. Can you think of more? In a paper, describe each of these and debate their relative heuristic value. For example, it will be clear from my description of the problem-historical method in chapter one that in my view an allegorical interpretation of the Bible, at a minimum, misreads the historical parts of Scripture.

3. Given what I have written in chapter three I feel the need to rehabilitate Augustine as a Christian. Whereas his *Confessions* shows a considerable influence of Neoplatonism, his later writings, notably *The City of God*, clearly demonstrate his adherence to the Christian faith. But I believe he showed his Christian colors throughout his life after his conversion especially by championing the primacy of love and will over reason. No staunch Neoplatonist would ever think of doing that. A good paper could be written about the struggle in Augustine's soul between Christianity and Neoplatonism.

4. One characteristic of the Middle Ages was surely the dominance of the Church and religion over medieval life. Today we experience a domination of business and economics. How do these differ, and how are they the same? Describe both these social powers and compare their effects on society. One effect of this dominance is that it shrinks the fullness of life to something less than it could be. What else can we say about them?

5. Connect the history of the theme of the *a priori* to the cognitive emphasis in contemporary psychology. What do these historical phenomena have in common? How do they differ?

6. Which areas of psychology lend themselves to quantification and which areas do not?

7. During the Renaissance period, man, according to Shakespeare, was "like a god," and yet, history, as the actions of humankind was described by him as "a tale told by an idiot." How can both be true?

8. Is the way boy meets girl today an example of romantic love? Or is it more like finding someone who has the same values as you have and who, therefore, belongs to the same subculture as you do?

9. Is the relative devaluation of women in our culture the product of a Christian or a Greek mind?

10. How does the Greek notion of faith differ from the Christian notion of faith? What are the similarities, if any?

11. Is the relation of the Divine to humankind one of logic, law, and order (if you obey the rules, if you are "good," you get rewarded, if not, you get punished), or is it a relation of love (in spite of the mess we make of our lives, God, like a loving parent, bails us out every time)?

12. In your opinion, is it possible to logically prove the existence of God? If it is possible, is it a valuable exercise?

13. Debate Aquinas's assertion that there are two equally valid sources of truth open to mankind, one based on faith and the other based on reason.

14. Was Scotus's and Ockham's attempt to safeguard the freedom of God any less an affront to God than Anselm's attempt to prove that he is real, since in both cases God's existence and nature depends on their arguments?

15. How radical was Descartes' radical doubting? The normal end product of an enquiry is a concluding judgment. But to doubt everything one needs to suspend judgment indefinitely. Is that possible? Consider the following counterargument: One can only doubt something in terms of something one does not doubt. We always question things in terms of what we do not question. Only those who firmly believe can afford to doubt. Inquiry has to start somewhere. Is that not what the pre-Socratic Greeks taught us when they posited the existence of the

four substances? One has to take a position to start an investigation. The Greeks called this one's *pou sto*, or one's "place to stand." What was Descartes' "place to stand" he did not question?

# 4. THE DEVELOPMENT OF SCIENTIFIC RATIONALISM: BRITISH EMPIRICISM, FRENCH SENSATIONALISM, AND POSITIVISM

## 4.1 *Intermezzo*

At this point I feel constrained to insert a few cautionary paragraphs between the previous chapter on the Middle Ages and the following two chapters that give a more detailed description of the modern period of Western thought. This period in our historical survey is a very complex period. It is not easily described in accurate detail. At the same time it is an important period because it immediately precedes the birth of psychology as a special science in both its experimental and its clinical forms. Also, during this period many of the notions that later became prominent in psychology were first formulated. In addition, some of the basic methodological principles operative in contemporary psychology find their origin here. For all these reasons and others we do well to spend some time describing this phase of the history of psychology.

It is customary for history of psychology texts to describe the modern period of philosophy in two chapters, the one recounting the development of empiricism and the other that of rationalism. I will also follow this custom, but I want to caution the reader that this procedure to some extent misconstrues the actual history of philosophical thought during the modern period. For it creates the impression as if these two schools of thought developed alongside one another, independently of each other's influence. In actual fact there was quite a bit of cross-fertilization between the schools (Critchley, 2001). To give two examples, Locke read Descartes and was influenced enough by him to be as much a rationalist as he was an empiricist. Another example is the fact that Bentham's utilitarianism as part of the development of empiricism shows a great deal of similarity to the emphasis on the utility of philosophy for every-day life that characterized some of the rationalistic philosophers of the continental mainland like Wolff and Kant.

Thus, the actual situation in modern philosophy is more complex than a division between two schools would make it appear. However, the aim of my survey of this period of Western thought is to show how historically contemporary psychology came to be separated into two approaches, the one experimental and the other clinical. For this reason I feel that it is important to follow the customary division found in history of psychology textbooks.

Moreover, there is considerable ground for describing the history of modern philosophy in this way. Due to Descartes' influence, philosophy in the modern period was primarily epistemological and rationalistic in character. That is, Descartes' emphasis was on discovering the certainty that human beings might have about their *knowledge* of themselves and of the world. His famous *cogito ergo sum* was designed to waylay the skepticism that had crept into late medieval/Renaissance philosophy regarding the question whether we can know anything for sure at all (Copleston, 1965, p. 20). However, Descartes was dualistic in his anthropology and this dualism also manifested itself in his theory of knowledge (Copleston, 1965, p. 23). For him self-knowledge was principally different from knowledge about the world. This dualism worked its way out in the two schools of modern philosophy. Empiricism in its search for certainty was more oriented to knowledge of the world and rationalism was by and large focused on self-knowledge.

This brings us to a discussion of these two schools of thought. I will first briefly describe the characteristics that these two schools had in common, which factors also sharply distinguished them from their medieval predecessors. Then follows a brief discussion on what I think is the essential difference between these two variants of the modern spirit.

In the rest of this chapter, I will outline the development of empiricism as a process that includes British empiricism and French sensationalism and that culminates in the nineteenth century philosophical school of positivism championed by John Stuart Mill and Auguste Comte. The latter school of thought was the predominant impetus in the birth of experimental psychology. In chapter five I will discuss the development of continental rationalism, which after Kant also included idealism and romanticism. The development of this line of thinking eventually led to a kind of anti-positivism; a philosophical attitude that probably became the major stimulus for clinical psychological thinking in the history of psychology.

It is generally recognized that the mindset of the modern period was to a great extent opposed to the Christian religion; this in sharp contrast to the veneration of the Christian religion during the Middle Ages. This anti-Christian characteristic is evident in both schools of modern thought. It represents a fundamental shift in focus and a clear illustration of the influence of periodicity on the history of psychology (Copleston, 1960, p. 40).

Why were the moderns generally so opposed to the Christian religion? I do not think it was because they were opposed to religion in general. Many of these opponents were themselves deistic or even theistic in their worldview, although there were also quite a few atheists among them. Furthermore, attempts to logically prove the existence of God, which were so prevalent during the Middle Ages, continued unabated during the modern period, albeit for different reasons. Thus, a general interest in religion continued during the modern period, so that a rejection of religion as such cannot be said to be the motivation for the anti-Christian attitude. I rather think that the definitive reason lies in the fact that a paradigm shift took place at the beginning of the modern period. Modern thinkers like Descartes and Locke and most of those who followed them were rationalist rather than Christian in their thinking.

What does this shift to rationalism mean? Earlier in the book (2.8) I indicated that during the modern period the theme of the *a priori* came to its full fruition. The ancient Greeks, the Hellenistic philosophers, and the sages of the Middle Ages all were keenly aware that they did their thinking within the context of a reality that existed independent from their thought. In other words, for them ontology preceded epistemology. During the modern period this order came to be reversed. For Descartes the world was a thought-up world. For Locke it was, for all practical purposes, a world experienced/perceived by human beings. For thinkers prior to the modern period reality transcended human thought and perception. For most modern philosophers reality was immanent to thought and perception. In their search for truth, medieval and also Renaissance thinkers tended to test the validity of their philosophical formulations against the tradition of an existing body of thought. They believed that it was important to know that their views were substantially in sync with writings of ancient authorities like Plato and Aristotle or with the authority of the Bible and church doctrine. For Descartes, Locke, and most modern thinkers after them, it was imperative to question every component of this tradition in terms of whether it could be clearly and distinctly thought or experienced. The paradigm shift that this entailed was truly revolutionary. The criterion for truthfulness was now no longer the tradition but one's own thoughts and experience.

Thus, I think it is important to note that compared to medieval philosophy both of these schools were rationalistic. That is to say, they did not base their search for truth on reason tested for its veracity by infallible church doctrine or the writings of the ancient philosophers. Instead they grounded their pursuit of truth in reason alone (rationalism) or in reason aided by empirical scientific verification (empiricism). This change in paradigm, I think, goes a long way toward explaining why the modern philosophers in both camps were on the whole so opposed to the Christian religion; why they chose for a deistic rather than a biblical picture of God; why they branded the Christian religion as sectarian; and why they deliberately opted for a more "reasonable" religion. Thus, the difference between these two schools was not that the one was rationalistic while the other was not. Both were rationalistic in the broadest sense of the word and to honor that fact I will re-baptize British and French empiricism as *(natural)scientific* rationalism and continental rationalism as *metaphysical* rationalism.

The founders of these two schools of modern thought had one more characteristic in common, a characteristic that was, paradoxically, at the same time what distinguished them from each other. This was the methodological conviction that the best way to think or perceive in order to gain clear and distinct knowledge via radical doubting was to think or perceive *mathematically*. It is noteworthy, but seldom mentioned in the history books, that Descartes never subjected this conviction itself to radical doubt (van Rappard, 1976, p. 29). He simply assumed the methodological superiority of thinking mathematically about reality because it was generally believed in those days that the order of reality was mathematical in nature (Galileo, 1623). Thus, the method he adopted for doing his philosophizing was one modeled on the discipline of geometry. In this manner he proceeded to deduce one clearly and distinctively self-evident proposition from another. This method of deduction was the method adopted by all metaphysical rationalists of the modern period (Tanney, vol. I).

While the method of metaphysical rationalism was deductive, the method of scientific rationalism was analytical. According to scientific rationalism, one understands complex experiences and phenomena only after they have been analyzed into more basic, simpler elements of experience and then synthesized in a mechanical fashion into wholes. This methodological difference, at the same time, documents the essential difference between these two schools of modern thought. Simply put this difference is as follows. For metaphysical rationalism the way toward truth proceeds exclusively via unbiased thinking, which inevitably leads one to clear and distinct, self-evident truth. In contrast, the way to truth for scientific rationalism requires observation in addition to thinking. Its critique of metaphysical rationalism is that something that is intuitively self-evident to us may nonetheless be factually incorrect. An imperative for scientific rationalists is that one always examines the validity of one's thought constructions in terms of the data of one's experience.

Earlier Francis Bacon (1561–1626) had expressed the same sentiments. He advocated the unbiased observation of the "Book of Nature" as the criterion for obtaining scientific knowledge. Verified observation came to replace the criterion of verification via an appeal to tradition. Bacon formulated a number of rules for unbiased observation that were designed to eliminate contamination by any factors other than the testimony of the senses, such as the influence of tradition, of prior experience, or of social convention. In essence, Bacon replaced the authority of tradition with the authority of what later came to be called the "scientific method" (Bacon, 1620). For this reason he is generally considered a forerunner of British empiricism. It is interesting to note that John Stuart Mill, whom I will describe as the endpoint of British empiricism, was preoccupied throughout his life with the very same questions of scientific methodology.

## 4.2 British empiricism

In this chapter I will attempt to draw a direct historical line from John Locke, the father of British empiricism, via the various theories of French sensationalism to the positivism of J.S. Mill and Auguste Comte, both of whom were the fathers of a hardnosed Scientism, which characterized the early history of experimental psychology.

### 4.2.1 John Locke: Father of British empiricism

Each of the schools mentioned above are characterized by empiricism. To understand various forms of empiricism, we must note a few things. The first is that all forms of empiricism are characterized by an ongoing skepticism. The empiricist mind is a suspicious mind. The central question for every empiricist is, "Prove it. Show me the money." The second characteristic is that all empiricists are mechanists and elementarists. They are primarily interested in how things can be taken apart down to their basic elements, how things can be put together, and how things (can be made to) work. Finally, with the rise of empiricism experimental psychology, as the study of the mind, became a respected field of investigation albeit for the first while as a sub-discipline of philosophy (Copleston, 1960, p. 5).

We begin the history of British empiricism with John Locke (1632–

1704), universally recognized as the father of this modern school of thought. He was a moderate, tolerant, reasonable man who, in line with the modern spirit, disliked all forms of authoritarianism and fanaticism. He was a rationalist in the sense that he believed that all beliefs ought to be tested by reason. But he was a *scientific* rationalist in that he tried to achieve true knowledge analytically, by taking things apart rather than by deducing self-evident statements from other self-evident statements. His chief method was observation for verification and his chief aim was to achieve factual correctness. He wanted to examine the mind's capacity and to "search out the bounds between opinion and knowledge" (Locke, 1671). He opposed metaphysical rationalism and its doctrine of innate *a priori* ideas on grounds that these ideas were neither universally accepted nor necessarily innate. Instead he argued that all ideas in the mind derive from experience. For Locke the material from which we derive knowledge is twofold. First we obtain knowledge from our sense perceptions of the world, and the second source of our knowledge comes from our reflection on those sensations.

Locke was a modern philosopher who, like Bacon before him, was a proponent of the natural scientific method. What does this mean in the context of modern philosophy? First, like his friend Newton, Locke strove to verify his hypotheses via observation. But, second, it also meant that he uncritically accepted Newton's mechanistic and atomistic view of the cosmos. More important for the history of psychology, since both he and Newton saw the mind as a mirror image of the world, Locke viewed the mind as a mechanism as well. His aim in all of this was to understand the mind, or what was then called "human nature," by reducing our everyday concrete experience of things to a natural scientific model of that experience. This model holds that experience consists of basic elements, which our minds combine or associate together to form the things of our everyday experience. With this view, Locke and the other British Empiricists like Berkeley, Hume, James Mill, and John Stuart Mill are forerunners of the experimental psychology movement started by Wilhelm Wundt in the nineteenth century.

Specifically, Locke held that the basic content of our knowledge consists of sensations that in turn are mirroring copies of material things in the outside world. Observing these external objects provides us with "ideas of sight" that are in essence elementary sensations of color, form, length, weight, etc. Inner observation, also called reflection or introspection, adds ideas about our own activities to these sensations. From this inner form of experience, we learn that the mind initially receives these simple elementary ideas of sensations passively but thereafter exercises activity in combining them to form the complex things of our every-day experience.

Implicit in the view that ideas are mirror copies of external things is the notion that there is an external world of material substances that is the ultimate source of all our knowledge. There is a longstanding doctrine that goes all the way back to Democritus's materialistic atomism (see 2.3.3), which Newton and Locke apparently accepted without question. This was the doctrine that reality consists of material elements each of which emit *eidola*, or bits of itself. Huygens, a contemporary of Newton and Locke, called these *eidolae* "vibrations." These vibrations were said to affect our sense organs to produce sensations that form the basic ideas of our minds. In this way the scientific rationalists explained how reality informs our minds about itself. This ancient, but now rationalistically updated, materialistic doctrine of Democritus was God-sent for these modern rationalists because they had a problem that the ancients did not have.

Prior to the modern times, most thinkers were Realists. They believed that what is in the mind essentially corresponds to what is in the world. They made no distinction between epistemology and ontology. For them, what we think equals what is. In such a situation there is no need to distinguish what is in the mind from what is outside of it. Descartes changed all that. He said there are two very different substances, mind and the world or matter (including our body). Thus he raised for the first time the distinction between inside and outside the mind. Inside are the innate ideas and thinking; outside are the mechanisms or the thought-about things. This is dualism (Descartes, 1649).

Once dualism has been established, it raises the question how inside and outside relate to one another, and more specifically, which is the origin of which. By embracing the doctrine of *eidolae*, Locke made it clear that he believed that reality outside the mind was the origin of what was inside the mind. At birth, he taught, there is nothing inside our mind, it is a *tabula rasa*, a blank slate, and as we experience the world, the outside world inscribes or impresses itself on our mind through the senses. Nothing exists in the mind that did not first exist outside the mind, or in the (Newtonian) physical world.

However, Locke also asserted that the mind knows nothing but its own ideas. We cannot assume, he stated, that what we have in our minds corresponds in all respects to what exists outside of it. All we have in our minds is our own ideas, which may or may not be true. Locke *believed* that the content of our minds corresponds to what is out there. And he *believed* that the *form* of our ideas corresponds to the form of external things. Locke *believed* that the ideas in the mind were true copies of the outside world because they originated there. But he confessed that he could not be sure because human beings are unable to perceive the things of the world *in themselves* (Locke, 1671).

### 4.2.2 *Berkeley: Doubt about an external world*

Anglican bishop Berkeley (1685–1753) who followed Locke in time, attacked Locke's doctrine of an unknowable material substance outside the mind as the origin of the mind's ideas. He argued that it is inconceivable that perceived beings like sensations should find their origin in an unperceiving substance like physical matter. So, he held that Locke's theory of a material substrate to sensation was both an unintelligible and an unnecessary hypothesis. Per definition sensible objects are only dependent on perceiving minds. To postulate some unknowable, unperceiving substance behind the sensations we experience makes no sense. Hence, Berkeley formulated his famous description of being: *esse est percipi* to be is to-be-perceived. Or more precisely *esse est aut percipi aut percipere,* to be is to-be-perceived or to-perceive. There is no other reality. The only things that exist are perceivers and their sensory perceptions.

Berkeley, quite properly raised the question how we can know for sure that there is a world outside of us independent of our sensory experience of it. And his answer was the same as that of Locke: we cannot know. He pointed to his pen and said, "I know that this pen exists *only* because I see it. I *believe* that it exists only because I associate different sightings of the pen over time and I *conclude* that it must therefore also exist when I do not see it. But I have no *proof.*"

By way of another example he asked, "How do I know that this pen is three-dimensional when all I see is only one side? To demonstrate beyond a doubt that it is, I would have to see the pen from all sides simultaneously. But I can't. I may *believe* that my pen is three-dimensional, but I have no *proof.* It is not self-evidently true for me that the objects of the world are three-dimensional." His solution to the problem of whether there is a three-dimensional outside world was to assert that there is no permanent material reality apart from my sense perception. There ain't no "out there" out there.

Berkeley then asked whether, if everything only has perceived being, there is *any* sense in which we can say that the world exists outside of us and that it exists in three-dimensional form. He then introduces God as the omniscient perceiver who by seeing all things all the time from all sides guarantees the continued existence of the things of the world.

Berkeley had his own agenda in questioning the existence of an external material world. He was a clergyman who wanted to refute the mechanistic materialistic worldview of Newtonian physics, which, he believed, was putting faith in God in peril. His solution was ingenious. He demonstrated the nonexistence of a Newtonian nature and made God indispensable to the structure of (sensorily perceived) reality. Where Locke had postulated some material substance as the origin of sensations, Berkeley postulated a spiritual or mental substance as their origin. For him reality consists of sensations that are dependent on some mind, either human or divine. Behind his phenomenalist analysis of material things lay a speculative Idealist or Spiritualist metaphysic (Berkeley, 1952).

### 4.2.3 *Hume: Doubt about the existence of causality*

Berkeley's phenomenalist or empiricistic analysis of experience proved to be more influential for the history of experimental psychology than his spiritualist metaphysics. David Hume (1711–1776), who followed Berkeley in time, rejected both the materialistic metaphysics of Locke and the spiritualist metaphysics of Berkeley. Instead Hume attempted to restrict himself exclusively to a phenomenalist analysis of experience. Empiricism rejects the doctrine that what we experience must necessarily be rooted in some unperceivable soul or in unknowable matter. It attempts to stick to what we can hear, see, touch, and smell in its search for true knowledge. Hume certainly was a prime example of such empiricism. He held that all we can know about reality is that it consists only of sensations. Our knowledge does not extend to the cause of these sensations. Sensations are of unknown origin.

Hume believed that the study of human mind, which for him was synonymous with the study of human nature, was the "capital center of all the sciences" since it is by means of the mind that we come to know the world. He wanted to apply the principles of (Newtonian) natural science to the study of mind. He wanted to study people via the experimental method, which under Newton had proved to be so fruitful in the study of the physical world. Consequently, Hume proposed to analyze experience down to its atomic constituents, i.e., its "impressions" or sense data, and their derivatives, our "ideas." The difference between these two constituents was not greatly important for Hume. He held that impressions are more vivid than ideas. Hume often referred to the constituents of the mind interchangeably as "impressions," as "ideas," and also as "perceptions." These are all what he refers to as the atomic constituents of the mind. The main importance of them is that they are contiguous to one another, i.e., they occur next to each other in time or space.

While these constituents of the mind are always singular, simple, and discrete, it is human imagination, according to Hume, that *associates* them into complex ideas in tune with certain "laws of association." We associate impressions, ideas, or perceptions together in our mind's experience, and we do so in three ways:

a)   Via *resemblance*: things that look like each other we group into "classes" (in our minds, apples belong to one class, oranges to another).

b)   Via *contiguity: we* view things and events that occur together in time and in space as "belonging together" (desks, students, a blackboard, and a teacher lead us to think "classroom").

c)   Via *cause and effect*: When two events occur one after the other, we readily conclude that the first must be the cause of the second. *Post hoc, propter hoc.*

With respect to the law of cause and effect, Hume questioned the self-evidency of the belief that everything must necessarily have a cause. He used the concept of association, which, following Newton, he called *mental gravity*, as an analytical tool to demonstrate that cause and effect are not basic constituents of our experience, because we can analyze the cause-effect *experience* further into the *experience* of temporal contiguity (one thing happening after another) plus the *feeling* of necessity that the first event must be the cause of the second event. Hume then questioned how valid this feeling of necessity is. We cannot demonstrate causality on the basis of our experience since all we can introspect is contiguity. Thus, belief in causality is only a conclusion, a generalization. Our belief that everything must have a cause is an *inference*. It may be wrong.

Hume applied this argument to all generalizations. For instance, based on our *experience* with swans, we may conclude to the generalization that all swans are white. But this general statement about swans is not necessarily true because there may be a black swan out there somewhere that we have not yet seen. Thus, Hume studied how the human mind works, and he came to the conclusion that the feeling we have of self-evidency regarding causality and the existence of general ideas is based on a psychological habit we have, one that animals have as well. Accordingly he rejected the notion that causality is an infallible *a priori* idea of the mind.

Furthermore, Hume argued, if causality does not exist as an *a priori* idea, then we cannot have any knowledge of the outside world either, because our conviction about the reality of an outside world is based on the belief that it *causes* us to have knowledge of itself. In the end Hume ironically came to the same conclusion that Berkeley came to on the basis of his reasoning. By applying Newton's natural scientific method to the human mind, he demonstrated the impossibility of a Newtonian physical universe (Hume, 1739).

### 4.3. *French sensationalism*

Before we complete our survey of British empiricism with a description of the theories of James Mill and John Stuart Mill, we must first make an excursion into French sensationalism. Like the British empiricists the French sensationalists, or "philosophes," were also thoroughgoing empiricists. These sensationalists had two main sources of inspiration: Locke's empirical psychology and Descartes' speculative view of the human body. On the basis of these two "authorities" they stated that animals and human beings do not differ in kind but only in degree because they are both simple machines. This view is not unlike the view of the later evolutionists and the behaviorists.

More so than the British empiricists, the French sensationalists opposed the influence of religion and metaphysics on human life. In their effort to ban these cultural forces from society they were motivated not so much by an antipathy for the church or a dislike for the theory of innate ideas as by a love for the natural scientific method. These French philosophers had a program of extending the sphere of empirically verified knowledge as far as it would go. They believed with all their heart that the wholesale application of the scientific method to everyday life was the only way to make progress in solving the problems of the world. They looked forward to the development of an empirical study of psychology and biology as well as to the development of studies in sociology and political economy. They wanted to scientifically understand humankind's psychological, social, and political life as much as possible without the input of religious and metaphysical presuppositions about human life. They wanted to do for mankind's mental and social life what Newton had done for the physical being of the universe. They worked hard at developing what Hume called "the science of man." In course of this attempt, they performed a number of tentative thought experiments that proved to be significant for the history of experimental psychology. In short, what they were after was a thoroughgoing natural scientific understanding of human nature (Copleston, 1960, pp. 57, 58).

### 4.3.1 *La Mettrie*

It is instructive to see how these sensationalists went about implementing their program. One such sensationalist was La Mettrie (1709–1751), who said that Descartes was in error by excluding human beings from nature. Like animals, he held, human beings are also machines. La Mettrie was a confirmed materialist, but unlike Descartes he did not think of matter as mere extension. He taught that matter possesses the power of movement. According to La Mettrie's view, motion in matter produces sensation in people, which in turn produces all the other forms of mental life. For him also, human beings, animals, and plants do not differ in kind but in degree (of motion) only. So, when La Mettrie stated that human beings are like animals he was not trying to lower human beings to the level of animals (as evolutionism and behaviorism does) but he was trying to raise animals up to the level of human beings. Animals, he said, are like human beings because they too have moral sentiments, like grief and regret (La Mettrie, 1748).

La Mettrie's thinking was natural scientific and anti-Aristotelian. To him the universe is not pulled up out of matter by an unmoved mover, but it *emerges* out of primordial matter. Note that in this view matter has become the *arche*, the creative source out of which everything else arises. This is the doctrine of *transformationalism*, which is a precursor of evolutionism. For La Mettrie matter is not dead but alive. Machines are not metallic gadgets, as we think of them, but vital, living, dynamic, integral parts of living nature. This view, which later the French philosopher Henri Bergson dubbed *vitalism*, made it possible for the emergence of biology as a special science and separate from physics (Copleston, 1960, p. 394).

### 4.3.2 *Condillac*

Yet another French sensationalist was Condillac (1715–1780). He was an even more pronounced representative of French sensationalism than La Mettrie. He was a great admirer of John Locke. "Immediately after Aristotle came Locke," he said. But where Locke had still distinguished between ideas of sensation and ideas of reflection, Condillac reduced everything that exists to sensations. The "stuff" of the universe is sensation. His motto was, "I sense, therefore I am." His sensationalism was an extreme form of empiricism. According to Condillac, all mental operations are reducible to sensations. They are all *"transformed sensations."* He started with sensations and tried to build up more complex mental activities from them. By way of experiment he hypothesized a person who only had one sense, the sense of smelling. When an odor occurred to him, it would capture his attention, or else he could not smell it. The presentation of two or more different odors would allow the person to distinguish between them and thus to form ideas. In this way the person would learn to abstract. In order to re-experience an odor that a person really liked he would attempt to recall that odor and thus memory was born. Memory, Condillac held, arises when we experience a sensation for the second time. But he cheated because he had to assume memory as an inner power to store the first sensation, which he was trying to demonstrate without the help of inner powers. When a desire for a particular sensation becomes dominant in a person's life, according to Condillac, we can speak of "passion." What people usually call "will" he defines as a desire or passion that has become absolute. These examples should suffice to illustrate Condillac's sensationalist interpretation of our mental life (Condillac, 1754).

### 4.3.3 *Helvetius*

Helvetius (1715–1771), a contemporary of Condillac, continued the latter's attempt to show that all psychological phenomena are in fact transformed sensations. He also applied this process of reductive analysis, i.e., the process of reducing everything to sensations, to humankind's ethical life. He identified self-love as the universal basis of human conduct, specifically the love of pleasure and the dislike of pain. People are most happy when they can acquire the pleasures they seek and avoid the pain they fear. Phenomena such as the love of power are secondary to this more basic seeking after pleasure and the reduction of pain, which motivating forces he called "corporeal sensibility." On this basis Helvetius also argued for the possibility of love for fellow human beings. A benevolent man is a person in whom the spectacle of misery in others produces a painful sensation. In the long run benevolent people try to relieve unhappiness and misery in others simply because this reduces the painful sensations that they feel.

Condillac had tried to give an empiricist theory of mind, but it went too far for him to strip human beings of their soul (Copleston, 1960, p. 34). This aspect of his views was of course in conflict with his empiricism. Helvetius had such scruples. He adhered to a complete environmentalism, which is in fact an extreme form of sensationalism. Environmentalism implies that human beings have neither a soul nor even a body like a biological structure that determines how we act (as La Mettrie still maintained). Human beings only possess senses, a passive mind capable of receiving sensations, and a body that is only capable of reaction. In other words, according to Helvetius, we are purely the product of our environment.

Thereby Helvetius unwittingly presented the crucial problem of the modern period, also called the period of the Enlightenment. The problem was that if human beings are part of the natural world, there is no basis on which to erect a system of ethics, or a theory about what human beings *ought to* do. In this sensationalistic view human beings are the slaves of their passions and they are determined by forces in their environment. Such a view leads to a complete hedonism.

For the rationalists, reason, or thinking as the activity of the mind, occurred prior to and independent of sensation. That view made hedonism only a temptation to be overcome. But the empiricists constructed reason or thinking *out of* (affectively charged) sensations. This made hedonism the directing force of thought. Thought here is a slave to passion. As we saw, Helvetius postulated a "pleasure principle" as the fundamental drive of human life. He also reduced all feelings, including feelings of love and altruism, to the egotistical pursuit of pleasure and the avoidance of pain. The logical outcome of this view is the "ethics" of the Marquis de Sade (Helvetius, 1772).

### 4.4 James Mill: Associationism

Now that we have looked at French sensationalism we are in a better position to understand later forms of British empiricism, specifically the associationism of James Mill and the positivism of John Stuart Mill. The various forms of empiricistic psychology of the eighteenth and nineteenth century, which were forerunners of contemporary experimental psychology, were all characterized by sensationalism, mechanism, elementarism, and associationism.

To understand James Mill's system, I must first devote a paragraph to Jeremy Bentham's utilitarianism. Like Helvetius, Bentham (1748–1832) held that nature has placed human beings under two sovereign masters, pleasure and pain (Copleston, 1966, p. 8). These govern all that we do. On this basis Bentham constructed his Utilitarian ethics. In his view, right action increases pleasure, wrong action diminishes it. Via this reductive analysis of human life, Bentham in essence defined a human being as a system of attractions and repulsions. His principles of pleasure and pain, which we first encountered in my description of French sensationalism, resemble Hume's laws of association. Bentham sought to quantify pleasure and pain and distinguished between simple and complex pleasures and pain, much in the line of Hume's thinking (Bentham, 1789).

James Mill (1773–1836) was a champion of Benthamism. By adopting Bentham's reductive analysis of human nature, James Mill was able to construct a completely mechanistic theory of the human mind. He followed Hume in distinguishing between impressions and ideas and in the view that causation is only a name we give to constant temporal contiguity. For James Mill ideas were just another form of sensations. He followed Condillac who thought of the higher functions of the human mind as transformations of sensations. Thus, Mill's view of human nature was also thoroughly sensationalistic.

Mill had what could be called a *"tinker-toy"* theory of the mind. In his view the mind is passive, a blank slate at birth and merely receptive of simple sensations throughout life. These simple sensations resemble the nodes of the tinker toy. Out of these atomic sensations complex sensations or ideas arise when associative links, i.e., the sticks of the tinker toy, are formed between these atomic units. Combined with the utilitarian hedonism of Bentham, the result of James Mill's conception is a completely mechanistic picture of the mind in which idea follows idea automatically with no room left for voluntary control by human beings over the process (James Mill, 1829).

### 4.5 *John Stuart Mill: Mental chemistry and positivism*

Mill's son, John Stuart Mill (1806–1873) found this model too sterile, narrow, and excessively calculating. Where Bentham and James Mill only allowed for quantitative distinctions, John Stuart Mill focused on qualitative distinctions within the human mind and, whereas his father was an elementarist, he was a holist. He also made room for the will as the director of human action next to the forces of pleasure and pain. He described the activity of the human mind as "mental chemistry" rather than mental gravitation. Elementary sensations, he said, are able to "fuse" into wholes, which are not reducible to the elements (J.S. Mill, 1843). Instead of association he emphasized that the mind is able to "coalesce" elementary ideas into new ideas. In all this he foreshadowed a debate later in the history of psychology – which especially involved the Gestalt psychologists – on whether consciousness consists of wholes or elements.

The other reason why the writings of John Stuart Mill are significant for the history of psychology is that he was one of the first to formulate rules for how scientific psychology ought to be practiced. By now many of these rules have become so much an integral part of the methodology of experimental psychology that we forget Mill was the one who formulated them. Mill drafted two global rules that have become commonplace today. The first is that scientific psychology may not be based on a priori theories but must be based strictly on empirically discovered facts. The second is that scientific psychology may not accept theories of psychology on the basis of their face validity but only on the basis of experimental research results.

These formulations seem like sound advice, but how does one go about implementing them? Because there is a problem in following these rules, a problem that Berkeley had already signaled earlier. He had pointed to the fact that what we perceive is not the result of observation only but the result of a *mixture* of observation and interpretation. In other words, what we think we see is partially affected by what we expect to see on the basis of past experience. In empirical research the part of our perception due to our expectancy would be considered a contamination of the data. It is for this reason that Mill argued that the data of scientific research cannot the observations of the researchers, but rather their *report* of their observations. This statement allowed Mill to formulate yet another rule. He believed that research reports or scientific statements in general cannot be considered factually correct unless they can be verified by other researchers. This means that research reports must be stated in such a way that other researchers can repeat the described research procedures and come up with the same results. They must be publicly formulated.

The question now becomes for Mill how these rules can be implemented in psychology, which studies "states of mind." States of mind are observed via introspection and are available for observation only to the person who does the introspecting. How can these introspection reports be formulated in such a way that they can be publicly verified? This can be done, according to Mill, by a formulation that shows under what physical conditions the introspected state of mind occurred. A mundane example of this would be that if a certain level of electromagnetic energy were directed toward the retina, any person who is not color blind would have the experience of seeing red. Thus, in this example the state of mind of seeing red is publicly verifiable because it is formulated as a function of the level of electromagnetic energy, a physical state of affairs (J.S. Mill, 1970).

### 4.6. *The positivism of Auguste Comte*

In drafting these rules John Stuart Mill showed himself to be an adherent of positivism, a movement, broadly speaking, that promoted the application of the natural scientific method to the social sciences and to psychology. During the nineteenth century there was great appreciation for the natural sciences and their technological applications, the telephone, the steam engine, and the chemical industry. People were impressed by science because of its power, instrumentaria, measurement ability, mathematical models, and ability to replicate physical phenomena in the laboratory. There seemed to be no end to the power of mathematics, observation, and experimentation in physics to break down complex systems into simple elements (Estes, 1979). As a result, many nonphysical scientists compared the state of their discipline with the state of the natural sciences and found their own discipline wanting. Thus, they pleaded for the application of the natural scientific method to their discipline. For example, in medicine the so-called *medical model* was adopted, which views bodies as the sum of physicochemical processes, i.e., it views bodies as complicated machines (Maher & Maher, 1979; Eisenga & van Rappard, 1987).

In this intellectual climate the "positive" philosophy of Auguste Comte (1798–1857) became popular. It stressed the historical development of human thought, which Comte divided into three phases.

a) *The theological phase*: During this phase thought looks for the cause and the purpose of observable events outside these events. For example, it explains earthly phenomena in terms of the actions of the gods.

b) *The metaphysical phase*: During this phase thought looks for the cause and purpose of events in the hidden powers in or behind the phenomena (platonism?). For example, it looks for the natural powers or properties of things, such as the sedative property of opium, the motivating properties of feelings, or the growth tendency of an acorn to become an oak tree.

c) *The positive phase*: Here thought restricts itself to the positively given phenomena, without looking in or behind things. Thought only deals with what is observable.

Two things should be mentioned at this point. First, Comte's theory of historical development implies a form of presentism. And second, given the history of empiricism and sensationalism, the concept of "observation" in Comte's system often means "reducing phenomena to sensations." In any case, as we will see, what it means exactly to scientifically observe things soon became a major source of contention in experimental psychology (Comte, 1868).

Comte's system resulted in a call for renewal in psychology. Many at that time saw psychology as *the* science of human nature. It was supposed to be the basis for all the social sciences and also a basis for the construction of a universal system of ethics. But these same people also saw the existing systems of psychology of that day as still far too metaphysical and divided among far too many points of view. Thus, the call went out to make psychology more reliable and unified by having it adopt the method of the natural sciences. It was this call for methodological renewal that caused experimental psychology to break away from philosophy and to establish itself as a special, empirical science, like physics, biology, chemistry, and physiology. From here on in, methodological questions related to psychology becoming a natural science become prominent in the history of psychology (Eisenga & van Rappard, 1987).

## References

Bacon, F. (1886). *Novum Organum*. 1620, London: Bell.

Bentham, J. (1948). *An Introduction to the Principles of Morals and Legislation*. Ed. by L. Lafleur, New York.

Berkeley (1952). *Philosophical Writings*. Selected and edited by T.E. Jessop.

Comte, A. (1868). *Principles de Philosophie Positive*. Paris.

Condillac, (1952). *Treatise on the Sensations*. Transl. by G. de Roy, Paris.

Copleston, F.C. (1965). *A History of Philosophy*. Vol. IV, Westminster: The Newman Press.

Copleston, F.C. (1965). *A History of Philosophy*. Vol. V, Westminster: The Newman Press.

Copleston, S.J. (1965). *A History of Philosophy*. Vol. VI, Westminster: The Newman Press.

Critchley, S. (2001). *Continental Philosophy*. New York: Oxford U. Press.

Descartes, R. (1879–1913). *Œuvres de Descartes*. Ed. by C. Adam and P. Tannery, 13 vols., Paris.

Eisenga, L.K.A. & van Rappard, J.F.H. (1987). *Hoofdstromen en Mensbeelden in de Psychologie*. Amsterdam: Boom.

Estes, W.K. (1979). Experimental psychology, an overview. In: E. Hearst, ed. *The First Century of Experimental Psychology*. Hillsdale: Lawrence Erlbaum, 623–668.

Galileo, G. (1623). *Il saggiatore*. [*The assayer*. Translated by Stillman Drake and C.D. O'Malley, in *The Controversy on the Comets of 1618*, University of Pennsylvania Press, 1960.]

Helvetius. (1777). *A Treatise on Man*. Transl. by W. Hooper, London.

Hume, D. *A treatise of Human Nature*. Introduction by A.D. Lindsay, 2 vols. London.

La Mettrie, J.O. (1912). *Man a Machine*. Translated and annotated by G.C. Bussey, La Salle, IL: Open Court.

Locke, J. (1894). *An Essay Concerning Human Understanding*. A.C. Fraser, ed. 2 vols., Oxford.

Maher, B.A. and Maher, W.B. (1979). Psychopathology. In: E. Hearst ed. *The First Century of Experimental Psychology*. Hillsdale: Lawrence Erlbaum, 561–621.

Mill, James. (1869). *Analysis of the Phenomena of the Human Mind*. 2 vols., London, 1869.

Mill, J.S. (1970). *A System of Logic Ratiocinative and Inductive*. London: Longman Group, Ltd.

van Rappard, J.F.H. (1976). *Psychologie als Zelfkennis: Het zielsbegrip tussen substantie en structuur in de Duitse rationalistische psychologie van Wolff tot Wundt en Brentano*. Amsterdam: Academische Pers, 29.

# SOME ISSUES TO STIMULATE DIALOGUE

1. In this chapter I take the position that there is a historical discontinuity between the Middle Ages and the modern period. I contend that a paradigm shift occurred between these two periods of Western thought. Medieval thinkers (both Christian and Renaissance thinkers) still assumed the identity of thinking and being (although one could argue that Ockham already began to call this dogma into question). For medieval philosophers, thoughts of whatever kind provided direct access to the way things are because they believed that being *informs* thinking. Philosophers of the modern period called this "naïve realism" into question. For Descartes only a certain kind of thinking provides access to being, i.e., only right thinking, only reason leads to clear and distinct knowledge. For Locke only that form of thinking that is rooted in sensation gives us insight into being. He held that, to gain access to the way things are, thinking must be augmented by observation. I believe that this difference between medieval and modern thought is pronounced enough to be able to speak of a paradigm shift. As a result of this shift, the question concerning *how* thinking relates to being moves to center stage during the modern period. When the relationship between thinking and being became problematic, philosophers began to search for the right *method* of investigating reality. Looking ahead, this emphasis on methodology came to be a major focus of concern during the nineteenth century of Western thought (see 6.1). At that time the idea became popular that only thinking in accordance with the "scientific method" would give us insight into reality. At about the same time, under the influence of evolutionism, Francis Galton offered the opinion that only people who are genetically gifted with intelligence are able to know what's what. This represented the beginning of I.Q. testing (see 9.3).

   In this chapter I argue in effect for a diachronic discontinuity between philosophers of the medieval period and philosophers of the modern period. This historical difference represents at the same time a synchronic commonality between scholars of the modern period. They were united in making the relationship between thought and being problematic. The question for you to consider is to what extent my construction of this time in the history of Western thought is valid. There are a number of historians of psychology who see a much greater continuity between the Middle Ages and the modern period. See, for example, Leahy (2000, p. 146), who paints Descartes as an apologist for medieval Roman catholicism.

2. An even more radical difference between the Middle Ages and the modern period is the fact that, for philosophers of the modern period, under the influence of the theme of the *a priori* (see 2.8; 3.13) reality became a *product* of the human mind. For Descartes the world we live in was a "thought about" world. For the empiricists and the sensationalists the basic elements of the world were "sensations." Other words for the basic building blocks of the world were "ideas" (as in Locke: "the mind only knows its own ideas"), "perceptions" (as in Berkeley: "to be is to-be-perceived"), or "impressions" (as in Hume: "impressions are more vivid than ideas"). In other words, modern philosophers, if I may be permitted to put it that way, *epistemologized ontology.*

They focused on the study of the mind because they saw the mind as the gateway to (physical) reality. They reasoned that if we understand how the mind works we would know how to gain access to (physical) reality. All this happened essentially because the Moderns lost faith in naïve realism. Modern philosophy is skeptical philosophy.

There were some positive aspects to this historical development. First, it allowed them to question the tradition of sterile dogmatism that held sway during the Middle Ages. It opened up scholarship to new ways of thinking about the mind and the world. Second, it affirmed the importance of empirically verifying our ideas about the mind and the world, and thereby gave impetus to the development of contemporary science. Finally, this historical development was important for contemporary psychology because via its exclusive focus on the study of the mind it made people in the Western world ready to consider psychology as a separate study of mental phenomena a viable enterprise. Can you think of other advantages of this historical development?

Unfortunately, there was also a considerable downside to this development. By focusing exclusively on the mind as the gateway to (physical) reality, these scientific rationalists came to doubt the independent existence of that reality. Locke still believed in the possible existence of a (physical) world outside the mind. Berkeley clearly did not. Hume, by raising doubts whether phenomena like causality and other generalizations have reference to anything outside the mind, even questioned the possibility of studying (physical) reality. This is ironic because the whole enterprise of scientific rationalism was to provide an epistemological basis for the physical sciences, specifically for Newtonian physics. Was this development inevitable or could it have been avoided?

Yet another downside to this development was that it estranged psychology as the scientific study of the human mind from every-day human experience. In order to study the mind as the gateway to physical reality, the scientific rationalists attempted to conceive of the mind as much as possible in terms of the vocabulary of (Newtonian) physics. So, they thought of the mind as a mechanism, consisting of elements that combine and recombine themselves automatically in accordance with certain laws of association, or mental gravity. The scientific study of the mind in this view consisted of analyzing or breaking down our everyday experience to its (sensory) elements and to demonstrate the ways in which the mind associates these elements into the wholes of our everyday experience. However, the scientific picture that results from this investigation bears next to no resemblance to what human beings experience. For example, no one would consider what actually goes on in his or her head as identical or even similar to the tinker toy model of the mind constructed by James Mill.

The problem of the estrangement of psychology from everyday experience is with us to this day. It is present, for example, in the models of mind constructed by behaviorism and cognitive psychology (see chapters 12 and 13). My question to the reader is whether this estrangement is an unavoidable byproduct of scientific psychology or merely a bias with which historically scientific rationalism saddled contemporary psychology. In other words, is it possible to scientifically study human experience in a way that avoids this estrangement?

3. Positivists like John Stuart Mill and Auguste Comte argued that psychology could only become scientific if it adopted the methodology of the natural sciences. For Mill this meant that psychologists would have to express their research findings in publicly verifiable terms. This in effect meant that mental states of affairs would have to be reported as variables dependent on physical states of affairs. Much of early experimental psychology was done in accordance with Mill's methodological rules (see chapters 6 and 7).

As I see it, the problem with this philosophy of psychological research is that under these rules a great deal of human experience cannot be scientifically studied by psychology (see chapters 6 and 15 for examples). Mindful of Vollenhoven's conviction that the methodology of a discipline must arise *out of* and be subservient to the study material of the discipline, I consider positivism's philosophy of research an unwarranted encroachment of the research methodology of one discipline (physics) on field of investigation of another (psychology). Do you know of a methodology that avoids this problem?

4. Why is it that under the philosophy of French sensationalism no system of ethics as it is usually understood is possible? Must one be a dualist to be able to have a system of ethics?

5. Since La Mettrie (4.3.1) and Leibniz (5.4) are both principally dynamic thinkers, but belong to different modern philosophical traditions, it would be worthwhile for someone to write a paper comparing and contrasting these two systems of thought.

6. What do you think of this argument? I believe that British empiricism, French sensationalism, and especially positivism are reductionistic. They reduce human being and action conceptually to something less (complex) than it is. When one does that, sooner or later, what one has chosen to ignore will rise up to refute one's reductionism. The classic example in psychology is the way behaviorism chose to deny the reality of mental states in its theories and practice. These mental states took center stage in the cognitive psychology that followed behaviorism in time. As soon as one decides to undo the reduction and acknowledge the complexity one chose to ignore, these factors become conscious and observable data that then enrich one's point of view.

7. One of the aims of this chapter is to show how British empiricism, French sensationalism, and positivism form the historical philosophical background for the various branches of experimental psychology. The vocabulary of this thought tradition appears to anticipate many notions found in contemporary experimental psychology. A good exercise to do would be to identify which notions of this philosophical tradition in the history of Western thought seem familiar to you based on your knowledge of courses like sensation and perception, learning and memory, cognition, brain and behavior, and research methods in psychology.

# 5. The Development of Metaphysical Rationalism: Rationalism, idealism, and Romanticism

## 5.1 *Introduction*

As I did in the previous chapter, I will start my description of the development of metaphysical rationalism with a few introductory remarks. These comments will take on greater relief as we deal in more detail with the various schools of thought included in this movement, those of rationalism, romanticism, and idealism. A description of the development of this movement of modern thought will show, I hope, how it forms the historical-philosophical background of clinical psychology. I believe this will become clearer when in Chapter 7 I give a description of the *Völkerpsychologie* of Wilhelm Wundt, who, we all know, was the father of contemporary psychology, and even more so in Chapter 8 with the discussion on the psychoanalysis of Freud, who arguably could be called the father of clinical psychology.

Even though metaphysical rationalism differs markedly from scientific rationalism, it too is a form of rationalism in that it represents an attempt to eradicate the dependence in philosophy, on existing authority, on religion, and on tradition, which tendency had dominated so much of prior medieval and Renaissance thought. Philosophy, in the view of this new movement, was to be critical of dogma and of any existing theory that could not be clearly and distinctly thought. In this conception philosophy was to serve as the sanitation of the soul or mind. This came about not by testing its contents for truthfulness in terms of the sensory experience of an outside world, but by bringing its own *a priori*, infallible powers to bear on its primary activity of thinking, or on its capacity for *representation* (Copleston, 1960, p. 34). The physical world was not much for this movement of modern thought. This form of thinking is quite properly called *meta*physical in that it was exclusively concerned with matters that were presumed to be *beyond* the physical world we inhabit. In true Cartesian fashion it only concerned itself with self-knowledge. In this view the mind has within itself the capacity to distinguish truth from error infallibly through reasoning and therefore it has no need for an external regulating criterion of truth. For metaphysical rationalism reasoning, or right thinking, is all there is and all there needs to be (Copleston, 1960, p. 71). There is no world outside the mind, and sensory perception is simply the lowest form of activity the mind can produce or the least clear and distinct way in which we are able to represent reality to ourselves.

Quite succinctly, in metaphysical rationalism the mind concerns itself exclusively with itself. It starts with self-knowledge that is dark and opaque and ends with knowledge that is clear and distinct. It patterns itself on the paradigm of mathematical thinking, specifically on geometry. From this starting point thinking proceeds deductively, in the tradition of geometric reasoning, and comes to rest when the results of thinking are formulated in self-evident propositions.

For the adherents to this movement of modern thought, the process of coming to know is one of self-clarification by the mind, or of explicating what is implied in thinking and of representing or "spelling out" what one really means. To use a more contemporary metaphor, it is a process of *consciousness-raising*. Thus, one can talk about *levels of clarity* or *levels of consciousness* in this representation, or consciousness-raising process. For example, the distinction between inside and outside the mind, which exercised the scientific rationalists so much, is not an ontological distinction for the metaphysical rationalists but an epistemological difference. The distinction refers to levels of clarity with which something is represented, contemplated, or introspected by the mind (van Rappard, 1976, p. 64). Similarly, the distinction between sense perception and thinking or reasoning is not one of qualitatively differing human functions, but it is one of gradually increasing levels of clarity of thinking by the mind. Thus, sense perception represents the initial activity of distinguishing dark, unclear, but basic knowledge. Thinking or reasoning, on the other hand, represents our capacity to see the unity of things. In addition to contemplating something in the most clear and distinct way, it also refers to the activity of unifying plurality. There is a persistent emphasis in the development of metaphysical rationalism on system building, on integrality and wholeness, and a focus on how elements hold together. In this process of clarification and systematization, the so-called *"faculties"* or functions of the mind also come in view. But these are always seen as specifications or sub-processes of the central function of the mind, i.e., of our capacity to think or to represent reality to ourselves.

As metaphysical rationalism evolves over time, different emphases come to the fore. At first the central focus in the clarification process is on logic and reasoning. Representations at this stage are referred to as the *contents* or *states* of mind. They are the *objects* of knowing. But quite soon, under the influence of Leibniz for example, representation becomes the *activity* of the mind. It becomes the activity of clarifying and of collecting diversity into unity. Thought at this stage comes to be seen as *dynamic.* This clarifying and unifying *process* of consciousness still later on comes to be seen as the movement of *progress.* To put it in contemporary terms, one not only maintains one's identity but also *improves* oneself via this clarification and unification process. Moreover, the final outcome of this development is that this consciousness-raising process becomes a way for human beings to *emancipate* themselves. But this last development reaches way past the scope of this chapter. A good deal of water has to have gone under the bridge before the history of Western thought reaches that end point. Under the influence of romanticism and in reaction to the unfeeling and ahistorical character of early metaphysical rationalism, the emphasis shifts from logic to feeling or intuition as the central function of the clarification and unification process.

What intrigues me about this historical development of modern thought is that it seems to carry faint sounds if not overtones of the central preoccupation of ancient Greek philosophy (see 2.3.1; 2.5; 2.6). The problem then, in one form or another, was how to relate the definite to the indefinite, or the finite to the infinite, or order to chaos, or unity to plurality. Is the fact that we see this problem reappear in the modern period perhaps an example of the persistence of typicality throughout the changes of periodicity?

After these introductory remarks I intend to walk us through the evolution of metaphysical rationalism in more detail and begin again with a few words about the father of this movement of modern thought, René Descartes.

### 5.2 *Descartes*

Descartes (1596–1650) was perhaps the first to view the process of coming to know something for sure as a self-clarification process. He held in effect that at first our knowledge of a thing is vague and uncertain. There is much darkness. We don't quite know what to think. But as we search our minds with questions such as "Is it this, or is it that?" we gain more clarity and understand better until we can say, "O, now I see!" What was to be known has now become clear and distinct. It is *evident*. Where there was darkness there now is light. The solution to a problem we might be struggling to solve may have become so clear and distinct, so *self*-evident that the need for more questioning and more doubt ceases. We are now certain we have true knowledge. The fact that the topic of our search has become perspicuous to us convinces us of its truthfulness. The end product of doubt is certainty (Descartes, 1637; van Rappard, 1967, p. 23).

### 5.3 *Pascal*

While this may have seemed true to Descartes, it was not so for his contemporary, Blaise Pascal (1623–1662). For him, doubt did not produce certainty, only more doubt. Most texts on the history of psychology make no mention of Pascal. I think that this is a mistake for at least three reasons. The first is that Pascal forms an essential link in the development of the importance of non-rationality in Western thought. This critique of reason by an emphasis on non-reason stretches all the way from Augustine, via Scotus and even Ockham, through romanticism, and finally to Wundt's voluntarism. In this development the terms of love, faith, will, heart, and feeling (or intuition) as *alternatives* to reason all have the common component of non-rationality. The second reason for Pascal's importance is that without reference to his notion of the "heart" the occurrence of romanticism's emphasis on feeling and intuition within metaphysical rationalism remains unintelligible. Historically Pascal's concept of the heart gave the Romantics the courage to oppose the intellectualism of the early Enlightenment period. Finally, Pascal was a Christian thinker who with Jakob Spener, the father of pietism in Lutheran Germany, was perhaps the only prominent Christian voice critical of the prevailing spirit of rationalism during the modern period of Western thought.

Throughout the history of Western thought, perhaps from the introduction of the Christian gospel into the Western world on, notions like *love, faith, will,* and *heart* were always present as alternatives to thinking, logic, and reason. It was not as if thinkers who championed these notions denied the importance of reason, but they wanted reason to be subordinate to these other notions as *Leitmotiv* for human life and action. When Pascal uttered his famous dictum, *"the heart has reasons of which reason knows nothing,"* he precisely intended to express this sentiment.

Reviewers of Pascal's thought generally have a hard time defining what he meant by the term "heart." It can mean intuition as the seat of feeling, or the embodiment of will, or the place where we lovingly apprehend and trust God. "Heart" can also mean a kind of instinctual, intuitive sense of immediacy, spontaneity, and directness. The most generally accepted description of the term is that the heart is a kind of instrument of knowledge next to reason. Some things can only be known by thinking them through, but other things we only know "by heart." We cannot prove this knowledge. We just know intuitively that it is true. In this definition "heart" is that which *precedes* "reason."

I think that the indefinability of the term "heart" is precisely what Pascal intended as the central characteristic of the term. The term is deliberately vague in opposition to the criteria for knowledge of clarity and distinctness associated with the term reason. Once again, the opposition of the indefinite to the definite in Western thought rears its head. I would not make so much of this theme if I did not see it played out again and again in the later critique that romanticism leveled against the intellectualism of the Enlightenment and in the fight between the Positivists and the Existentialists. More to the point, I believe that this spirit of opposition is also very much with us today in psychology between experimental and clinical psychology.

I would be amiss if I failed to mention Pascal's motivation for positing the heart as the central notion in his critique of Descartes' reason. Pascal was a Christian thinker and, like Augustine's (partial) opposition to neoplatonism in his time (3.2.1), he was opposed to the rationalistic spirit of the modern times because of its anti-Christian tenor. He was particularly opposed to the speculative proofs for the existence of God prevalent in both the medieval and modern periods. He put it this way: People are both wretched and great. They are wretched because they are sinful and cannot save themselves; they are great because, unlike the animals, they *know* (by reason) that they are wretched. Furthermore, to have knowledge of God (via the proofs of reason) without an awareness of our wretched, sinful state leads us to unwarranted pride; an awareness of our wretchedness without knowledge of God leads us to despair. Pascal, much like Augustine ages before him, confesses that both kinds of knowledge can only be found in a relationship with the God-man, Jesus Christ.

In its most general form, Pascal's opposition to rationalism pleaded for the necessity of two kinds of knowledge: existential and intellectual knowledge. The need for existential knowledge arises out of the problems of living we face. The need for intellectual knowledge arises when we attempt to solve these existential problems of living. But to *define* existential problems of living *as* intellectual puzzles represents the aberration of rationalism. It betrays the ideology that holds that we live to think, whereas in actual fact people think to live. That is to say, abstract thinking is only valuable insofar as it helps us to live life better (Pascal, 1662;

Copleston, 1958, p. 153 – 174).

The *function* of thinking for living is also the central theme of another kind of Christian critique of the intellectualism of the modern period's rationalism, that of pietism. This variant of Christianity arose at that time in the Lutheran church and presented itself as a renewal movement aimed at combating dead scholastic orthodoxy in that denomination. As I remarked in 3.9, second-generation Reformers, the Lutheran Melanchthon in particular, sought to systematize Reformed theology by using scholastic (i.e., Greek-Aristotelian) logic. For many Lutheran churchgoers, the result was that their religion became little more than an adherence to a set of abstract doctrines that seemed to have little relevance to the way they lived their lives. Jacob Spener started the movement that came to be called pietism within Lutheranism, by emphasizing a return to the text of the Bible, by stressing the necessity of a personal relationship to Jesus Christ, and by focusing on the need for repentance to good works for the less fortunate in society. Pietists also sought to gauge the genuineness of their faith by how they *felt* about their relation to God rather than what they *thought* about him. In the main, pietism sought to make the doctrines of the church more relevant to the lives of its members (Spener, 1675; Hazard, 1963, p. 422–424).

Jakob Thomasius (1622–1684) was a philosopher, and he is important for our survey because he was one of Leibniz's teachers. His views also show a decided appreciation for pietism as well as for French sensationalism. Thus he had several reasons to be opposed to the intellectualism of the modern period's rationalism. To him metaphysics and natural theology were useless as preoccupations of philosophy. The chief motive for philosophical reflection, he held, should not to be contemplation of the truth for its own sake, as was the aim of metaphysical rationalism. Rather, the function of philosophy was to be its utility for life. According to Thomasius, the value of philosophy lay in its tendency to contribute to the common good and to the happiness or wellbeing of individuals. In other words, philosophy was to be an instrument of *progress*.

This bourgeois idea of progress with its aims of the promotion of the common good and the happiness and wellbeing of individuals was in fact a secularized version of the outlook of the Protestant Reformation. The Reformation had held that true service of God was to be found in the ordinary forms of social life, not in the secluded contemplation of eternal verities. Nor was it to be found in turning away from the world in asceticism and mortification. The secularization of this notion entails the elimination of the necessity of being of service to God. When that motivation is eliminated one is left with the bourgeois notion of progress or with the ethical notion that one ought to be kind to one's neighbor and that one should strive to better oneself. The value of philosophy from here on in came to be seen as its usefulness for the promotion of these ideals. As we will see, the successors of Thomasius within metaphysical rationalism reaffirmed their belief in the value of metaphysics and abstract philosophy. But they also adhered to the idea that the value of philosophy lies in its utility for ethics. Thus, even metaphysics according to these thinkers is only worth pursuing insofar as it enriches the practice of living. Within the history of Western thought a decided turn in emphasis occurred during that period from intellectualism to practicalism (Copleston, 1960, p. 101–105).

### 5.4 *Leibniz: Monadology*

You'd never know that Leibniz (1646–1716) was a pupil of Thomasius. He was certainly not a pietist. Most of the characteristics of metaphysical rationalism described above, perhaps without a pronounced emphasis on the practical use of philosophy, are to be found in the philosophy of Leibniz. It is especially his famous *Monadology* that is important for the history of psychology. For one thing, Leibniz was the forerunner of German Act Psychology, which championed the notion that persons are agents, or centers of action; this was a notion that was important for the development of personality theory. For another, his emphasis on the dynamic nature of human life helped to foster the idea of stages in personal development. Finally, his notion of what today we would call "subliminal perception" set the stage for the idea that some of the functions of the mind are unconscious.

Perhaps the best way to introduce the monadology of Leibniz is to refer to the debate between metaphysical rationalism and scientific rationalism during the modern period about the character of the things in our world, or about the question whether the basic building blocks of the cosmos are mechanisms or monads. The key element in this debate was whether things are externally or internally caused. Are they objects or subjects, atoms or energy points? Are things inert, and put in motion by other things (think of billiard balls)? Or do they move themselves (think of living beings)? This early discussion anticipated a later debate between mechanism and vitalism.

The metaphysical rationalist Leibniz influenced later faculty psychology, according to which the mind has inherent "powers" and actualizes itself toward more and more complex, higher organization (compare

Leibniz: petit perceptions→perceptions→apperception, etc.). By way of contrast the scientific rationalist Locke influenced later mechanistic psychology, according to which the mind is a mechanism acted upon by the outside. Here complexity is explained via the association of elements (compare Locke: tabula rasa→impressions/sensations→association→ideas, etc.).

The best way to understand Leibniz is to say that he was a metaphysical rationalist. What does this mean? In a time when many scholars were trying to understand Mind in terms of nature, Leibniz interpreted nature in terms of Mind. We might put it this way: Mind is not natural, but nature is mental. That is to say, one has to think in terms of epistemological notions like perception, thinking, representation, and consciousness when trying to understand Leibniz's ontology. His conception of reality is exclusively in terms of the functions of Mind and the most characteristic function of mind is that it is ceaselessly engaged in a process of self-clarification, which for Leibniz is a process of self-perfection, or of perception, by which he means that Mind has a natural tendency to represent external things. This process is not random but has direction. To use some terms of Aristotle's philosophy, who had a marked influence on Leibniz, Leibniz subordinated efficient causes to final causes. Finally, there is an emphasis on unity, harmony, and organization in Leibniz's worldview. The more Mind clarifies, perceives, and apperceives itself, the more unified and organized it becomes.

The basic building blocks of Leibniz's worldview are perceptions, which he calls "monads." More precisely, monads are not defined by what they are as much as by what they do. Monads "strive toward" perception, which Leibniz defined as the representation or the "gathering together" of the "diversity" of the "outside world" into the unity of the "soul" or into "thinking." The basic question for him was not, How does what we think correspond to what is out there? But, how can what is out there be represented or collected or perceived into what we think?

According to Leibniz, what exists does not consist of atoms lying next to each other in space but consists of monads that exist "inside" one another. "Inside" must not be taken in a literal spatial sense, because according to Leibniz monads have no extension. Rather, monads exist inside one another in the sense that they differ from one another in terms of complexity or in terms of "levels of perception." Simpler monads are included in more complex monads. Monads are unique. No monad is the same as any other. All monads strive for self-perfection or its highest possible level of perception. This urge toward perfection is what Leibniz calls "appetite." Monads are a world unto themselves. They have no windows to reality, no contact with one another, and do not interact with one another. Each monad expresses or reflects the whole of reality in its own way. This act of representing external things is called "perception."

If monads are worlds in themselves, are windowless, and do not affect one another, how do they differ? They differ from one another in terms of the level of perception or complexity they have achieved. For example, rocks and plants have achieved a low level of perception. They function at the level of petit perceptions and are said to be in a state of swoon. They are less clear than animals, which have achieved a higher level of perception or complexity. They function at the level of perceptions. By contrast to all of these, human beings have achieved the highest level of perception, called "apperception" or "consciousness," which is the reflective knowledge of one's level of perception.

To sum up, monads are unique and a world in themselves. Each monad is not externally motivated to change but contains its successive variation in itself. Monads do not interact with one another but relate to one another via a harmony pre-established by God, who has achieved the highest level of perception and therefore includes all other monads in itself.

To say all this in yet another way, we can say that entities do not consist of inert matter (i.e., atoms in space) which is externally changed by contact with other atoms; entities consist of energy (non-spatial) *points*, called monads, that change themselves spontaneously. The fundamental characteristic of these points is perception. They are literally "points-of-view." Therefore, each monad (and not just human beings, or animals) has/is perception and each monad has/is its own point-of-view. Monads are subjects, rather than the objects of other monads. Monads are unique and have no connection with, openness to, or effect on other monads.

The basic unit of analysis (the first principle or "stuff") for Leibniz is the monad. Like the atoms, monads are uncreated and indestructible. Although they do not interact, they change or develop in harmony with other monads (in accordance with a harmony pre-established by God). Monads have inner change as their basic characteristic. They are therefore *energy, rather than matter* principles.

In distinction from Descartes, Leibniz was a monist. Like Plato, the dualist Descartes made a sharp distinction between mind and matter, or between thinking and sensation. For Leibniz the difference between mind and matter, or between thinking and sensation, is merely one of degree. He considered matter and sensation a lower level of perception than mind and thinking.

On this basis, Leibniz solved the infamous "mind-body" problem created by Descartes. For Descartes, mind and body are separate substances that are qualitatively different. This formulation raises the question of how these two different entities relate to one another. Descartes suggested that they cannot interact because this would mean that, to put it in contemporary terms, something mental is able to change something physical. The solution that Descartes' followers devised was called *occasionalism*. According to this theory God sees to it that when a bodily event occurs, so will a mental event and vice versa. The problem with this view is that it has God running around forever trying to keep mind and body coordinated. By contrast, Leibniz held that there is a pre-established parallelism between mind and body, which relation is a special case of monads changing according to a pre-established harmony. Consciousness or mind mirrors exactly what happens in the body but does not interact with the body.

This problematic of the relation between mind and body also raised the whole question of the nature of causality. Materialistic mechanists (atoms in space) held to only efficient causes in the material world, which means that atoms affect and move one another externally. Leibniz said that monads are internally motivated to perfect themselves, to actualize their potential. In this view change is spontaneous and natural. It is not caused by anything outside the monad. Monads are energy principles. (Compare the notion of "maturation" in developmental psychology.)

Leibniz also believed that many ideas we have are (virtually) innate. That is to say that many ideas are in principle present in a child at birth but require experience to activate them, i.e., to make the child aware of them. As example he used the idea of a block of marble containing the statue of Hercules (in its veins). It may take a sculptor to bring it out, but it is there already (compare the nature vs. nurture debate in developmental psychology).

Leibniz' view of perception has petit perceptions as the basic units. By themselves petit perceptions are so weak that they are not perceived. They are not clear and distinct. We are not aware of them. It takes many petit perceptions combined for us to perceive anything. By way of illustration, we do not hear the sound of a single drop of water. However, we do hear the sound a wave makes, which consists of many drops of water. Leibniz was probably the first to speak of an "unconscious" or a "preconscious."

According to Leibniz, petit perceptions lead to perception, which in turn leads to apperception. That is to say, for Leibniz perceptions are raw, confused ideas. They are not really conscious; animals also have them. They consist of many petit perceptions. However, a person can refine or sharpen perceptions and become reflectively aware of them in consciousness via apperception. Apperception unites petit perceptions into perceptions that are the most clear and distinct, like ideas. This process is not aggregation; ideas are emergent properties that come from masses of petit perceptions. For example, blue and yellow combined becomes green. Green is an idea.

Attention is a major component of apperception. Leibniz distinguished between passive attention (absorbed in one activity, we do not notice a stimulus until it becomes so strong that it draws, demands our attention) and active attention (we may actively focus on one thing and ignore the other). Leibniz sometimes ties active, voluntary attention to apperception. He sees apperception as an act of will. Memory is also involved in attention; something must be stored in memory to be attended to (Leibniz, 1714). ♦

## 5.5 Wolff

Christian (von) Wolff (1679–1754) was the second major figure after Leibniz in the history of metaphysical rationalism. He represented the high point of German philosophy and dominated that scene until the rise of the critical philosophy of Immanuel Kant. He is important for the history of psychology because he first coined such presently familiar terms as *consciousness, representation, faculty, person,* and *psychometrics.* In addition he was the founder of German faculty psychology.

Like Leibniz he was a student of Thomasius. Like Thomasius also he believed that philosophy should be an instrument of progress and that the chief motive of reflection should be its utility for ordinary life. Unlike Thomasius, however, he was not a Pietist but believed passionately in the power of reason. In that sense he represents continuity between his time and that of the later Scholastics and the philosophers of the Renaissance during the Middle Ages. He believed that people are capable of right rea-

---

♦There is one aspect of Leibniz's system that will prove to be important for our later discussion of cognitive psychology. This is his assertion that, while monads change in harmony with one another, they do not interact with one another. Leibniz's way of saying this is, "Monads have no windows to reality." Later I will point out that the computer based notion of cognition in cognitive psychology also has no windows to reality (see 13.2).

soning and of making the right moral choices. He had a bourgeois concept of morality, i.e., believed that human beings have the ability to perfect themselves and therefore a moral obligation to strive for perfection. His ideal was to harmonize all human affects under the rule of reason. He held that reason should be the judge of what is an acceptable belief in God. Like his French contemporaries he was a deist who believed that the key to right religion is tolerance. He also believed that reason should be the criterion for judging proper aesthetic taste and just government.

The goal of his philosophy was the promotion of self-perfection for individuals and of the common good for humankind as a whole. To that end he held that we should work on the initially clouded field of our experience by our reason in order to obtain clear knowledge. The method he used was for the mind to think about itself via deductive reasoning so as to ferret out statements that are implied in prior statements.

Unlike Descartes there was no dualism in his worldview between sensation and thinking. Wolff considered them the opposite poles of a continuum of representation, which consists of levels of clarity. In that continuum sensation represents the least clear, rather vague knowing, and reasoning represents clear and distinct knowing.

Similarly, Wolff distinguished between empirical psychology, which collects data, or "possibilities" as he had it, and rational psychology, which looks for the coherence of these data, or looks to determine whether these possibilities are actually logically true. In any case both sensation and thinking are functions of the human mind and both approaches to psychology have to do with what happens *inside* the mind. These notions of thinking and sensation and of inner and outer perception are epistemological distinctions for Wolff that have no reference to ontological differences. The terms "inner" and "outer" perception refer to distinguishable levels of perception in the mind, not to ontological states of affairs. In essence there is only inner perception possible in Wolff's system since for him nothing exists outside the mind. Moreover, minds or souls have only one power. That is the power to reason or to more or less clearly represent reality. All the distinctions presented here are none other than specifications or differentiations of the one power the mind has, which is to think or to represent reality unto itself. Wolff calls these differentiations of the function of the mind "powers," or "faculties" of the mind. This is why he is called the father of German faculty psychology (Wolff, 1713; van Rappard, 1976).

## 5.6 *Kant*

In many ways the philosophy of Immanuel Kant (1724–1804) represents a *crisis* in the thought world of the modern period. The term "crisis" must not be taken to mean that with Kant things fell apart but rather that Kant's philosophy represents a *turning point* in the history of philosophy and psychology. Kant's philosophy constitutes a confluence between scientific and metaphysical rationalism. That is to say, he provided a *synthesis* between the viewpoint that knowledge results from sensation and the viewpoint that knowledge originates in thinking abstracted from sensation. Initially Kant was a proponent of metaphysical rationalism and followed the giants in that tradition, Descartes, Leibniz, and Wolff religiously. This meant that he believed that knowledge about reality is possible without the benefit of sensation, provided only that we think straight. However, after being exposed to Hume's skepticism he began to doubt the possibility of obtaining knowledge purely on the basis of deductive reasoning. At the same time Kant was not willing to accept the empiricist's view that all knowledge originates in sensory experience, and thus that thinking is only secondary to sensation. He was critical of both traditions in modern philosophy and over time he formulated his own unique view on the relation between experiential and intellectual knowledge.

Kant was especially upset by Hume's arguments that on the basis of experience causality does not exist, because without causality the whole enterprise of Newtonian science, which Kant greatly admired, would be in jeopardy. Now, Kant agreed with the empiricists that science can only deal with reality *as it appears to us*, or with the "phenomenal world," the observed world. Science cannot deal with the things of the world as they are in themselves. It can only deal with phenomena experienced via the senses.

However, over against Hume, Kant argued that this world of phenomena, the world as we experience it, must be such that every thing and every event has a cause. For Kant to experience meant ordering the phenomena of our experience directly, immediately in terms of a set of *categories* of the mind, which are his terms for what others called *a priori ideas*. These are categories such as *time, space*, and also *causality* that are innate to our minds. Our minds are so constructed that we cannot *not* view the things that appear to us as existing in time and space and as causally related to other things.

Kant put it this way:

That all our knowledge begins with experience there can be no doubt . . . .
But though all our knowledge begins *with* experience, it does not follow that
it all arises *out of* experience. (Kant, *Critique* I, 1933)

Another quote from Kant is also revealing:

Hitherto it has been assumed that all our knowledge must conform to
objects. But all attempts to ascertain anything about them *a priori* by
concepts, and thus to extend our knowledge, came to nothing on this
assumption. Let us try, then, whether we may not make better progress
in the tasks of metaphysics if we assume that objects must conform to
our knowledge. This at all events accords better with the possibility we are
seeking, namely of a knowledge of objects *a priori*, which would determine
something about them before they are given to us. (Kant, *Critique* XVI,
1933)

It should be noted that Kant's "Copernican revolution" does not
imply the view that reality can *be reduced to* the human mind and its
ideas. What he was suggesting is that we cannot know things, except
insofar as they are subjected to certain *a priori* conditions of knowledge
on the part of our minds, to wit, the categories. According to Kant human beings as experiencing and knowing subjects are so constituted that
they necessarily synthesize the ultimately given data, or sensory impressions in certain ways. The world of experience, the phenomenal world,
or reality-as-it-appears-to-us, is not simply our construction, a dream as
it were, nor is it simply something given. It is the result of an application
of *a priori* forms and categories *to* what is given. Kant agreed with the
metaphysical rationalists that the mind is active, but not in the sense that
it creates reality. Rather, the mind imposes on the ultimate material of
sensory experience its own forms of cognition (Copleston, 1960, p. 225).

Previously, the empiricists and also the old realists assumed that human beings have knowledge because objects impose themselves on our
understanding, which conforms itself to them. Hume's philosophy is the
endpoint of this assumption. Kant held that the mind actively structures
experience in an organized shape. Only thus, he believed, can human
(scientific) knowledge be rescued from skepticism.

The implication of Kant's thought revolution was that true knowledge of the world can only be gotten by science, i.e., by a kind of knowledge acquisition that is based on empirical observation of phenomena.
Metaphysics, which pretends to obtain knowledge of the world purely by
means of deductive reasoning and in the absence of sensory experience, is
on that basis a pseudo-science.

At the same time, Kant held that the scope of science is restricted. It can only deal with the phenomenal world. There is a part of human reality beyond the phenomenal world that is for that reason beyond the reach of science. Kant agreed with Locke that behind the phenomenal world there is an unobserved world of things-in-themselves, called the "*noumenal world*," or the world of the *noumena* rather than of *phenomena*. These two worlds are fundamentally different. In the phenomenal world, all events are perceived to be caused. Thus according to science all behavior is caused, for science rests on phenomena. In the noumenal world, however, there can be uncaused events. Furthermore, in the phenomenal world all events are perceived to be ordered and predetermined. Thus, the world according to science is deterministic. In it there is no room for choice. But the noumenal world is the world of human freedom. People can be *phenomenally* determined (subject to causality) and *noumenally* free (uncaused). In fact they must be free if moral responsibility is to have any meaning.

Kant was trying to do three things. First, he attempted to safeguard the validity of science. Second, he also attempted to limit science to the realm of the phenomena. Finally, he tried to protect human nature, including morality and the concept of freedom it requires, from the onslaught of a mechanical Newtonian-Cartesian worldview that seemed about to engulf and alienate humanity. Kant believed he had accomplished these aims by positing a phenomenal and a noumenal world.

In his conception the noumenal world is not based on observation and scientific reasoning but on the fact that human beings have a will and a sense of obligation. To use a phrase coined by the psychotherapist Carl Rogers, people are perpetually "up to something" and feel obliged to do the right thing. They believe that in order to live the good life they ought to live life in a certain preferred way. This formulation implies the necessity of choice, which implies human freedom. The notions of will and moral obligation also entail a belief in God, Kant argued, since someone must be present to reward good choices and good behavior and to punish immoral choices and behaviors. Thus, Kant rescued ethics and theology from the threat of being extinguished by the deterministic, materialistic, mechanistic, and atheistic tendencies inherent in the Newtonian scientific enterprise of the modern period.

Even though Kant tried his utmost to unify the two world-and-life views of the modern period, he left us with a bifurcated picture of reality in which reason and will, determinism and freedom, science and morality are each other's opposite. As we will see presently, both idealism and romanticism tended to accent the will, freedom, and morality side, whereas positivism, as we saw in Chapter 4, tended to emphasize the reason, determinism, and science side. Furthermore, it is noteworthy that with Kant, as with so many others before him in various forms, the old dichotomy of the definite and the indefinite reappears. Moreover, it will not be the last time that this theme surfaces in the history of philosophy and psychology. The form of the bifurcation may have changed over time. At one time it was called mind versus matter, then reason versus faith, then, as with Pascal, it was will/feeling/heart versus reason, and now with Kant, phenomena versus noumena. But the theme or the issue remains the same. So, once again we have an example of typicality and periodicity in the history of philosophy and psychology (Kant, 1902–1942).

### 5.7 Reid

Before we move on to a discussion of idealism and romanticism in our historical survey I need to discuss the neo-realism of Thomas Reid (1710–1796). It is a moot point whether he should not rather be discussed in the chapter on scientific rationalism since most of his philosophy was a polemic against the empiricism of Locke, Berkeley, and especially Hume. But since there are many similarities between Reid and Kant, Reid's philosophy can also quite naturally be presented here, immediately after Kant.

The historical setting for Reid's neo-realism runs as follows: As a result of the empiricism of Locke, Berkeley, and Hume there arose doubt about three things in academic circles. First, there was doubt about the existence of an outside world. Newton's "nature" became defined as a figment of our imagination. This implied that science, and specifically physics, is an exercise in futility because it is the study of "nothing." Second, doubt arose about the reality of complex objects, like three-dimensional objects. It was suggested that they are only artifacts of our minds, the product of a psychological habit we have to associate sensations. Finally and most perniciously, empiricistic philosophers became skeptical about people's ability to apprehend self-evident truth and began to doubt the human ability to know the world as it really is. According to the empiricist's view, our feelings of self-evidency are based on faulty associations. Thus, our intuition of self-evident truth is a feeling only and not based on reality.

All this resulted in far too much doubt about reality for the Scottish Presbyterian minister Thomas Reid. Over against empiricism Reid posited his form of (neo-)realism, which states that our minds are capable of apprehending reality directly. Thus, Reid reaffirmed the old realist doctrine that knowing equals being.

Reid found Hume's conclusion offensive to common sense. He repudiated the "way of ideas" as he called the empiricism of Berkeley and Hume and supported realism, i.e., that perceived objects are real. According to Reid, Locke claimed that there are four elements to any perceptual act: the perceiver, the act of perception, the idea that is the immediate object of the perception, and the real object that the idea represents. Over against this Reid posited his common sense philosophy (which really ought to be called a common perception philosophy). Reid held that there are only three elements to perception: the perceiver, the act of perception, and the real object. Our perceptual acts make direct contact with objects, not just with their representative ideas. Hume and Berkeley held to a content version of Locke's "idea," Reid to an act psychology version. He said, "I cannot see without seeing something." In stating this, Reid prefigured what Brentano much later was to call "intentionality." Our primary experience, he also stated over against Hume, is not one of a compound of simple sensations but of complex impressions. Experience is always an organized whole. Complex experience cannot be reduced to atomic sensations without robbing it of its meaning.

To back this up, he put forward the view that we are naturally endowed with certain innate faculties and principles of mind that allow us to know the world accurately and that furnish us with essential moral truths as well. These are, said Reid:

> the inspirations of the Almighty . . . they serve to direct us in the common affairs of life where our reasoning faculty would leave us in the dark. They are the common sense of mankind. Knowledge of the world is secure because of our innate constitution that delivers it. The Almighty is not a deceiver. (Reid, 1975)

Both Reid and Hume wanted a science of human nature along Newtonian lines. Both elevated psychology (understood as the study of the content, or the workings, or the acts of the mind) to the position that metaphysics and theology enjoyed in previous times, namely, that of being the queen of the sciences. Their desire was based on their common assumption that what goes on in the mind determines what goes on in the world. However, this formulation led Hume to deny causality and therefore the independent existence of the world. But this was going too far for Reid. Therefore he posited the common sense, native ability of our minds to know the world as a world of objects rather than of impressions.

This common sense ability consists of a number of "fundamental judgments" *by means of which* we reason. They are operative in the way we perceive reality. They are part of the

> furniture which nature has given human understanding. . . . [A]ll
> the discoveries of our reason are grounded upon them . . . and what is
> manifestly contrary to any of those first principles is what we call absurd.
> (Reid, 1975)

Thus, it makes no sense to believe that these natural faculties, by which we distinguish truth from error, should be fallacious.

Reid believed that human beings were constitutionally able to have direct and infallible contact with the things of the world. That makes him a Realist. But he was a *neo*-realist in that he grounded this ability not in the way the world is structured but in the way human nature is structured, better yet, in the ability of human nature to structure reality. His fundamental judgments are the equivalent of the Stoics' *logos spermatikos*, of the Rationalist's *a priori ideas*, of Pascal's *heart*, and of Kant's *categories*. It appears that the theme of the *a priori*, according to which the human mind or human nature structures reality and gives it coherence, is alive and well in these philosophies of the modern period.

### 5.8 *Idealism*

Johann Fichte (1762–1814), who followed Kant in the history of metaphysical rationalism, tried to overcome the bifurcation in Kant's philosophy and in the course of this effort he started a school of philosophy called "idealism." Kant had taught that human beings order their experience, such that it is not nonsense to say that objects conform themselves to human knowledge. But he also believed in the existence of an unknowable world of things-in-themselves, a noumenal world that provides us with phenomena to be ordered, thus with a situation in which human knowledge conforms itself to the objects of our knowledge. In order to overcome this dichotomy, Fichte rejected the Kantian doctrine of an unknowable world of things-in-themselves. This only left him with the structuring activity of the human mind as the source of all knowledge and reality. In fact, Fichte and the succeeding idealists after him believed that the objects of the world were the products of the *con*structing, creative activity of the mind. Fichte referred to this constructing mind as the *Ego*. To avoid the charge of solipsism he pronounced this Ego to be a universal Ego. This meant that for him all individual things, including individual human beings and minds are the product of this one creative, producing universal Ego. In this manner Fichte overcame the dualism of Kant, but it will be clear that his formulation also turned idealism into yet another form of metaphysics. What for Kant had been part of how we come to *know* reality, namely the structuring activity of the mind, Fichte viewed as a constituent aspect of reality itself. In idealism the universal Ego is an ontological principle, whereas for Kant it had been an epistemological principle.

In emphasizing the constructive character of the Ego, Fichte and the other Idealists who succeeded him was more in line with the philosophies of previous metaphysical rationalists than Kant was. For one thing, Descartes, Leibniz, and Wolff, like Fichte, were all system builders and metaphysicians. They all believed in the constructive powers of the mind and de-emphasized the importance of sense-perception in coming to true knowledge. Moreover, they were all speculative, deductive thinkers rather than critical, analytical thinkers. But there was also a fundamental difference between the pre-Kantians like Descartes, Leibniz, and Wolff and the post-Kantians like Fichte and the other idealists. Succinctly put, the pre-Kantians epistemologized ontology and the post-Kantians ontologized epistemology.

Translated into more understandable English, this means the following: For the pre-Kantians what people normally think of as reality or the world is immanent to the mind. For philosophers like Leibniz and Wolff, it makes no sense to talk about inside and outside the mind. For them reality is a function of the ability of the mind to represent the world. Similarly, the difference between thinking and sensation for these pre-Kantians is not that sensation is somehow primarily in touch with the world, whereas thinking is only secondarily aware of it *via* the function of sensation. For them the distinction is one of levels or stages of clarity in the self-clarification process of the mind.

On the other hand, the idealists who came after Kant, believing themselves to be followers of Kant, took what for Kant was clearly an epistemological principle and turned it into an ontological principle. For Kant the mind or Ego orders the raw sense data of experience and in this way we come to know reality. For Fichte the mind, or Ego, *produces* reality. That is to say, for Fichte the nature of reality is such that it is constructed by the universal Ego. Kant wrote about how people come to know the world. Fichte, using Kant's insights, wrote about how the world we come to know is constructed.

The contribution that idealism made to the history of psychology and to clinical psychology in particular is its emphasis on the active, creative, productive character of human personality and human cognition. For example, the central notion in the current theories of cognition, of perception, and of memory is that they are active and productive of their own contents. Our current understanding of reality in contemporary cognitive psychology is that it is a function of human cognition (Copleston, 1960, p. 148, 210, 430–435; Fichte, 1794).

### 5.9 *Romanticism*

Romanticism arose in Germany, where Leibniz and Wolff, as well as Kant, had been more influential than Locke, Berkeley, and Hume. Romanticism, therefore, is part of the development of metaphysical rationalism. The Germans rejected the Empiricist view of mind, holding that the mind is active and autonomous with respect to experience and sensation. Psychology, they said, should not only study the *content* of the mind, but also the energetic *activities* of the mind that unify and process sensation.

As we saw earlier, the vision of the British empiricists and, especially, of the French sensationalists was to apply Newtonian reason to human affairs, i.e., to psychology, ethics, and politics. They wanted to banish superstition, religious revelation, and historical tradition and replace these, in their view "outdated" notions, with laws for human conduct discovered through natural scientific reason, which enlightened despots could use to create a perfect society. They were intolerant of cultural diversity because cultural traditions, they said, are not products of scientific reason. These traditions all fall short of the present enlightened, rational ideal. They were scornful of history, calling it "the gossip of the past." Talk about Whig historiography!

Some eighteenth century thinkers found this view horrifyingly inhuman; in reaction, they set the autonomy of *culture* over against the imperialism of *natural science*. Over against the excesses of (mathematical) reason, they placed (the feelings of) the heart. Much earlier, Pascal had argued that "the heart has reasons of which reason knows nothing." This was certainly the sentiment of the Romanticists (Copleston, 1960, pp. 135–149).

### 5.9.1 *Vico:* Geisteswissenschaft

I will discuss three examples of romanticism's objection to the Spirit of the Enlightenment, the objection of Vico, of Herder, and of Rousseau. These three figures may also be called the fathers of romanticism.

Giambattista Vico (1668–1744), for example, stated that knowledge of nature is inferior, secondhand, compared to knowledge of society and of history. He used a criterion of knowledge used regularly during the Middle Ages, which stated that one cannot really know something unless one has made it. God made nature, said Vico, so only God knows the natural world. To human beings, nature is given only as "brute fact." We can only observe it "from the outside in." But we see our own lives "from the inside out," and via sympathetic understanding we understand the lives of men and women in other cultures and other historical times as well. History is the greatest science. History is the process of human self-creation. Human life is a project. Human beings make themselves through history. As Dilthey was to call it later, history is a *Geisteswissenschaft*, literally a "science of the human spirit," rather than a natural science (Berlin, 1977). The distinction between the "natural" and "social" sciences started with Vico. This raises the question whether psychology is a natural or a social science. Most people feel that psychology straddles the two.

### 5.9.2 *Herder: Human heart vs. artificial reason*

Another example of romanticism was Herder (1744–1803). He rejected the modern period's worship of mathematical and empirical reason and its claim that the enlightened culture of the eighteenth century was the only culture worth having. Herder was for romanticism's trust in the human heart and its historical reverence for many human truths. His motto was that we live in a world that we ourselves create. He stressed the absolute uniqueness of each culture and each historical period. He detested the tendency of the French sensationalists to caricature the past and presentistically to hold out their own times as the universal model for humanity. He stressed the degeneracy of the Age of Reason, as the Enlightenment period or the modern period has been called. It is artificial, he said; it apes the Greeks and the Romans and is altogether too insufficiently spiritual. He called the modern critics "masters of dead learning." He advocated Heart! Warmth! Blood! Humanity! Life! Descartes had said, "I think therefore I am." Condillac had said, "I sense, therefore I am." Herder said," I feel, I am" (Berlin, 1977). Thus ended the rule of abstract reason, of the geometric spirit, and of reasonable emotion. Instead, organic development led by empathic emotion was the base of the new romanticism.

### 5.9.3 *Rousseau: Nature vs. civilization*

Yet another figure who rebelled against the Age of Reason was Rousseau (1712–1778). He did this by placing nature *over against* civilization. That was something new for that time in history. Rousseau's famous phrase was, "Man is born free, and everywhere he is in chains." He championed the noble savage, man before the coming of society, in a state of nature. Note that "nature" here is the exact opposite of Newton's nature. It is indeterminate, uncaused, uncultivated, and uncivilized. For Rousseau to exist is to feel; the first impulses of the heart are always right. He rejected mechanism because it cannot explain free will. He denied that mankind had benefited from scientific and technological advances. To him, contemporary French civilization was artificial and excessively rational (Rousseau, 1974; 1762).

Romanticism was a general revolt against the Cartesian-Newtonian worldview. Above all, it wanted there to be something more in the universe than atoms in a void, something transcending material appearance. Romanticism worshipped emotions. It stressed *vernunft* (i.e., intuitive reasoning that is capable of transcending appearances) rather than *verstand* (i.e., logical, analytical reasoning). It saw the unconscious as more important than the conscious; it posited the will as a noumenal reality behind the appearances; it celebrated mental activity and freedom; and it was a voluntaristic, rather than a deterministic philosophy. This view of human beings and of the human mind must be seen in contrast to the *tabula rasa* and the passivity view of associationism.

Romanticists also rejected the idea that the universe is a machine. They were vitalists and teleologists. To them nature is not dead matter but something organic, growing, and improving itself with time. According to their view, biology rather than physics should be the model for thinking about things.

In summary, they opposed mechanism and promoted individual freedom, voluntarism, and holism. Instead of association as the law of the mind they stressed "coalescence." By this they meant to emphasize that active imagination can synthesize atomic elements into something that is more than the sum of its atomic parts. With respect to the world outside, they stressed vitalism and teleology. As we will see presently, romanticism initially did not influence psychology a great deal. However, in the later stages of the development of psychology its influence can scarcely be overstated. Think, for example, of its influence on Gestalt psychology, psychoanalysis, and humanistic psychology.

## References

Berlin, I. (1977). *Vico and Herder: Two studies in the History of Ideas.* New York: Vintage.

Copleston, F.C. (1960). *A History of Philosophy.* Vol. VI, Westminster: The Newman Press.

Descartes, R. (1939). *Discours de la Methode.* 1637. Text by E. Gilson, Paris.

Fichte, J.G. (1794). *Basis of the Entire Theory of Science.*

Hazard, P. (1964). *The European Mind, 1680–1715*. N.Y: Meridian Books.

Kant, I. (1902-42). *Gesammelte Schriften*. Berlin: Prussian Academy of Sciences.

Kant, I. *Critique of Pure Reason*. Transl. by N.K. Smith, London, 1933, I, XVI.

Leibniz, G.W. (1930). *The Monadology of Leibniz* [1714], translated by Herbert Wildon Carr, Los Angeles: University of Southern California.

Pascal, B. (1950). *Pensées*. Ed. by H.F. Stewart, London.

Reid, T. (1975). *Thomas Reid's Inquiry and Essays*. K. Lerner and R. Beanblossom, eds., Indianapolis: Bobbs-Merrill.

Rousseau, J. (1750–1762). *Social Contract and Discourses*. Ed. by G.D.H. Cole, London.

Rousseau, J. (1762). *Emil.* N.Y: Dutton, 1974.

Spener, Ph. J. (1675). *Pia Desideria.*

van Rappard, J.F.H. (1976). *Psychologie Als Zelfkennis: Het zielsbegrip tussen substantie en structuur in de Duitse rationalistische psychologie van Wolff tot Wundt en Brentano*. Amsterdam: Academische Pers, 29.

Wolff, C. (1713). *Gesammelte Werke*. Hildesheim: George Olm Verlag, 1965.

# Some Issues to Stimulate Dialogue

1. One of the aims of this chapter and also of the part of Chapter 6 that deals with anti-positivism is to show how metaphysical rationalism, idealism, romanticism, and irrationalism form the historical philosophical background for the various branches of clinical psychology. The vocabulary of this thought tradition appears to anticipate many notions found in contemporary clinical psychology. A good exercise would be to identify which notions of this philosophical tradition in the history of Western thought seem familiar to you based on your knowledge of courses like personality theory, psychotherapy, counseling, abnormal and clinical psychology.

2. By way of demonstrating synchronic differences and commonality, compare and contrast scientific and metaphysical rationalism.

3. By way of demonstrating diachronic differences and commonality, compare and contrast Aristotle's great chain of being with Leibniz's monadology, since both define the difference between the "kingdoms" of the world (rocks, plants, animals, and human beings) in terms of a hierarchy of complexity (Aristotle in terms of the actualization of matter and Leibniz in terms of levels of perception).

4. The adherents to metaphysical rationalism all thought of the activity of the mind as a form of therapy. Thinking for them was a process of internal housecleaning. They viewed philosophy as the "sanitation of the soul." For them the process of coming to know oneself was a process of "self-clarification." The term we would use today is "consciousness-raising." The other aspect of coming to know yourself in their view was that of "unifying plurality," i.e., of systematizing or "whole making." Today we might call that the "integration of experience." They held that the inevitable result of this reasoning activity would be self-improvement. The path to self-knowledge was a path of liberation, of emancipation. Moreover, they viewed this process to be spontaneous and self-correcting. Which contemporary approaches to therapy, do you think, echo these sentiments the most, and why do you think so?

5. It would be good for someone to research the motivation behind romanticism's reaction against the intellectualism of the Enlightenment movement as well as its preference for feelings, intuition, and empathy over reason and logic as pathways to knowledge and action. In my view their reaction was rooted in a love of individual persons rather than a preference for social or intellectual systems. When I discussed Duns Scotus's voluntarism in Chapter 3, with its idea that will and choice transcend reason and logic, I argued that the notion of will is of Hebraic-Christian rather than Greek origin. I further argued that this emphasis on choice does not lead to arbitrariness because in voluntarism will is rooted in love. We find this same idea back in Pascal's notion of the heart and the romanticists' celebration of intuition and empathy. The basic idea in all this is that will and choice are best governed by love rather than logic. To my mind this notion of will ruled by love derives from the unique contribution that Christianity (its central teaching, not its actual practice during the Middle Ages) has made to the development of Western thought. What do you think?

6. Perhaps the most dominant notion of metaphysical rationalism, idealism, and romanticism alike is the idea that human beings are active vis-à-vis their experience, that they order or construct their reality, or that they live in a perceived environment. Which systems of contemporary psychology continue this tradition and which systems don't?

7. One way to gain an appreciation for the historically constructed nature of contemporary psychology is to take a notion such as the relation between the definite and the indefinite, to identify its historical origin, and to trace the historical development of this notion in all its different forms up to the present in contemporary psychology. Other examples of this process would be to trace the history of will-ruled-by-love from Augustine, through Scotus, Pascal, romanticism, and anti-positivism into current theories of personality and psychotherapy. Yet another interesting historical investigation would be to trace the Protestant notion of vocation, and to show how it was reformulated by Spener's pietism. The next step would be to demonstrate how in this form it was secularized to become the bourgeois notion of progress and later emancipation. The final leg of this research could be to illustrate the way this idea of progress and liberation operates in contemporary forms of psychological counseling.

8. Which specific notions in Leibniz's *Monadology* and of La Mettrie's *Man a Machine* can be said to have influenced theories of evolution,

and specifically theories of developmental psychology? You can of course ask similar questions about the influence of Locke, Hume, and J.S. Mill on branches of experimental psychology.

# 6. PRELUDE TO PSYCHOLOGY AS A SEPARATE DISCIPLINE

## 6.1 *Introduction*

We are about to begin a discussion of the development of schools in psychology during the last 150 years. But before we do that, we must first deal with two historical developments usually neglected in *Introduction to the History of Psychology* textbooks. The first is the historical reason why psychology became a special science during the nineteenth century. The reader will recall my argument in Chapter 1 that it is historically incorrect to discuss the question whether or not psychology is a special science in the first chapter of a history of psychology text. You will recall my objection that this practice distorts the actual history of thought leading up to the start of psychology proper (1.6). But having arrived at this stage of our historical survey, it is imperative that we answer this question. There is a historical reason why contemporary psychology is regarded as a separate discipline of study rather than a sub-discipline of philosophy; this reason is to be found in the development of Western thought during the nineteenth century.

This period of philosophical thought is characterized by a nearly universal intense preoccupation with methodology. We already saw this perhaps most clearly in the positivism of Auguste Comte and of John Stuart Mill as heirs of French and British empiricism. But this obsession with method is no less present in the neo-kantianism of Windelband and Rickert, in the historicism of Dilthey or in the phenomenology of Brentano and Husserl, who find their origin more in metaphysical rationalism (Polkinghorne, 1983, pp. 20–47).

It should be noted that this quest for the right method represents a retrenchment in the rationalism of the modern period. Under the influence of Ockham's nominalism and other forms of philosophical criticism, these rationalists had given up for good the notion of naïve realism that thought equals universal Being. But they certainly celebrated the ability of right reason with or without the aid of sensory experience to bring people in touch with reality. This was because they firmly believed in the *constitutional* hypothesis. This widespread belief in human rationality held that all human beings are endowed with certain "germs of truth" that guide them infallibly to know reality as it is, provided only that they think and see straight.

The preoccupation with methodological issues by philosophers of the nineteenth century represents a loss of faith in this rationalistic doctrine. During this period of Western thought thinkers shifted their trust to the *methodological* hypothesis. According to this doctrine even clear thinking human beings can only get at the truth they need to live provided they use the right *method*. For the natural scientific rationalists this was the *experimental* method. For the metaphysical rationalists this was the method of *hermeneutics*. Looking ahead and anticipating a later discussion in this historical survey I will mention yet another retrenchment of rationalism in the early twentieth century. One form of this takes the shape of the romantic *irrationalism* of Schopenhauer, Nietzsche, Bergson, and the existentialists who held in essence that life is always bigger than thought. So why bother? The end result of this retrenchment is the postmodernism of today in which the key phrase is "Whatever!" (Copleston, 1963). The other form of retrenchment is the evolutionistic irrationalism of Charles Darwin and others such as Francis Galton, who adhere to the *hereditary* hypothesis according to which only a few above-average people are intelligent enough to get at the truth, and this depends strictly on their biologically inherited genes (9.7).

It may not be inspiring to note this, but psychology as a special, independent discipline of inquiry was born in this climate of rational retrenchment. We may wonder, therefore, whether the birth of psychology represents a celebration of human ingenuity or a loss of nerve. During the first few decades of its existence, psychology was preoccupied with finding the right research method. This was so much so that what constituted the subject matter of psychology for the early psychologists, and also which data were to be accepted as evidence, was entirely determined by the research methodology they chose (Boring, 1929; Eisenga & van Rappard, 1987; Koch, 1959; Sanders et al., 1975).

### 6.2 *The rise of experimental psychology*

This historical fact can be demonstrated most clearly in the experimental branch of psychology. Psychologists professing this brand of psychology adopted the natural science approach as their research methodology in order to bring scientific rigor to the discipline. But in the pursuit of this ideal, they narrowed the field of investigation considerably. They decreed that only those phenomena that could be clearly observed could count as evidence in psychology. This entailed for them that the only legitimate objects of study for psychology were sensations and their derivatives. Other aspects of psychology, such as thoughts, feelings, drives, intentions, moods, plans, decisions, and acts, all had to be converted to sensations before they could be studied with scientific rigor. For example, the philosopher Ernst Mach held that memories, representations, feelings, concepts, and will processes are all composed of traces left behind by previous sensations. Carl Stumpf, another philosopher-psychologist, suggested that psychology could legitimately deal with feelings only by viewing them as "feeling sensations." Moreover, the famous researcher of memory Hermann Ebbinghaus taught that drive processes were really sensations of unpleasant feelings, and that will is nothing more than a drive or unpleasant feeling that anticipates the future (Muller-Freienfels, 1938, pp. 39–41; Lersch, 1960, pp. 77–79).

These experimental psychologists prided themselves in being objective. This meant, among other things, that they believed their approach to research to be free from philosophical presuppositions. But this belief is hardly tenable. For implicitly or explicitly these early experimental psychologists worked with a view of mind as the subject matter of psychology that shows a decided affinity to the view of mind operative in natural scientific rationalism. They adhered to an atomistic, mechanistic, and sensationistic conception of mind that excluded emotions and will processes. They believed that the mind is a mirror image of the outside world that inscribes itself on the mind with very little input from the mind itself. In this process the mind is relegated to the role of spectator. It was viewed as the sum total of sensations caused by external stimuli, which are reproduced in the mind as representations and are put together by a mechanical association process into a totality of consciousness. In this view the mind itself does not act but is merely a succession of states of consciousness that depend for their existence wholly on physiological processes in the central nervous system. The aim of this type of experimental psychology was threefold. It was to reduce immediate experience to ultimate elements believed to be the building blocks of the mind. Also, it aimed at producing a natural scientific picture of the mind by converting qualitative differences to quantitative differences and by localizing psychological processes in specific areas of the central nervous system, such as the brain (Muller-Freienfels, 1938, pp. 18–26, 35, 39–46; Sanders et al., 1976, pp. 121; 237; Lersch, 1960; Polkinghorne, 1983, p. 15). Whatever merit this conception of psychology might have, it was not hailed with enthusiasm by scholars who stood in the tradition of meta-physical rationalism.

### 6.3 Anti-positivism

This brings us to the second philosophical development during the nine-teenth century: the push to develop an alternative method of investiga-tion. It was to be a method that differed from the experimental approach and was thought to be more adequate for dealing with the subject matter of the *Geisteswissenschaften* (also called the *human sciences*, roughly iden-tical to what today we call the *social sciences*). It is regrettable that most introductory texts to the history of psychology pay so little attention to this movement, since it was highly significant in the development of the clinical branch of psychology. It was also very important for the develop-ment of another, relatively recent approach to psychology, the so-called *narrative psychology* (Sarbin, 1986). For these reasons we will deal exten-sively in this survey with this movement.

The predominant method in psychology during the second half of the nineteenth century was the experimental method. It seemed that the push by the positivists to make psychology a *natural* science had won the day. However, toward the end of that century it also became more and more evident that this approach had some major deficits. Furthermore, at about the same time two other movements in psychology became popu-lar. These were psychoanalysis and characterology, which later became known as personality theory. Neither of these movements fit easily in the experimental approach to psychology. It is for these and other rea-sons that an anti-positivistic reaction arose that promoted an alternative method of study for psychology (Muller-Freienfels, 1938, pp. 13–16).

To the reader who just finished reading the previous chapter the de-scription of this anti-positivism movement will seem strangely familiar. This is no accident because every one of the proponents of this move-ment stand in the tradition of metaphysical rationalism, and thus betray the influence of Leibniz, Wolff, Kant, Herder, and Fichte, among others, in their systems of thought.

The anti-positivists were opposed to treating psychology as if it were another natural science like physics. They argued that an experi-mental approach to psychology that views the mind as one physical sys-tem among many fails to deal adequately with the higher functions of the mind like thought, judgment, and valuation; it completely ignores other equally important psychological functions such as feelings, affects, emotion, and motivation altogether. So, a natural scientific, experimental approach excludes from the purview of psychology the very essence of psychological experience.

According to the anti-positivists, psychological reality is of an entirely different kind than physical reality. It is a subjective rather than an objective experience. It deals with experience that is always connected to an individual subject, or to an "I," or a mind, or some kind of personality structure. For one thing, the psychological experience that psychology studies always presents itself to us as an organized, integrated structural whole. The elements of this experience can only be understood in terms of that whole, as manifestations of this holistic experience. For another, the experience of one individual differs fundamentally from that of another, so that a general theory of subjective experience is an impossibility. For this reason an anti-positivistic approach to psychology generates typologies rather than theories. Furthermore, according to the anti-positivists the mind, which is the subject pole of experience, is always active. It *generates* experience. The structure of the mind is *intentional,* teleological or goal directed, and *dynamic.* It is a structure of motives, purposes, ideals, and goals. To use a favorite phrase of Carl Rogers, about whom later, the mind, or human person is always "up to something" (Van Belle, 1980, p. 70).

Finally, a natural scientific, experimental approach to psychology is in the nature of the case compelled to view human experience as a mechanism of causal relations, the elements of which are entirely determined by external forces. Thus, it is unable to deal with what are possibly the most essential characteristics of subjective experience, such as spontaneity, choice, creativity, imagination, meaning, and value (Muller-Freienfels, 1938, pp. 27–35; Lersch, 1960, p. 32, 39, 40, 67, 68, 79; Polkinghorne, 1983, pp. 24–32).

It will be clear that the anti-positivists stand squarely in the metaphysical rationalist tradition. One finds in their view of subjective experience conceptual elements also found in Leibniz's notion of *monad,* Pascal's notion of the *heart,* Wolff's notion of *consciousness,* Kant's notion of *noumena* that generate *phenomena,* Herder's notion of *emotion* and *intuition,* Rousseau's notion of *nature* as opposed to *civilization,* and, finally, Fichte's notion of *Ego.*

Saddled with this view of subjective human experience as the subject matter for psychology the anti-positivists could hardly be expected to endorse the use of the experimental method. Instead they argued that the aim of psychology is not to experiment with human experience but to *understand* it. In order to describe what the anti-positivists meant by "understanding" I will introduce the technical term *verstehen*, and un-pack the various meanings this term acquired in the development of anti-positivistic thought. The term was first coined by Johann Gustav Droy-sen in 1858 when he contrasted *verstehen* (understanding) with *erklären* (explanation) (Polkinghorne, 1983, p. 22). For him these were two dif-ferent approaches to two different kinds of knowledge, based on Kant's distinction between practical reason and theoretical reason.

"Verstehen" first of all has the meaning that we already find with Descartes in metaphysical rationalism, namely that of the "self-clarifica-tion of the mind" (5.1). Another meaning of "verstehen" is the one used by Dilthey (1833–1911). His use of the term was probably the most in-fluential in anti-positivism and is similar to the term *hermeneutic method* in biblical or literary interpretation. As used in psychology it views hu-man experience as a text that needs to be expounded. This means that the elements of human experience can only be understood or interpreted correctly in terms of the whole of human experience. Implied in this view of understanding is the conviction that we already find in Thomas Reid and is reiterated by Dilthey, that human experience, or "the life of the soul is not composed of parts . . . but is always and immediately an integrated whole" (Lersch, 1960, p. 33; Polkinghorne, 1983, p. 26).

Yet another meaning of "verstehen" is based on the fact that expe-rience is always individually different. This meaning refers to Wilhelm Windelband's distinction between a *nomothetic* approach to psychology and an *idiographic* method (Polkinghorne, 1983, p. 23). The nomothetic approach aims to formulate general theories about human experience that are applicable to all human beings. The idiographic method is more typological and attempts to formulate a personality description of indi-vidual persons in an effort to clarify their unique way of experiencing the world. By extension, what the experimental approach describes as quan-titative differences between people are viewed as really qualitative differ-ences. From the point of view of *idiography* human beings differ radically rather than by degree. They are incomparably unique (Muller-Freienfels, 1938, p. 33; Lersch, 1960, p. 77).

So, what does one do when one adopts "verstehen" rather than "erklären" as a research method in psychology? Essentially, one attempts to understand what makes a person tick. Specifically, to understand a person's subjective experience one must discover the reasons for, or the motives behind, the experience. There are many different ways to express this idea. Anti-positivists hold that sensations and thoughts are the prod-ucts of needs and drives rather than the results of the impact of external stimuli. The picture human beings have of external reality never corresponds completely to what in fact is out there. We see what we need to see and think what we want to think. To understand subjective experience means to look for the activity of the will, the emotions, the affects, and the drives that determine our experience. It means that we search for the noumenal structures *behind* the phenomena of our experience. It means that we identify a person's personality, which determines the manner in which he experiences the world. Dilthey states that to understand someone's experience in the sense of "verstehen" one must penetrate his spirit down to his structure of choices, purposes and ideals, values and meanings. The essence of understanding (*verstehen*) a person's experience (*erlebniss*) is to empathize with (*nacherleben*, literally "experience along with") that person's experience (Copleston, 1965, pp. 371–372). The end product of such an exercise is that one is truthfully able to say: "Now I know why this person looks at the world the way she does, thinks the way she does, and acts the way she does."

What I have tried to describe so far is the manner in which one person attempts to understand another. Clinical psychologists will recognize this method as a staple ingredient in *psycho-* or *personality diagnostics*. The product of such activity is usually a psychological report. However, when the focus is instead on a person attempting to understand him- or herself, with or without the help of a psychologist, this process is more likely to be called *psychotherapy*. Psychotherapy is a process of self-clarification, of self-understanding, that is often healing for a person's emotional life as well. But this process hides an interesting puzzle. One might ask the question, "Doesn't an individual understand his own mind, his own needs and drives, his own emotions and intentions?" Apparently not, at least according to one movement in psychology, the clinically most influential school of psychoanalysis, which holds that people are mostly unaware of what really motivates them. The motives that really move us to see, think, and act the way we do are hidden from us in the *unconscious part* of our minds. This way of thinking about subjective human experience has a long history, which demonstrates the influence of romanticism on anti-positivism.

The reader will remember that romanticism was really a kind of anti-intellectualism. Ellenberger calls it the "cult of the irrational," and writes that it had "mystical tendencies" (1970, p. 199). It celebrated feeling and intuition rather than logical analysis. In a later phase of history, romanticism indeed evolved into a kind of *irrationalism* as is illustrated in the philosophies of Schopenhauer, Bergson, Nietzsche, and the Existentialists. This development represents a loss of faith in the capacity of reason, or of knowledge in general, to comprehend life. However much these thinkers may have differed from one another on their definition of life, they were united in the conviction that life is bigger and much more powerful and mysterious than the knowledge we have of it. Schopenhauer's *transcendental voluntaristic idealism*, as Copleston calls it (1965, p. 286), is a prime example of this irrationalism. The main idea of his philosophy is that of a universal *will to live*, which is the blind impulse and dynamic force of the world. This force is constantly at work propelling the universe into a process of infinite becoming and permanent change. This universal life impulse, in which human beings participate, is a *noumenal* force in the sense that it lies behind the phenomena of our everyday experience of reality and dominates our conceptual knowledge of it. Thus, there is no such thing as a total grasp of life. At best we have a partial, intuitive knowledge of it. This is mostly the reason why anti-positivists promote methodological pluralism. From their perspective, the positivistic belief that one scientific method is able to capture the infinite variety of life is ludicrous.

Schopenhauer's pupil, Friedrich Nietzsche, is another example of irrationalism. He turned Schopenhauer's will to live into a *will to power*. Schopenhauer was a pessimistic thinker, because for him this blind will to live rules the universe and also mankind like the Greek *ananke* or fate, so that human beings have very little capacity to influence the situation. With his will to power, Nietzsche is far more optimistic about the chances of human beings to make a living. He exhorts people to free themselves from conventions and traditions, especially from religion. He also calls people to affirm life by becoming their own creators of values in order to exercise their will to power. Asserting our will to power by creating our own value systems is the only thing that matters in life for Nietzsche. One of his more well-known quotes is, "This world is the will to power – and nothing else! And you yourselves too are this will to power – and nothing else" (Copleston, 1965, p. 407). Even knowledge itself must be the servant of this calling. Truth is only a fiction, and theories are only good or bad in so far as they do or do not advance one's will to power, which for the individual culminates in becoming a *Superhuman.*

Perhaps as an appeal to authority Nietzsche, who loved the culture of ancient Greece, refers to two streams of thought in that culture: A Dionysian and an Apollonian stream. Throughout history these two streams have been identified with passion and reason. For Nietzsche, Dionysus is the symbol of the stream of life; he is the symbol of a place where boundaries fall away and individuals become united with this stream into a primordial unity. Apollo, on the other hand, is the symbol of light, of measure, and of restraint. He represents the principle of individuation and separation (Ellenberger, 1970, pp. 529, 542; Copleston, 1965, p. 397). Once again the tension between the indefinite and the definite appears in the history of Western thought.

The Dionysian stream is full of horror, terror, and danger, but it is also the place of vitality, creativity, and constant renewal. For this reason Nietzsche wants to get us in touch with this stream by uncovering the many conceptual masks that civilization has placed upon mankind. Thus, we have arrived at a further elaboration of the method of "verstehen" (which, incidentally, betrays the influence of Rousseau). It has now become an action in which we unmask the usual ways in which we apprehend the world. One gets at this deeper, hidden Dionysian layer of our experience via imagination, intuition, and empathy rather than by logical analysis. But getting at this unconscious layer also requires the acceptance of the fact that none of us are who we think we are. It also requires adherence to the view that what we hold for truth is really a fiction, which serves to contain the Dionysian beast, that all of us are, hidden down in the deep unconscious recesses of our mind. Thus, what Nietzsche advocated was in essence a philosophy of suspicion, which requires a constant questioning of the viewpoints that we take for granted and of the values that we hold dear. It is not difficult to discern in Nietzsche's philosophy elements that were later to come to fuller fruition in the psychoanalysis of Sigmund Freud.

### 6.4 *Methodological changes that prepared the way for experimental psychology*

In the last section of this chapter, we look at some historical changes that prepared the way for the emergence of psychology as an empirical discipline. The earliest form of psychology as a discipline separate from philosophy during the nineteenth century was mostly experimental psychology. This was the kind of psychology that was envisioned when psychologists began to look for a radical change in the methodology of their discipline. However, it was one thing to call for a change of psychology from being a philosophical sub-discipline to becoming a special empirical science like physics. It was quite another to actually do it. Psychology had no measuring instruments and no experimental methods. How was one to go about becoming an empirical science?

The change from philosophical to (natural) scientific, experimental psychology became possible when a number of people demonstrated that the research procedure of the natural sciences was applicable to psychology, i.e., when they showed that it was possible to apply counting, measuring, analysis, quantification, experimentation, and observation to the human mind. Those who demonstrated this were not themselves all psychologists, but without them psychology would not have been able to become experimental, and that was the main thing most psychologists of the late nineteenth century were after (Eisenga and van Rappard, 1987, p. 20).

### 6.4.1. *Helmholz: Measuring the human mind*

Historically there had always been a hesitancy to make human beings the object of empirical research. By the middle of the eighteenth century, scientists had barely begun the systematic observation of the human body. Such research did not really blossom until the nineteenth century under the influence of physiologists like Muller and Helmholz. But even then it was still quite a step to move from research on the human body to research on the human mind. Physiologists could make that step more easily than psychologists could because they viewed the brain as the seat of the mind. They saw the mind as the as yet mysterious link between sensory input and motoric output. This link was mysterious because sometimes this process seemed to run automatically, as in the case of reflexes. In other cases, the mind seemed to intervene. Take, for example, the case of individual differences in reaction times, which astronomy found to occur when different telescope observers reported different times at which a star passed by the center of the visual field of the telescope. Even though their eyes were stimulated at the same time, their motoric reactions differed individually by as much as a full second. Many physiological theories tried to explain this phenomenon. So did psychological theories, employing what today we would call differences in attention and expectancy as explanatory constructs.

In 1850 Helmholz (1821–1894) was able to determine the speed with which an impulse travels the length of a neuron. This was quite a discovery because this speed could be considered pure physiological reaction time (R.T.). Now scientists could study the individual differences in R.T. experimentally as deviations from physiological R.T. These differences were then attributed to psychological factors. For example, they could now determine the time it takes a person to make a choice. Whatever the value of this research, it demonstrated that the human mind could be measured; that is why R.T. experiments became important to psychology (Helmholz, 1886).

## 6.4.2 *Fechner: Quantifying the human mind*

Fechner (1801–1887) was a physicist who found a method to quantify states of consciousness. He was interested in the phenomenon that there is no one-to-one relationship between the sensory stimulus and our (subsequent) psychological perception of it. For example, our impression of light does not double in its intensity when we change the light source from a 60-watt bulb to a 120-watt bulb. Even though the amount of physical light energy increases by a factor of two, our corresponding sensation of light intensity increases by a much smaller amount. Phenomena of this sort were already known at that time. What Fechner wanted to know was, exactly by how much less? Fechner tried to answer this question via his method of psychophysics. In psychophysics one presents an experimental subject with a physical stimulus and watches what sort of sensations the subject experiences as a result of this stimulus. In this way one can define a sensation, i.e., an element of the mind, in terms of a physical event outside the mind. Fechner defined a unit of sensation in terms of how much physical energy is necessary to double the intensity of that sensation. On the basis of his experiments, he formulated the "law": $S = k \log R$, i.e., the intensity of a sensation increases logarithmically with a linear increase of the physical stimulus.

The important thing to note is that via this experiment Fechner demonstrated that we can *quantify* psychology. We can express psychological laws mathematically and manipulate these statistically. Therefore, it seemed that it was possible to quantify that mysterious thing called the human mind, and therefore apply natural scientific methods to it (Fechner, 1966).

## 6.4.3 *Lange/Muller: Observation of the human mind*

F. A. Lange (1828–1875) was a physicist-philosopher who criticized the psychology of Herbart (1776–1841). Herbart had said that his psychology was natural scientific because he had "based it on observations of consciousness." Lange argued that Herbart's psychology was not natural scientific at all. Herbart states, said Lange, that he observed this or that psychological event, but he never spells out *under what concrete conditions* he observed it. He has not specified how he went about doing it, what his method of observation was. Therefore we are unable to check the validity of his observations. Another observer cannot repeat his observations. His observations are not *replicable*; therefore they are scientifically useless.

But is replicability possible in psychology? Are psychological phenomena observable under specifiable and replicable conditions? Lange argued that they are, and he cited Muller's experiment as proof for his assertion. Muller had demonstrated that what we hear or see is not caused by external events but by the specific nerve that is stimulated. We see sights and hear sounds because in seeing the optic nerve is stimulated and in hearing the auditory nerve is excited. According to Lange, his finding shows that controlled observation is possible in psychology, because Muller described a psychological event as it occurs under replicable physical-physiological conditions.

For this reason Wundt, who is known as the father of scientific psychology, later called his experimental psychology "physiological" psychology because it was a psychology in which observations could be replicated. Moreover, Wundt went one step further. Not only can we in this way reliably *observe* consciousness, he said, but we can also *manipulate* it. We can evoke psychological phenomena at will by presenting the experimental subjects with certain physical-physiological stimuli of our own choosing. Once we can do this, the road to experimentation with the mind is wide open (Lange, 1873).

### 6.4.4 *Ebbinghaus: Experimentation with the human mind*

A common practice in those days was to classify the functions of the mind as central or peripheral functions. Central functions were what we call cognitive functions today, while perception and sensation were considered peripheral functions. Though he was the father of experimental psychology, Wundt had argued that only those psychological processes directly related to physical-physiological stimuli such as sensation and perception are replicable under controlled conditions. For the investigation of the higher functions, psychology must use another research method, which Wundt dubbed the *genetic* method.

Ebbinghaus (1850–1909) showed that these "higher" psychological processes, i.e., the central functions of learning, remembering, and forgetting, were also open to experimental research. He criticized the psychology of his day because it had many theories but no method to verify them. For example, the psychology of his day was unable to describe forgetting something as a function of the time it took to learn it, the speed or ease with which it was learned, or the interference of other events on the learning process. The psychology of his day could not describe *exactly* what happens when we forget something.

Current theories of memory and forgetting have no standardized procedure for collecting data, he said. At one time researchers talk about remembering or forgetting poems or prose, at other times the stuff to be remembered are names of places or dates. What is needed is a standard-ized form of learning material. This is why Ebbinghaus constructed and used an enormous list of nonsense syllables, which per definition are not connected to anything else because they have no meaning. In his mem-ory experiments, in which he used himself as the experimental subject, he systematically varied length of lists of nonsense syllables to be learned, the speed with which they were read, etc.

The psychology of Ebbinghaus was an associationistic psychology. It was basically an attempt to establish quantification in habit formation. According to associationism single elements A and B are associated after they have occurred a specified number of times in consciousness. Ebbing-haus wanted to know exactly *how many times* they had to be presented. For example, one of his research questions was, *How many times must one read a series of discrete nonsense syllables out loud before one is at the first attempt to reproduce them able to do so fluently, at a certain rate, and with the certainty that the reproduction is correct?* Note that in this type of psy-chological research the overriding focus is on what we today would call scientific rigor (Boring, 1929).

### 6.5 *A new formula for psychology*
All these methodological innovations provided psychologists with a new formula for doing psychology. This bit of (pre)history of psychology also demonstrates that, in actual fact, empirical, experimental psychology had more than one founding father. Wundt just synthesized what was already there. The "new formula," which started experimental psychology, was actually formulated by Oswald Külpe and Edward Titchener, who were students of Wundt, rather than by Wundt himself. This approach to psy-chology contained a number of fundamental principles:

1.  Stick to what is positively given, to what is observable, repli-cable, and controllable. Older definitions of psychology as the science of mind, or of the human spirit or soul, are unaccept-able on methodological grounds. Psychology cannot deal with such unobservable entities as the "I ," the "soul," or psychologi-cal "faculties." New formula psychology practiced what Lange had called a "psychology without a soul."

2.  According to this formula, psychology is the science of *conscious experiences*, or of those experiences of which people are conscious when they say that they observe a book, are sad, worry, etc.

3.  To answer the question what "conscious experience" is, psy-chology must analyze "*moments of consciousness*" into their

constitutive elements. Once these elements are found, we can then set out to discover the laws by which these elements are synthesized into the larger wholes we are familiar with in our experience (the "moments"). This model of consciousness is much like the medical model where the "body" is the sum of its separate elements. In the same way, the formula viewed "I hear a melody" as an aggregate concept for an as yet to be discovered number of separate contents in consciousness.

4. According to the adherents to the new formula, the research method of psychology is *introspection,* or "inner-observation-under-experimental-conditions." Moreover, they stipulated that introspection reports must be so detailed that everyone can reconstruct them in their own consciousness, like builders read the blueprints of an architect. This principle of the formula was especially emphasized by Titchener, who is the father of the school of psychology known as structuralism.

## References

Boring, E.G. (1929). *A History of Experimental Psychology.* New York: Century.

Copleston, F.C. (1965). *A History of Philosophy.* Vol. VII, London: Burns and Oates.

Eisenga, L.K.A. and van Rappard, J.F.H. (1987). *Hoofdstromen en Mensbeelden in de Psychologie.* Amsterdam: Boom Meppel.

Fechner, G.T. (1966). *Elements of Psychophysics.* New York.

Helmholz, H.F. von. (1886). *Handbuch der Physiologischen Optik.* Leipzig.

Lange, F.A. (1873). *Geschichte des Materialismus und Kritik seiner Bedeutung in der Gegenwart.* Iserlohn: Baedeker.

Lersch, Ph. (1960). *Algemene Psychologie.* Translated into Dutch from the German *Aufbau der Person.* Utrecht: Het Spectrum.

Müller-Freienfels, R. (1938). *De Voornaamste Richtingen in de Hedendaagsche Psychologie.* Translated into Dutch by P.H. Ronge, Utrecht: Erven J. Bijleveld.

Polkinghorne, D. (1983). *Methodology for the Human Sciences, systems of inquiry.* Albany: State University of New York Press.

Sanders, C., Eisenga, L.K.A., and van Rappard, J.F.H. (1976). *Inleiding in de Grondslagen van de Psychologie.* Deventer: Van Loghum Slaterus.

Sarbin, T.R. (1986). *Narrative Psychology: The Storied Nature of Human Conduct.* New York: Praeger.

Van Belle, H.A. (1980). *Basic Intent and Therapeutic Approach of Carl R. Rogers.* Toronto: Wedge.

# Some Issues to Stimulate Dialogue

1. Now that you have read this chapter, revisit questions three and seven in the Dialogue part of Chapter 5.

2. One of the things this book does not provide is a *Zeitgeist* analysis of changes in the history of psychology. That is to say, it does not give explanations of paradigm shifts on the basis of changes in society as a whole. Even so, this form of analysis and explanation is a legitimate topic for dialogue. It is said that the near universal focus on methodology in academic circles during the nineteenth century was a product of the Industrial Revolution. If this explanation is valid for nineteenth century psychology, what are the effects of globalization and the information processing revolution of our time on contemporary psychology?

3. Ultimately the opposition between anti-positivism and positivism is rooted in the opposition between will and logic. In what ways does this opposition manifest itself in contemporary psychology? (To give you a hint of what I am after, think of the opposition between freedom and determinism.) This opposition between will and logic is a historically grown reality in Western thought. For that reason it is also part of the enterprise of contemporary psychology. But the question can be debated whether there *ought* to be an opposition between will and logic.

4. Describe in detail the impact of romanticism on psychoanalysis. Pay special attention to the influence of later romanticists like Schopenhauer and Nietzsche (see H. Ellenberger, *The Discovery of the Unconscious*).

5. The main reason why those early psychologists spent so much time and effort on methodology was to eliminate controversy from psychology. They wanted to create one unified empirical system of psychology in which debates were settled exclusively on the basis of research results. As we will see in the following chapters they failed in this regard. Controversy and school formation continued unabated after psychology became a separate empirical discipline and adopted the new formula approach to research. From your own knowledge of

psychology, is there more unity in our discipline today than there was before? Given that a unified research methodology is a prerequisite for unity in psychology, must this be a natural science method of research? Is there perhaps another approach to the study of psychology that is likely to have more success because it is more in line with the subject matter of psychology? This, after all, was the argument put forth by the anti-positivists for adopting the method of *verstehen*. Should psychology has a unified field of investigation? Perhaps the field of research in psychology is so diverse that it requires a multiplicity of methodologies. What do you think?

# 7. THE PSYCHOLOGY OF CONSCIOUSNESS

## 7.1 *Wundt's voluntarism*
The earliest experimental psychology was the psychology of consciousness. The method of this psychology was that of systematic introspection-under-experimental-conditions, much in line with the research principles listed at the end of Chapter 6. Generally speaking, an assertion in psychology about human beings was deemed to be true if people repeatedly could look inside themselves and verify the assertion as present in their awareness.

### 7.1.1 *Experimental psychology*
When it came to a general understanding of the business of psychology, Wundt (1832–1920) did not differ much from his contemporaries. It was commonly accepted that one tried to understand consciousness by breaking it down to its elements and then finding the laws of consciousness. However, Wundt did have his differences on a number of issues with mechanistic British empiricists, who also pursued this goal. For the British empiricist tradition, the basic elements of consciousness were thought to be discrete, passive sensations. For Wundt these elements were *impulses*. The basic elements we are aware of, he held, are mental or physical *activities* that are purposeful. They aim at something and are up to something. Wundt's psychology was a *dynamic* psychology, in which the basic elements of consciousness are inherently (pro)active, rather than re-active. The basic elements of human life, according to Wundt, are creative acts of will. This is why his psychology is called *voluntarism*. Looking toward the outside, these acts of will are behaviors. Looking inside at them, introspecting them, they are bits of consciousness.

Moreover, for Wundt, "will," or "inherent activity" as he also called it, is not just a characteristic of consciousness but of all living matter (Leibniz? La Mettrie?). Wundt was not a dualist where mind acts *upon* matter, or on the body. Rather, he was a parallelist. For him, what happens in the mind also simultaneously happens in matter, or in the body.

Wundt maintained that the laws of consciousness were not forms of association as they were for the British empiricists but forms or levels of creative, whole-making *apperception*. He stated that in our conscious-ness human actions consist of three components inextricably united with one another. These components are sensation, emotion (or feeling), and movement. It is only via abstraction that we can become aware of these by themselves. For example, it is only when we abstract feeling and move-ment from human action that we become aware of something like sensa-tion. Sensations are not the basic elements of consciousness at all; rather, they are the product of abstraction. Apperception unifies or organizes incoming sensory information *immediately* so that we are only aware of wholes in consciousness.

Wundt conducted reaction time experiments to demonstrate his theories and modified his theories on the basis of experimental results. In that sense he was truly an *experimental* rather than a *philosophical* psy-chologist. But this did not entail that he had to become an elementarist or a sensationalist, as the positivists with their new formula approach intimated.

Historically Wundt did not stand in the empiricistic tradition, as so many of his time did, but in the rationalist tradition. Intellectually he was a descendent of Leibniz's monadology, which stressed that elements of re-ality are inherently active, and also a descendent of Leibniz's view of (ap) perception. Furthermore, like Leibniz, Wundt adopted parallelism as his view of the relation between mind and body. Next, Wundt was also influ-enced by Kant's emphasis on the constructive character of consciousness. Finally, Wundt was heavily influenced by the German idealism of Fichte, with its emphasis on the will. However, this focus on volition goes back much farther in history than Fichte. In that sense we can say that Wundt was also influenced by Duns Scotus.

### 7.1.2 Völkerpsychologie

In addition, romanticism put its stamp on Wundt. The influence of romanticism comes especially to the fore in Wundt's *Völkerpsychologie*. For Wundt, as with most of the Rationalists, the intellect or the mind consists of the higher functions (thought and judgment) and the pe-ripheral functions (sensation and perception). Wundt, with most other Rationalists, held that natural scientific or experimental psychology is incapable of studying the higher functions. In order to investigate these higher functions Wundt believed that one needed a *hermeneutic* method. In Wundt's time this was called the *historical* or *genetic* method. This was a method that saw individuals as part of a historically grown culture or "*volk.*" Wundt spent the last two decades of his life writing ten volumes of *Völkerpsychologie*. This work was part of the movement of *anti-positivism*, which promoted a form of scholarship called *Geisteswissenschaften* (Wundt, 1873; Rieber, 1980).

### 7.2 *Titchener's structuralism*
Much of what was said under the "new formula" applies to Titchener's structuralism. A student of Wundt, with ambitions to be his successor, Titchener (1867–1927) was an Englishman and a positivist. He stood in the line of British empiricism. He is credited with bringing the psychology of Wundt to America with the intent of co-opting Wundt's psychology for British empiricism. In the process of doing this he unfortunately totally distorted Wundt's voluntarism, because Wundt simply does not stand in the English empiricist tradition.

For example, Titchener claimed that Wundt's notion of "apperception" is identical to John Stuart Mill's notion of "mental chemistry." But during his lifetime Wundt explicitly distanced himself from this view of consciousness. Also, Titchener downplayed Wundt's *Völkerpsychologie* because it did not fit in his structuralistic vision of psychology. Titchener held that the mind consists exclusively of sensations and of images of those sensations. He rejected apperception on grounds that it can only be inferred, not observed (Rieber, 1980).

According to Titchener, experimental psychology has three tasks:
1. To reduce complex contents of consciousness to sensations. The method of analysis used to perform this task in structuralism was a complicated form of introspection.
2. To determine how these sensations are connected.
3. To explain the workings of consciousness. Here Titchener appealed to the physiological substratum of consciousness for answers. Consciousness, he held, is physiologically caused.

In essence, these tasks are an expression of the new formula approach to psychology. It is generally agreed that structuralism was a dogmatic and a sterile school of psychology. Its influence on psychology essentially died when Titchener died. We will pick up structuralism again when we discuss functionalism (Titchener, 1897).

### 7.3 *Response to the new formula in psychology after Wundt: The Wurzburg School*
Generally speaking, the students of Wundt were far more influenced by positivism than Wundt himself. Hence most of them adopted the new formula in psychology. However, in using the formula they demonstrated

its limitations and paradoxically contributed to its demise.

In terms of method the new formula promoted introspection of consciousness under experimental conditions. In terms of content it saw consciousness as consisting of discrete elements or sensations that are mechanically associated via laws of association (i.e., temporal and spatial contiguity) to form more complex conscious contents. How did all these notions stand up in the research?

The new formula was more a guideline for doing research than a full-fledged research program. It said: "*Analyze consciousness down to its irreducible elements and search for the laws that synthesize these elements into larger wholes.*" However, the definition of what these psychological elements were, as well as the definition of their synthesis into wholes, was as yet unclear. Most psychologists used the visual perception of color or form as examples of such psychological elements. A visual perception is simple and observable. Therefore, it can function as a building block for complex perceptions. It is also repeatable and controllable. In addition, it only occurs under the bodily condition of stimulation of the retina, and finally, in the visual perception of color and form there is a 1 to 1 relation between the psychical and physiological (which is called "the constancy hypothesis" in psychology). Thus, a visual perception appeared to be the ideal candidate for what a basic element of consciousness was supposed to look like. Most psychologists pictured the synthesis of these elements in consciousness as the association of loose elements brought about by habit formation. They viewed consciousness as a train and its elements as the cars of the train connected to one another.

### 7.3.1 Von Ehrenfels: Form qualities

How did new formula psychology fare experimentally? At first it seemed to be the way to go in psychology. But fairly soon the experimental re-sults of Christian von Ehrenfels' experiments in auditory perception be-gan to cast some doubt on the new formula approach. Von Ehrenfels (1859–1932) found that in listening to a melody like "Mary had a little lamb" we not only hear the separate elements and the tones that are then joined together in our minds associatively; we hear their relation to one another as well. In short, we always hear a melody as an organized unit, not as the association of loose elements. This is clear from when we play it in a different key. The elements are physically different, yet we hear the same melody. Therefore, said von Ehrenfels, we cannot reduce a melody to its elements. There is something more to consciousness than *psychic* elements (sensory qualities). In addition, there are also *form* qualities

(German: *Gestalt Qualitäten*) (von Ehrenfels, 1890). This discovery did not necessarily invalidate the new formula approach. It could still picture these form qualities as psychic elements next to the other, more familiar sensory qualities. Nevertheless, it had some explaining to do.

### 7.3.2 *Külpe: Directed, imageless thought*

The results of the experimental research done by Oswald Külpe (1862–1915) on thinking, judgment, and understanding were, however, much harder to harmonize with the new formula. New formula psychology assumed that the cognitive processes involved in thinking unfold associatively. Thinking is simply the sum of psychic elements A, B, C, and D, associated successively with one another over time in consciousness. In thinking, problem P evokes concept A, which leads to concept B, which leads to C, which leads to D, which mechanically leads to solution S, eventually.

If this view were correct, then it would be easy to observe and describe these steps as they occurred in consciousness. Remember that the new formula dictated that only observable phenomena were to be included in their scientific psychology. What Külpe found, however, was that certain crucial steps in the cognitive process appeared to be unobservable. For example, in judging two weights, trained subjects could readily report which one of the two was heavier, but they could not introspect the process that led them to this judgment. They just "knew." So, the question arose whether there are also *un*observable elements in consciousness, which of course would be against the new formula view of consciousness.

To settle this question, Külpe began to study the "knowing" or "understanding" or "comprehension" process more minutely. He divided the process into four phases and asked his experimental subjects to report what they could observe in their consciousness during each phase. For example, he had them tell out loud what they were thinking 1) before he presented them with a problem, 2) immediately after he presented the problem, 3) during the time when they were looking for a solution to the problem, and 4) when they had found the solution. He discovered that they could observe and report on phase 1), 2), and 4), but not phase 3). Apparently, the activity of comprehension in the problem solution process during phase 3), which is the key to the whole knowing process, was unobservable. Külpe also found that the first phase of the process directed the entire problem solving process from beginning to end.

Thus, he found that thinking does not proceed mechanically, associatively, but that it is observably goal directed. Based on these findings

Külpe expanded the new formula view of consciousness. He stated that consciousness also contains *un*observable content, or *"imageless thought."* Moreover, in addition, it contains intentional or goal directed acts of synthesis (Külpe, 1912).

Needless to say, this put the new formula view of consciousness, and therefore the positivistic psychology of that day, on a very shaky footing indeed. This situation led Titchener, the other person who with Külpe had formulated the principles of new formula psychology, to reject Külpe's experimental results. Rather than admit that the formula needed drastic revision, he chose to discredit Külpe by criticizing him on methodological grounds. In doing this, he pretty well set the tone for the debate in psychology at that time. Since 1910 a fierce battle raged among psychologists about these unobservable elements and these goal directed activities. The discussions among psychologists took on the character of trench warfare with each school defending its own view rather than helping each other clarify the vagueness of the formula for psychological research.

At this point it should be noted that the central aim of psychology going empirical, natural scientific, and experimental was, you will remember, so that there would emerge one unified theory of psychology. It appears now that this aim was not even realized within one school of psychology, i.e., the new formula school of psychology. To put it succinctly, different people using the same experimental method came up with different and conflicting results!

## 7.4 *Gestalt psychology: Wertheimer, Kohler, Koffka*

This brings us to Gestalt psychology. The critique of Gestalt psychology was that the new formula rests on an outdated view of science. It did not reject the new formula approach outright but it sought to renew and to expand it.

Gestalt psychology is chiefly based on one insight. This is the discovery by von Ehrenfels of "form qualities" (*Gestalt Qualitäten*) in human perception. Based on this insight, the school of Gestalt psychology practiced psychology as an empirical science and it did many classic experiments.

The proponents of Gestalt psychology were schooled in the natural sciences and they were very well-informed about the latest developments in theoretical physics. Wertheimer and Kohler, for example, were close friends of the prominent physicists Max Planck and Albert Einstein, both of whom rejected the classical Newtonian view of the natural physical world, i.e., the view that reality consists of material elements (atoms), the mutual pull and push of which wholly determines their motion. Clark Maxwell, another physicist, had shown that this classical theory does not always hold. Sometimes the dynamic "field," which exists independent of the atoms, determines the movements of the atoms. Consider, for example, the pattern of iron filings that is formed not by the interaction of the filings but by the magnetic field of a magnet.

A change in point of view in physics had, therefore, occurred since Newton regarding the physical world, in that it now recognized the existence of wholes that are independent of the parts, wholes that cannot be explained as the mechanical sum or aggregate of its elemental parts.

Gestalt psychology's critique of new formula psychology was that it was based on and continued to cling to an old view of the world that was no longer tenable. If physics accepts the existence of wholes, Wertheimer and Kohler asked, is it not time for psychology to do the same and to question the view of consciousness as consisting of discrete elements plus their association? Furthermore, can psychology continue to ignore the teleological "determining tendencies" that Külpe had discovered, or von Ehrenfels' discovery that a melody is an organized whole, a *Gestalt*, that exists in our consciousness independent from the elemental perceptions we have of the separate notes?

The conclusion of Gestalt psychology was that the natural scientific model does not distort psychological phenomena, provided that this model is expanded and corrected to include the latest discoveries in theoretical physics. In this way, Gestalt psychologists argued, we can have a natural scientific psychology that does not distort the uniquely wholelike character of the human mind.

All of the experiments of Gestalt psychology were done to drive home this point. Their experiments were mainly polemic. Their goal was to demonstrate that new formula psychology was no longer tenable. As their field of experimentation Gestalt psychologists chose the field of visual perception, since this was *the* area in which traditionally the existence of discrete mental elements (remember the perception of color or form) had been "demonstrated." The aim of these experiments was to show that the visual world does not consist of mental elements plus their association but that it is an organized whole. We will look at three examples of these experiments:

### EXPERIMENT I: PHI PHENOMENA
Present two lines, A and B, after one another. Repeat and vary the time interval between the presentation of A and B. The results are that at a certain time interval the subjects see one line moving from

top to bottom while the physical stimulus itself is not moving. Reduce the time interval, and the subjects see the two lines simultaneously. Increase the time interval, and the subjects see the two lines appearing one after the other in a stationary position. When subjects are given the instruction not to see the line moving, they still have the same experience. At the right time interval they see one line moving from position A to position B, and nothing else. This is an indisputable fact of perception, but it does not square with the new formula view. Wertheimer accused the new formula adherents of prejudice because they refused to accept an observable, replicable fact of observation (Wertheimer, 1912).

## Experiment II: Good Form

Draw six lines 11  11  11

When instructed to see the lines as two groups of three, subjects find it impossible to do so. Seeing the lines as three groups of two is dominant. As perceivers we cannot resist the "organization principle" (*Prägnanz-prinzip*) that forces us to order our perceptions into "good," "harmonious," "symmetrical" form. This experiment demonstrates that perception involves more than what is physically available to the retina. Another example of this same phenomenon is that we regularly see objects, tables, doors, and windows as rectangular, while in (physical) reality (i.e., on the retina) they seldom are (Wertheimer, 1923).

## Experiment III: Insight

Kohler's experiments with chimpanzees demonstrated that learning does not occur by trial and error, as the new formula psychologists maintained. When chimpanzees were presented with a problematic situation, they surveyed the situation and then they had a sudden insight (an *Aha Erlebnis*) after which they solved the problem immediately. At later trials they were able to solve the problem directly. The chimps appeared to "let themselves be governed by the meaningful, goal-directedness of the problem situation" (Kohler, 1927).

The experiments of Gestalt psychologists demonstrated that the new formula was untenable, but they did little to develop their own Gestalt formula. These experiments did not explain, for example, *how* insight into the problem-situation comes into being. They might have ascribed the organization of consciousness, about which they had so much to say, e.g., to *psychic activities* (von Ehrenfels), or to *goal-directed psychic acts* (Külpe). This would have fit the metaphysical-rationalistic view of human beings as active, meaning-giving beings.

But they chose not to do this. Instead they looked for the explanation of the organization of perception and cognition in the structure of the brain. They feared the notion of psychic activity because such activity appeared to be unobservable. It occurred in the dark part of the mind, of consciousness, or of the psyche. It was understood to be an *un*conscious psychic process. As empirical scientists they feared that "unconscious" meant the same thing as "non-empirical" or "non-observable." They were afraid that by accepting a *psychic* activity they would be introducing a *homunculus,* i.e., a hidden, invisible, inner man, whose activity would then provide the explanation for observable processes. Instead they accepted the "*isomorphism thesis,*" which holds that psychological and physiological processes run parallel and stand in a one to one relation to one another. They stated that in the brain there are, in principle observable, structures whose form corresponds to the form of the perceived object or perceptual field. The analogy they used for the relation between these brain structures and the perceptual field was that of a map and its correspondence to the geography of the land (Eisenga & van Rappard, 1987, pp. 46–53).

With the acceptance of the constancy hypothesis, Gestalt psychology opened up a discussion about the causes of observable behavior and of the introspected content of consciousness. So the question became: What explains, what accounts for, or what are the "causes" of these phenomena? Are they unconscious and therefore unobservable "psychic activities," or are they in principle observable physiological brain processes?

## References

Eisenga, L.K.A. and van Rappard, J.F.H. (1987). *Hoofdstromen en Mensbeelden in de Psychologie.* Amsterdam: Boom Meppel.

Kohler, W. (1927). *The Mentality of Apes.* New York: Humanities Press.

Külpe, O. (1922). "Über die Moderne Psychologie des Denkens," in *Vorlesungen über Psychologie.* Leipzig: Hirzel.

Titchener, E.B. (1897). *An Outline of Psychology.* New York: MacMillan.

Rieber, R.W. ed. (1980). *Wilhelm Wundt and the Making of Scientific Psychology.* New York: Plenum Press.

von Ehrenfels, C. (1890). "Über Gestaltqualitäten," *Vierteljahrschrift für Wissenschaftliche Philosophie.* 14, 249–292.

Wertheimer, M. (1912). "Experimentelle Studien über das Sehen von Bewegung," *Zeitschrift für Psychologie,* 61, 161–265.

Wertheimer, M. (1958). Principles of perceptual organization [1923], in *Readings in Perception.* Eds. D.C. Beardslee and M. Wertheimer. New York: van Nostrand, 115–135.

Wundt, W. (1873). *Principles of Physiological Psychology.* New York: MacMillan.

# Some Issues to Stimulate Dialogue

1. See if you can list the historical-philosophical influences on Wundt's voluntaristic view of mind/consciousness, on his preferred research methodology, on his experimental/physiological psychology, and on his *Völkerpsychologie*.

2. In view of the fact that all kinds of experimentation occurs today in the realm of cognition, Wundt's belief that one cannot experiment with the so-called "higher" functions would appear to rest on philosophical bias rather than psychological evidence. However, there is more to this problem than meets the eye. The interesting thing about psychology is that in distinction from other disciplines it does not study the world but the way we look at the world. In essence psychological research is looking at looking at, or the perception of perception or thinking about thinking, etc. Introspection or thinking about thinking *is* really impossible because in introspection thinking is both subject and object. I have to use the function of thinking to observe the thinking I am trying to observe. At best I can only think about what I just thought, which is really remembering rather than thinking, right?

3. My guess is that Wundt was not so much concerned with the impossibility of experimenting with the higher functions as with the impropriety of it. Being an anti-positivist he probably considered this type of research an affront to humanity. Is there any validity to the sentiment that the psychological study of human beings somehow devalues their humanity?

4. In the psychology of consciousness, which per definition studies by means of introspection that of which people are aware, unconscious factors are problematic because they cannot be introspected or observed. They can only be inferred. It is for this reason that Gestalt psychologists adhered to the isomorphism thesis rather than explain the perceptual data they demonstrated as the result of psychic activity. Later in the history of psychology psychologists tried to solve this problem by means of operationalization. Find out what this means.

# 8. The Psychology of the Unconscious Mind

## 8.1 *Freud's psychoanalytic psychology*

For Gestalt psychology the question became: What explains, what accounts for, or what are the "*causes*" of the Phi phenomena, of good form and of insight, observed in our experiments? Are they unconscious and therefore unobservable "psychic activities," or are they in principle observable physiological brain processes? We meet the same problematics in psychoanalysis.

Sigmund Freud (1856–1939) has been called both a mechanistic, biologistic materialist, akin to the new formula approach, and an archeologist or hermeneutic of human experience à la Dilthey's method of *Verstehen*. But he fits in neither camp. Hence, like Gestalt psychology, psychoanalysis is best viewed as an attempt to expand and correct the new formula.

Freud was a medical doctor who accused his fellow MD's of showing a lack of respect for the facts. He said that their lack of respect was due to them having turned medicine into a natural scientific discipline. This mechanistic turn of medicine on the one hand advanced medicine considerably; on the other hand, it closed the eyes of MD's to the most important and most difficult problems of their practice.

Many MDs, Freud said, believe that they can only accept as fact that which has absolute certainty. They do not take the observable suffering of hysteric patients seriously because the symptoms that these patients suffer are inexplicable in terms of anatomical or physiological causes. Therefore they interpret the *observable* symptoms of hysteric patients as dissimulation, or as plain trickery. "It's all in your head," they say, "quit complaining, there is nothing wrong with you (physiologically)."

My fellow MD's, said Freud, refuse to even entertain the notion that these symptoms may have a *psychic* cause. They are afraid that this kind of talk is metaphysical, mythological, and nonscientific. Their fear is understandable because historically psychic causes have been associated with demon possession, cosmic magnetism, mesmerism, and spiritualism. However, Freud continued, this attitude of my fellow MD's regarding hysteria and other inexplicable neurotic phenomena is nevertheless in conflict with the essence of the natural scientific approach, which states that we must study all potentially observable phenomena. To separate observable phenomena into those that are explainable and those that are inexplicable and then to refuse to study the ones that you do not understand is unscientific, according to Freud. So, he advocated an expansion of the current view of the scientific method.

Granted, Freud said, the current view of science gives us knowledge that, as far as it goes, is quite reliable. But it has not always been that way. The current view of the scientific method itself has been a long time in coming. It came about as a result of people for a long time being willing to be empirically open to all kinds of new and as yet inexplicable phenomena, rather than rejecting them dogmatically. If we stay open to currently unknown phenomena, Freud said, we may ultimately discover a set of natural laws that reach wider and dig deeper than do the currently known physicochemical laws (of Newtonian physics).

Granted also, Freud continued, we currently do not have neurophysiological explanations for hysteria (as is required under the medical model). But from that it does not follow that these symptoms are purely random products of a sick mind. Hysteric symptoms may be *psychically* determined rather than physiologically. At least, the data that result from hypnosis and free association seem to point in the direction of that hypothesis. The behavior of hysterics appears exaggerated to us outsiders, because we do not know any of the determining motives out of which this behavior arises. But if we knew the motivating causes of this behavior, we would be able to explain it. These arguments led Freud to the following principles of psychoanalytic research.

## 8.2 *Principles of the psychoanalytic formula for psychology*

1. A variety of inexplicable phenomena, such as neurotic symptoms, dreams, (Freudian) slips of the tongue, etc., become intelligible when we view them as products of psychic activities. For example, we understand the inexplicable behavior of a person when we know that he or she is acting under the influence of posthypnotic suggestion, which is a psychic influence.

2. To accept the existence of psychic activities means that the human mind is not completely free in its creative activity. Under posthypnotic suggestion, a person may *believe* that he is acting freely, but in reality his acts are determined by the suggestion of the hypnotist. His behavior is motivated, even if he does not

know what motivates him.

3.  Psychic acts do not have to be conscious. On the contrary, most of the things that motivate us are unconscious, i.e., they occur outside our capacity for introspective observation. We are mostly oblivious to their influence. They exist in the *dynamic unconscious*.

4.  "Unconscious" does not mean "inactive." Even though we repress the awareness of a certain motive from our consciousness, it still influences our behavior. This is why the unconscious is called *dynamic* (i.e., active). A repressed motivation can enter our awareness *symbolically*, i.e., as a dream, as neurotic symptoms, or as obsessive acts and thoughts. But whether we become conscious of this motivation or whether it remains hidden, it is still active.

Freud wanted to expand new formula psychology, which on methodological grounds restricted psychology to consciousness, or to the introspectively observable contents of consciousness. He wanted psychology to study the *un*observable (read: the unconscious) contents of the mind *next to* observable (read: conscious) psychic contents. Moreover, he assigned an active, behavior-influencing role to these unconscious factors. (Compare with von Ehrenfels and Külpe, who talked about the unobservable content of consciousness that nevertheless *forms* the melody and *directs* problem solving.)

According to Freud, the reason why psychologists and philosophers cannot accept the idea of the unconscious is that it implies that human beings are not exclusively rational and that they are in some ways like an animal. Tradition had always held that on the basis of reason human beings can control their drives and emotions. But, according to Freud, this only holds true when a person is fully aware of his or her drives and motives; it does not hold when a person is not aware of his or her unconscious drives. Therefore, the stumbling block of accepting unconscious content is that it means that human beings are not completely lord and master in their own house, and that idea was threatening to Freud's contemporaries, most of all to the metaphysical rationalists of that time.

Freud himself was ambivalent about the issue of whether human beings are in control of themselves or not. To Binswanger, an existentialistic psychiatrist, in an interview later in his life, Freud said:

> I know that the whole of man is (rational) spirit (*Geist*/Ego/Consciousness) and that this is the essence of man. But the people know that already. I

had to show them that man is also driven (id). Constitutionally man is a *dualism* (both free/ego and driven/id). But man's task is to form himself into a unity. What is id must become ego (*Wo Es war soll Ich werden*).

## 8.3 *The history of psychotraumatology and psychoanalysis*

One way to understand Freud is to see him as a child of his time. Freud lived in an age when the two intellectual movements that had shaped Western civilization and those living in it for several centuries, the Enlightenment (comprising scientific and metaphysical rationalism) and romanticism, were losing their grip on how people lived, thought, and felt. What was beginning to replace these two spiritual movements were Darwinism, Marxism, and positivism.

During the modern period of history, the Enlightenment had celebrated (natural) scientific reason. Historically earlier than romanticism, it was an upbeat movement born in reaction to the superstitions of the Middle Ages. It promised that human beings could solve every problem they faced provided they thought straight, kept their eyes open to reality, and did not let their passions get the best of them. It promoted a practical, down-to-earth style of living in which emotions were things one needed to control by clear thinking and by keeping a level head (Ellenberger, 1970, pp. 193–199).

In time romanticism replaced the Enlightenment as the cultural-intellectual spirit dominating Western civilization. It was precisely this unfeeling character of the Enlightenment spirit to which the romanticists reacted. Instead of the cold reason of the head they celebrated the warm feelings of the heart. They gave a central place to passions in the economy of human life. They were impressed with the way things felt rather than with the way things looked. Empathy rather than "empiry" became the way toward knowing what to do. One could come to understand the nature of things, not by looking at them and by thinking about them, but by *living into* them. Being in touch with nature, with other people, or with other cultures, and especially being in touch with one's own inner self were considered the most important in life (Ellenberger, 1970, pp. 199–222, 278–291).

The people of Freud's time had inherited these two contradictory cultural styles of living. These had become part of their psyche. It was in terms of these contradictions that they experienced and expressed their personal problems. Whoever sought to help them would have to reckon with this fact. Somehow these two opposing tendencies needed reconciliation within these people.

### 8.3.1 *Pierre Janet's environmental dynamics and the Enlightenment*

The Enlightenment had more influence in France than it did in Germany (Ellenberger, p. 193). This is why Pierre Janet (1859–1947), a French medical doctor based in Paris, who worked to heal people suffering from hysteria, essentially took an Enlightenment approach to therapy (Ellenberger, 1970, p. 331). For Janet, hysteria was the result of an individual experiencing a traumatic experience. This experience, he held, threatens to overwhelm the individual who is organically already predisposed to be overwhelmed. For this reason, this experience is automatically dissociated out of ordinary *narrative* memory, where things make sense, into the subconsciousness of *habit* memory, where things do not make sense. There the traumatic experience takes on a life of its own in the form of becoming a *fixed idea* that the patient is doomed to repeat in action over and over again as a symptom, all the while not being aware that this is happening. By means of hypnosis Janet also changed the idea of the experience in his patients' mind so that it no longer seemed traumatic to them and therefore no longer overwhelmed them.

It is noteworthy that Janet's *"psychological analysis"* of hysterics is all about thinking and not about affect (Ellenberger, 1970, p. 401; Janet, 1889). Janet stressed that as a result of a traumatic experience a patient initially loses her ability to think about the event, that is, she does not remember or *dissociates.* She also is disturbed in her thinking about the experience and in her actions with regard to the experience (repeated fixed idea and compulsion). As a result of therapy the patient is taught to think straight about the experience again and in this way the symptoms disappear. However, Janet said little about what all this does to the patient emotionally or about what role her emotions play in the etiology and the cure of hysteria. In some sense both the cause and the cure are externally and rather mechanistically induced (Ellenberger, pp. 331–417).

### 8.3.2 *Psychotraumatology: Posttraumatic stress disorder*

Janet is the father of an approach to psychopathology that today is called psychotraumatology. It studies the effects of traumatic experiences (war, holocaust, natural disasters, accidents, and sexual assault) on a person's psyche. The DSM-IV category it works with is *"posttraumatic stress disorder,"* the symptoms of which are hypermnesia, amnesia, flash backs, memory recovery, etc. (Herman, 1992; DSM-IV, 1994).

### 8.3.3 *Sigmund Freud's psychodynamics and romanticism*

In his adherence to the Enlightenment ideal, Janet differed fundamentally from Freud. Throughout his life Freud remained a romanticist at heart (Ellenberger, 1970, pp. 331, 465/6, 532, 542). Above all else he wanted to do justice to what happens inside people and especially to what and how they feel. His passion for giving psychological, and within that, *affective* explanations for human behavior led him to divorce affect from cognition and both of these from reality. Consequently, his explanations lost much of their "ecological validity" (Neisser, 1976). Explanations of human behavior were now given exclusively in terms of the interaction of affect and cognition. They were purely *psychological* explanations.

By doing this, Freud refocused our attention on what after all is the area of research for psychology, namely how people are affected by, react to, and process influences from the outside. Outside influences such as traumatic events or actions by others now were no longer seen as causes but only as *occasions* for hysteria and other psychopathologies. Not the environmental dynamics but the internal psychodynamics were placed center-stage. And whether events or experiences were to be called traumatic at all could now only be determined by their relation to these inner dynamics.

For Janet environmental dynamics determined psychodynamics, i.e., the nature of outside influences determined the nature of inner conflicts. For Freud the reverse was the case; he believed that life is governed by (the resolution of) inner conflicts between the energy-less structuring ego and the structure-less energizing id (Eagle, 1987, p. 76), between conscious plans and unconscious impulses, between the reality principle and the pleasure principle, between a censoring super-ego and a licentious id, between the height of values and ideals and the depth of wishes, drives, and passions, between control and letting go, between cognition and affect, between life and death.

Throughout his life Freud was a confirmed anthropological and psychological dualist. This not only meant that for him life or the human psyche consists of a duality but also that the two components of the duality are each other's opposite. For each of the above pairs, the essential characteristic is that the one is not the other in the sense that being *un*conscious means *not* being conscious. This is the reason why the components of this dualism are in conflict. Living means attempting time and again to resolve this conflict or to overcome these irreconcilable differences without ever fully succeeding. Environments are considered traumatic by Freud only insofar as they contribute to these conflicts.

Freud was a dualist because the people he treated were the recipients of two opposing cultural-historical Spirits, those of the Enlightenment and of romanticism. In Nietzsche's terms, the former was Apollonian, the latter Dionysian (Ellenberger, 1970, pp. 529, 542). The old struggle of ancient Greece between *the definite* and *the indefinite* reappears here, as it did so often in the history of Western thought. Furthermore, ever since the Greeks these Spirits had also been identified the one with reason and the other with passion. Today we may identify them with cognition and with emotion.

Freud wanted to confront the people of his time, and us by implication, with what it *felt* like to live. He wanted to confront people with the raw passion of the depth of their inner life, *before* reason or cognition had a chance to sanitize it. He wanted to confront people with the irrationality, the strangeness, and the unpredictability of their affective life. He wanted his contemporaries to feel *before* they thought. And he achieved that goal by shocking them with his theories of infantile sexuality. Hence, he told his audience that boys *wish* to put their penis into their mother's vagina. He said that because of this wish, boys fear that their father will cut off their penis with a kitchen knife, blood spurting all over the place, so to speak. Was anything more repulsive to the Victorian male? Is there an image that evokes a more visceral emotion in *any* male?

Freud deliberately sought to provoke his contemporaries. He did this, for instance, by publishing his *Interpretation of Dreams* (1900). The German title, *Traumdeutung*, was intriguing and shocking to Victorians. It had the connotation of being associated with magic and witchcraft. Moreover, at the beginning of this book Freud placed a motto borrowed from Virgil's *Aeneid*, which said, "If Heaven I cannot bend, then Hell I will arouse." He also revealed to his friend Fliess that he enjoyed the thought of "all the headshaking" of his countrymen over the "indiscretions and impudences" of the book (Ellenberger, 1970, p. 452). He loved to shock people.

Freud anticipated much of what modern popular music is all about when he recognized the shock value of certain images, and when he understood that shocking people puts them in touch with their guts. To put it bluntly, he rubbed our noses into our shit (*anal-erotic*, for goodness' sake!) in order to make us feel our bodies.

Ernest Becker, in *The Denial of Death* (1973, p. 33), continues this tradition by quoting one of Jonathan Swift's poems about a lover who exclaims about his beloved:

> Nor wonder how I lost my Wits;
> Oh! Caelia, Caelia, Caelia shits!

Whereby Swift meant to indicate that there is an absolute antithesis between the state of being in love and the awareness of the excremental function of the beloved. Becker also shocks his readers by quoting Montaigne (31), who said "on the highest throne in the world man sits on his arse," a crude, but effective way of putting us in touch with that part of our reality that we normally tend to ignore. What Freud and Becker were saying is that one does not understand the life of passion by reasoning about it or by cognitively processing it as information. That part of our reality must be felt *before* it is cognitively processed *if* qua feeling it can be processed at all.

### 8.4 *Freud's models of mind*

Yet another way to summarize psychoanalysis is to discuss a series of successive models of mind, which are evident in the development of Freud's thought (Monte, 1995, p. 101–150).

#### 8.4.1 *Depth psychology model: Conscious vs. unconscious*

According to this model the human psyche or mind is like a gestalt in which the figure is the conscious and the ground the unconscious. In this model Freud comes closest to the views of Gestalt psychology. In this model the human mind is like an iceberg: 10 percent conscious, 90 percent unconscious. The unconscious is a can of worms. It is a cauldron full of insistent drives and base passions. The conscious is the lid. Normally a person desperately tries to keep the lid on, but one is not often fully successful. Some unconscious material escapes and appears in consciousness in a distorted, symbolic way as slips, as physical symptoms, dreams, and as obsessions. These are a compromise between the conscious and the unconscious that allows us to live with our unacceptable biologically-based urges. Freud taught us that there is a depth to our minds, an active, motivating part we are not aware of. He showed us that we have passions, drives, longings, and desires. He made us realize that we have a body, feelings, emotions, and affects.

#### 8.4.2 *Developmental model of libido displacement: Oral, anal, phallic, latency, genital*

According to this model, the psycho-sexual stages of life are determined by the movement of the libido across the surface of our body. The libido as the pleasure principle consists of biologically-based *psychic* energy. Freud's libido concept is an adapted version of the law of conservation of energy. This law states that energy can neither be created nor destroyed;

it can only be transformed. According to Freud, the libido similarly *displaces* itself from one body zone to the next, from the mouth, to the anus, to the genitals, to nonspecific places on the body surface, and finally to the genitals again. Its location in a zone creates tension feelings, and these feelings turn that zone into an *erogenous* zone. This tension is released by stimulation (mouth-suck, anus-defecation, genitals- masturbation, or intercourse). When the tension in a given body zone is released via stimulation, the libido flows to another zone. The successive displacement of libido from one body zone to another determines the stages of psychosexual development, the oral, anal, phallic, latency, and genital stages. Fixation of the libido on a body zone thus causes stagnation in a person's psychosexual development.

### 8.4.3 *Structural model: Id, ego, superego*

(a)   Origin: id, superego, ego

According to this model, a human being originally is an *it* (Latin: id). The id is a depository of desires and drives. It says, "I want, I want." The id comes in contact with "society" that says, "You can't, you can't." Society places sanctions on our desires. A human being introjects these sanctions as a superego. *Inside* a human being the id and the super ego are in conflict with one another. This creates anxiety in a person, which in turn necessitates a mediator, the ego. This ego says to both the id and the superego, "Come now, let us reason together." The ego is the reality principle. It is more realistic than either the id or the superego.

(b)   Relation id, ego, superego

With that the relation between the three is also stated. The id and the superego are both out of touch with reality. They are in conflict. The ego is in touch with reality, and mediates between the id and the superego.

(c)   My interpretation of why Freud came up with this structure

Freud was an MD, specifically a healer of the mind. To heal people he needed a view of human nature or a view of the human mind. Where was he to go to get the material for his view? What was historically available to him?

There was the Enlightenment view of the mind and of human nature. It preached salvation through natural science, through exact methods of thinking and research. It was the view of "civilized humankind," against which Rousseau fulminated so much; it was "polite society." In Freud's time this took the shape of the industrialist *bourgeoisie*, the Victorian man or woman, who preached total control of life for the purpose of material gain, for profit.

There was also the romantic view of human life. It celebrated personhood as passion, feeling, emotion, impulse, guts, and glory—the Bohemian life. This view led to fierce nationalism in Germany and ultimately to the bloodbath of World War I, the war to end all wars. Freud knew these historical strands intimately from experience and became disillusioned with both. He asked, "Which of these two is on the side of reason?" and concluded, "neither." The Victorian man or woman he encountered in his practice was a product of both conflicting views. In such a situation, Freud decided that reason and realism is at best served by a compromise between the two. Reason is a balance between the two. Therefore, reason is on the side of the ego, the mediator. As Freud said, "*Wo Es war soll Ich werden.*" What is id must become ego. The same could be said about superego. Both should become more *reasonable* by becoming part of the ego.

### 8.4.4 *Cultural model: Thanatos vs. Eros*
Later in life, as can be seen in his book, *Beyond the Pleasure Principle*, Freud had experienced World War I and had lost faith in the power of the ego to balance the conflicting forces of the id and the superego. At that point in his life he came to view human nature, or the mind, as a product of a death-instinct, *Thanatos*, which seeks to reduce a person downward to the state of matter, and a life-instinct, *Eros,* which bubbles upward out of matter. His main point here is that human beings are doomed to be a house divided against itself. A human being, according to Freud at this point in his life, is a tragic figure (Freud, 1905).

### 8.5 **Conclusion**
Like everyone else, Freud experienced evil in his life and he had a profound sense of it. More than any other psychologist I know he took evil seriously. But like everyone else also, he had to account for it. How was he to do that? If he had been a humanist or a Christian he might have said that evil is a temporary aberration of the world. He could have said that there was a time when there was no evil in the world. Then something went wrong. But some day, through some form of redemption, salvation, or self-actualization, everything will become good again. However, Freud was neither a Christian nor a humanist, but a dualist. He could only say that we are *constitutionally* evil. In effect he held that evil is a (created) flaw in human nature. Dualists believe that there is an evil *part* in us that

must be redeemed or saved by the good part. But this raises the question of which part is good.

One could say that the superego as the deposit of "polite," "civilized" society has the task of saving the id as the passionate, selfish, "I don't care" part of us, by controlling it via introjected social sanctions. One could also say that the id, as the deposit of all creative life forces, must save the superego or society by opening it up, by freeing it, by erasing the barriers on the road toward self-actualization, etc.

The profundity of Freud is that he did not, and could not, buy into either solution. He lived with the tension all his life. At best, he stated, we can hope for a *compromise* between the two. Freud had a profound sense of the irony of human life. Our best intentions notwithstanding, we cannot seem to save ourselves. This is certainly one of the reasons why he has had, and still has, such an incredible influence on the culture of Europe and North America.

## References

American Psychiatric Association (1994). *Diagnostic and Statistical Manual of Mental Disorders* (4th ed.) Washington, DC: Author.

Becker, E. (1973). *The Denial of Death.* New York: Free Press.

Eagle, M.N. (1987). *Recent Developments in Psychoanalysis.* Cambridge, Mass: Harvard University Press.

Ellenberger, H.E. (1970). *The Discovery of the Unconscious.* New York: Basic Books.

Freud, S. (1896). *Collected Papers.* London: The Hogarth Press.

Freud, S. (1900). *Interpretation of Dreams.* London: The Hogarth Press.

Herman, J.L. (1992). *Trauma and Recovery.* New York: Basic Books.

Janet, P. (1889). *L'automatisme Psychologique.* Paris: Alcan.

Monte, C.F. (1995). *Beneath the Mask.* Toronto: Harcourt Brace.

Neisser, U. (1976). *Cognition and Reality.* San Francisco: Freeman.

# Some Issues to Stimulate Dialogue

1. Over the years, I have come to realize that many people – myself included – experience a sense of uneasiness when reading Freud. What he writes all seems to be a bit too shocking, a bit too scandalous, too disturbing. It creates in me at least an urge to dismiss him and to go on with my ordinary, normal life. I think this feeling of uneasiness has to do with the peculiar relationship between thought and feeling. In a sense they are each other's opposite. When we are overly disturbed in our emotion we cannot think straight. On the other hand, the quickest way to kill a feeling is to analyze it. Thinking has a way of taking the passion out of what we feel. I believe Freud was on to that and he found a way to make us feel without thinking. Implicit in his view is the conviction that feeling is pre-logical and more basic than thought.

2. It is a fact that Pierre Janet is the father of the psychological treatment I have called psychotraumatology, which focuses particularly on the alleviation of the DSM condition "posttraumatic stress disorder." A worthwhile investigation would be to research the connection between Freud's psychoanalysis and other DSM categories.

3. Freud is often seen as an oddball in relation to mainstream psychology, whereas this chapter attempts to show that he like others was wrestling with the problems within the psychology of his time. It would be a fruitful exercise, I think, to show the connections of psychoanalysis to the other schools of psychology, structuralism, Gestalt psychology, and the Wurzburg school.

# 9. THE PSYCHOLOGY OF ADAPTATION: GALTON AND THE MEASUREMENT OF INDIVIDUAL DIFFERENCES

## 9.1 Evolutionism

Before I can properly describe the psychology of adaptation, we must first deal with the various theories of evolution found in the history of Western thought. According to the Newtonian/Cartesian view of the world, the world is a mechanical, static world in which nothing essentially changes. God, or some creator, has constructed the world as a marvelous machine perfect in conception and endless in time. Each object, each biological species in this world is fixed for eternity, changelessly perfect in obedience to fixed natural laws. The various theories of evolution that arose during the eighteenth century drastically changed this conception. We will mention two theorists: Lamarck and Darwin.

### 9.1.1 Lamarck and vitalism: Matter is self-perfecting

According to Lamarck (1744–1829), living matter has an inherent capacity to change and to improve itself. It is intelligent, purposeful, self-directing, and self-perfecting (influence of Leibniz?). This conception called *vitalism* is essentially the worldview of romanticism. What is interesting is that, according to this view of the world, not only the hereditary traits but also the characteristics of parents acquired during their lifetime are passed on to their offspring.

### 9.1.2 Darwin: Principle of natural selection

Charles Darwin (1809–1882) mechanized or de-romanticized Lamark's theory of evolution, and recaptured it for the Newtonian-Cartesian worldview. Darwin asked the question: Why should there be improvement in the species if, contrary to Aristotle, there is *no* unmoved mover perfecting them and if, contrary to vitalism, matter is *not* self-perfecting? Darwin's answer was as follows. As the species or life forms in the world multiply, a scarcity of resources arises. The species tend to outgrow their food supply. This forces them into a struggle for survival. Some species are fitter, or better adapted to survive in a given environment than others.

The fitter ones survive, but the weaker ones die off. This is the principle of *natural selection,* or the way nature, as it were mechanically, improves the species.

Furthermore, Darwin stated, environments change over time and require new traits for survival of the species in them. As environments continue to change the species in them will attempt to adapt themselves to these changes and thus diverge more and more from their parent forms. In this way Darwin was able to explain the observed diversity of nature as the result of a few mechanical principles operating over long periods of time as species evolve from species (Darwin, 1897).

### 9.2 *The psychology of adaptation*

Darwin's evolutionism sparked the psychology of adaptation. The history of psychology has known three major movements: a) the psychology of consciousness, b) the psychology of the unconscious, and c) the psychology of adaptation. The psychology of adaptation was basically the application of the theory of evolution to psychology. Historically, this application took two directions:as functionalism and later behaviorism, and as the psychology of *individual differences.* The latter is inextricably connected with Francis Galton.

What is the psychology of adaptation? It is a shift in the history of psychology from a focus on consciousness to a focus the relation between consciousness and behavior, which eventually led to a focus on behavior itself. But what do we mean by "behavior"? Behavior is the way life forms or the species (specifically, human beings and animals) adapt themselves to an environment; in the process of adapting, they change as well. Behaviors are responses to environmental stimuli. Behavior is doing rather than thinking. Behavior is action that makes one species, or one individual within the species, different from another. Adaptation is the evolutionary way of viewing human and animal action. It focuses on differences. The psychology of adaptation is a psychology of differences.

The adherents to the psychology of adaptation did not focus their attention on *between species* differences, for they considered these differences negligible. The biologist Spencer, for instance, stated that animals and human beings learn the same way because all brains work the same whether they are animal or human (1897). This fact, therefore, makes cross-species research possible and allows one to extrapolate from research results in animal behavior to the behavior of human beings. Instead of focusing on between-species differences, the psychology of adaptation focused on *within species* differences, or (between) *individual* differences.

Discovering individual differences became *the* methodology of the psychology of adaptation. This is the psychology of Galton and later Cattell.

### 9.3 *Francis Galton*

Galton (1822–1911) was born the last child of a large well-to-do family of nine children. Precocious as he was, he could read fluently at the age of three. Yet, he only showed mediocre school performance, and he never pursued a university degree or a teaching career. The fact that he had inherited money made it possible for him to live the life of a free ranging scientist. He had many and varied interests. He was a cousin of Darwin and, at one point in his life, became singularly interested in Darwin's theory of evolution.

Psychology owes a great deal to Galton. He is rightly called the father of mental testing for two reasons: first, for focusing on individual differences rather than on general laws as Wundt had done, and secondly, for showing that individual differences could be measured objectively. By focusing on individual differences, Galton made testing as we know it today possible. Most modern tests do not measure how well people score on a given characteristic but how well they score *in relation to other people taking the test*, i.e., their test scores show how they differ from one another. The concept of individual differences is the central concept of test theory. Without it we would have no tests, no way of determining correlation, reliability, or validity, and we would have no way of doing factor analysis. In general, Galton is important for the history of psychology because of his focus on individual differences, because of his work on the measurement and the correlation of individual differences, and because of his views on the origin of individual differences. We will look at each of these in more detail.

### 9.4 *Focus on individual differences*

Before Galton came on to the scene, Wundt was already acquainted with the phenomenon of individual differences or with the "*personal equation*" in the context of astronomy. But he considered individual differences a source of error to be controlled. In contrast, Galton made individual differences the centerpiece of his work. Prior to Galton, others had focused on individual differences. For example, Gall's phrenology compared people's personality and intelligence in terms of the shape of their cranium. Similarly, Lombroso tried to differentiate criminals from non-criminals on the same basis. Lastly, of course, Darwin with his concept of variation between and within species had stressed the notion of individual differences. But none of these did as much for the psychology of individual differences as Galton did.

## 9.5 *Measurement of individual differences*

There has always been resistance to measuring human uniqueness, the "soul," or the "higher functions," especially among Rationalists. Galton was one of the people who showed how it was done.

In evolutionary theory, the problem of eugenics arose. Darwin had proposed that all living organisms, including human beings, differ individually on a large number of characteristics. Some of these characteristics are more conducive to survival than others, which explains why some organisms or species that have these features survive while others who do not. The theory of evolution held that these differences are genetically based or that they are biologically inherited. The question of eugenics vis-à-vis the human race was: How can we increase the pool of characteristics with high survival value in a given population? The answer the theory of evolution gave was that we can accomplish this by getting individuals who have high survival value characteristics to mate and by keeping individuals with low survival value characteristics from mating. This is what the proponents of eugenics were proposing to do.

But this policy required the classification of people in terms of these high and low survival value characteristics. One needed to discover who had more of the good characteristics and who had fewer. One needed to find out who had desirable and undesirable qualities. What's more, to be fair to everyone involved, one had to do this in an objective and replicable manner. Francis Galton set out to do just that.

He demonstrated that individual differences exist and can be measured fairly and objectively as well. Furthermore, Galton believed that not only "physical," but also "mental" characteristics are genetically based, and he demonstrated that these mental traits could be measured indirectly via reaction time and sensory discrimination scores. It was Galton's belief that tests of sensory discrimination could serve as a means for gauging a person's intellect. In this respect, he was influenced by Locke and by empiricism. Thus, he wrote:

> The only information that reaches us concerning outward events appears to pass through the avenue of our senses; and the more perceptive the senses are to difference, the larger the field upon which our judgment and intelligence can act. (1907)

In the course of pursuing the objectification of individual differences, Galton recorded a large amount of data on physical differences, on reaction times, on sensory acuity, and other measures. He established what may be called the first mental testing center. He also developed a great number of testing tools, such as the questionnaire, the Galton whistle (to measure sensitivity to high-pitched tones), the Galton bar (to measure perceived visual distance), and the Galton weights (to measure just noticeable differences, as indicators of kinesthetic discrimination ability in psychophysics experiments).

### 9.6 Correlation of individual differences

Not only did Galton measure all kinds of human physical and mental characteristics, including indirect measures of the so-called higher functions, but he also was able to demonstrate that almost all human characteristics are normally distributed, with most scores on them clustering around the arithmetic mean. He already knew that physical characteristics are normally distributed. This had been shown earlier by the Belgian astronomer Jaques Quételet (1796–1874). In addition, Galton showed that this also held true for mental or psychological characteristics. Furthermore, he was able to demonstrate that the distributions of certain characteristics co-varied with one another, and that this co-variation could be mathematically expressed as correlation. One of his students, Karl Pearson, refined his concept of correlation into the Pearson product-moment coefficient of correlation that allows for a precise mathematical expression of the relationship between two distributions. This $r = -1.00 \rightarrow r = 0.00 \rightarrow r +1.00$ formula is familiar to us all.

### 9.7 Origin of individual differences

It was Galton's conviction that differences in intelligence were based on inheritance. Some people, he believed, were born to be geniuses, born to *eminence*. Others were born to lives of insignificance, never to amount to much. He espoused the *hereditarian* hypothesis. Essentially this a form of nativism as opposed to environmentalism.

Nativism was well known in his time. Reid and the Scottish Realists had decreed long ago that at birth the Creator endows every human being with certain intellectual faculties to see the world aright. This, they believed, was the common sense of mankind and part of the constitution or makeup of every human being. Reid and the Scottish Realists adhered to the *constitutional* hypothesis.

For Galton, influenced by evolutionism, the inheritance of intelligence was a matter of biology. Parents passed their intellect, or relative lack thereof, to their offspring *via their bodies*. Biology, he believed, differentiated people into smarter or dumber persons, into people who had more sense and people who had less. Biology was destiny for Galton. Learning and experience added little to one's intellect. Galton viewed intelligence as *biologically* innate. Intelligence, or eminence as he called it, is not a matter of *social* inheritance, as if those born into a privileged family could count on an environment that motivated one into intellectual pursuits. There was only one way to increase the pool of eminence in a group of people, he felt, and that was by means of eugenics described above.

Galton sought to demonstrate the biologically inherited origin of intelligence by selecting a pool of eminent people and then inspecting their family trees to show that they were invariably connected by birth to other eminent people. He also sought to demonstrate the same via twin studies, in which he showed that the intelligence of identical twins is more similar than that of fraternal twins. Lastly, he sought to demonstrate the biological origin of intelligence by anecdotal descriptions of the national character of countries like the United States, which he considered to be less intelligent than the nation of Great Britain, because all the riffraff of Britain had immigrated to U.S.A. (Galton, 1869, p. 1907)!

## References

Darwin, C. (1897). *The Origin of the Species by Means of Natural Selection.* New York: Appleton.

Darwin, C. (1872). *The Expression of Emotion in Man and Animals.* New York: Philosophical Library.

Galton, F. (1907). *Hereditary Genius: An Inquiry into its Laws and Consequences.* New York: Dutton.

Galton, F. (1907). *Inquiries into Human Faculty and its Development.* New York: Dutton.

Spencer, H. (1897). *The Principle of Psychology.* New York: Appleton.

# SOME ISSUES TO STIMULATE DIALOGUE

1.  It seems to me that with the psychology of adaptation a fundamental shift occurs within psychology. Its research program is now no longer focused on describing the characteristics of being human or even how these factors relate to one another. Instead the question becomes how (much) people differ from one another in the characteristics they share. This focus began in earnest with Galton. The other shift is one from an emphasis on the nature of human characteristics to their *function,* i.e., what good they do in human life. This emphasis comes to the fore in the psychologies of James and Dewey, discussed in the next chapter.

2.  Galton is rightly called the father of psychological testing. In psychological testing, the focus on individual differences is further refined to a quantitative comparison between human beings. In intelligence testing, for example, the question is not how much intelligence a given individual has. Rather, the question is how much *more or less* intelligence *than others* she has. The factor of inter-individual comparison, even competition, is intrinsic to the concept of intelligence.

3.  The motivation of Galton's life work was to demonstrate what I have termed the *hereditarian hypothesis.* This is the doctrine that how much intelligence a person has, or how much more of it he has than others, is entirely genetically determined. One inherits one's level of intelligence from one's ancestors. What for millennia was deemed to be the common good of humankind (the *germs of truth)* is now reserved for the privileged few. This view is inherently elitist. This doctrine has had evil results in the history of psychology. It gave rise to the practice of *eugenics.* It also led to the wholesale practice of racial discrimination, when people were stereotypically judged to be intellectually inferior purely on the basis of the color of their skin.

4.  With Galton, we also see the beginning of a misuse of methodology in psychology that carries on to this day. This is the practice of allowing psychology's methodology determine the subject matter of psychology. By way of illustration we can ask, "What is intelligence?" The answer that is often given in textbooks is "intelligence is what intelligence tests measure." In this definition the measurement of the

quantity of this human ability to solve problems defines the nature of that ability. Reductionism is built into all forms of psychological measurement and most certainly into psychometrically based tests.

# 10. THE PSYCHOLOGY OF ADAPTATION: THE FUNCTIONALISM OF JAMES AND DEWEY

During the 1920s a uniquely American psychology arose, the fathers of which are William James and John Dewey. This was the school of functionalism. It borrowed from new formula psychology, but also from the evolutionary theories of Herbert Spencer and Charles Darwin. It was not just a straight mix of these two sets of theories; it also gave these theories its own American twist. It was more technologically oriented than German (N.F.) psychology and by using evolutionary theory as a means it turned psychology into a program for realizing the *"American dream."* Its main focus was on "outer" behavior rather than on "inner" experience. More specifically it viewed consciousness as directly *related to* behavior, and it sought to investigate the *function* of consciousness *for* behavior. That is why this school came to be known as functionalism. It was a forerunner to behaviorism.

This movement is historically very important because, due to Hitler's reign of terror in Germany during the 1930s and World War II, many German (Jewish) psychologists fled for their lives to the United States. As a result, German psychology declined and psychology in the U.S.A. grew from 1930 on. By 1945 the U.S.A. was the acknowledged leader in psychology and since that time psychology everywhere has acquired a strong American, technological bent.

## 10.1 *James' critique of new formula psychology*
William James (1842–1910) traveled to Europe where he studied German experimental psychology under Wundt. His verdict of new formula psychology was that for two reasons it was not *"natural."* By "not natural," James meant first of all that new formula psychology was not natural scientific. Against the dogmatism of Titchener's structuralism, which held that the N.F. was the only method for psychology, James advocated methodological pluralism. Psychology, he said, is too young to be definite about its research methodology. James said that ". . . at a certain stage in the development of every science a degree of vagueness is what best con-

sists with fertility" (James, 1950, p. 6).

Following Einstein and Maxwell, the German view of the aim of science was to gain a comprehensive theoretical insight into nature. Following Edison, Bell, and Westinghouse, American scientists viewed the aim of science as the comprehensive technological control over nature. To them science meant instrumental, practical control over nature for human ends. For them, knowledge of a phenomenon meant the ability to predict and to control it (Eisenga & van Rappard, 1987, p. 63). This was James' own view of psychology as well. He believed that German experimental psychology (N.F.) was too theoretical and too impractical because it did not teach people how they could improve their thoughts, their behaviors, and their lives. Angell, another leader in the school of functionalism, later remarked that N.F. psychology talked a lot about "inner" states, but never showed to what action or behavior these inner states lead people (Eisenga & van Rappard, 1987, pp. 32, 64). Thus, for James and other functionalists N.F. psychology was not natural because it did not live up to the American view of natural science.

Second, James also felt that new formula psychology was artificial. He was disappointed in the new formula because it promised to break clear from philosophy, whereas in fact it did not. What James meant by his critique was that in real life, thinking and doing, motive and behavior, are always related. Everyone knows that thinking most often occurs in the context of action. Yet philosophy treats them as two fully independent, separate parts. It separates human science into psychology and physiology, where the one deals with the soul and the other with the body. It is true that new formula psychology did use the psychophysics method and in that way acknowledged the relation between the mental and the physi(ologi)cal. But it only used the physical and the physiological to study the mental. It used the "body" and "matter" only to study the "soul" or the "mind." N.F. psychologists did not make the relation between mind and body the object of study, probably because they feared getting caught in a mind-body or mind-matter dualism. In any case, it is this fear that James identified as the root of the lack of practicality in new formula psychology.

So, what was needed, according to James, was a psychology "*with which one could get to work.*" What was needed was a pragmatic, anti-intellectualistic psychology. Angell, James' fellow Functionalist, once again echoed this sentiment when he stated that people need practical advice on how to cope in this vale of tears, not information about a "disembodied soul" (Angell, 1907).

## 10.2 *The cultural setting of James' critique*

To understand James' critique we must know something about the cultural context in which it occurred. The U.S.A. at that time was a country of pioneers who all had the *"American dream"* of overcoming the shortcomings of the Old World (Europe) by creating a new world in America. The three schools of American psychology, functionalism, behaviorism, and humanistic psychology all agreed that the task of psychology is to serve as a means of creating a better world. Psychology must not just be the servant of the status quo; it must present us with a formula for realizing the American dream.

The American dream is embodied in the constitution of the U.S.A. and consists of a set of social-ethical values originally drawn up to join a heterogeneous collection of ethnic groups into one unified nation. Some of these values are, respect for the dignity of the individual, a belief in human beings as rational creatures who can actualize their own potential, the ideal of universal equality, and the defense of a set of democratic rights, such as freedom of speech, freedom of religion, the right to a fair trial, etc. (De Tocqueville, 1845).

Now we can understand James' disappointment with the new formula psychology better. It promoted a disembodied consciousness that only *mirrors* present-day, imperfect reality, he said. It cannot picture a better world, nor does it have the instruments to realize that better world. Hence, James went shopping for an approach to the study of human nature that would better serve the realization of the American dream, and he believed to have found it in the evolutionistic formula of Herbert Spencer (1820–1903), which stressed the adaptation of inner consciousness to external events (James, 1890, I, p. 6).

## 10.3 *Spencer's evolutionistic worldview*

There were all kinds of evolutionistic theories around in the nineteenth century. Spencer's was one of them. He applied the notion of Lamarckian evolution to human life. His worldview stated that all of reality, from the amoeba through society and political systems to God, is involved in an evolving process toward utopia. He believed that this is a natural phenomenon like gravity and it is cosmic in scope. Nothing that exists can escape it. The key concept of this evolution process is adaptation. Each organism adapts itself to a changing environment by actively developing and using those of its organs that are especially suited to its environment. For example, an antelope develops long legs to escape the dangers of predators. The highest ethic in life is to adapt inner relations to external relations. Applied to human life this theory decrees that human beings must adjust their wishes and desires to the existing circumstances. If people want to survive in life, they must get their behavior in tune with the course of nature. They must let their goals be determined by the opportunities that arise.

This view of human life is also called "Social Darwinism." Adaptation is the core concept of social Darwinism, which starts with the premise that each individual in society has equal opportunity to better him, or herself. The success of one person and the failure of the other is therefore due to the presence of or a lack of adaptation and effort. Those who through ignorance, misconduct, or laziness fail are, according to Spencer and social Darwinism, like weak organs in a body. It is their own fault if they do not survive, because "nature" tests everyone without respect for persons. This law of nature, Spencer said, is the way in which God will create a new world (Spencer, 1897)!

Thus, Spencer's theory gave human beings a way of improving their lot. However, it also created a problem for the adherents to the American dream because Spencer believed that the ideal of the dignity of individuals and their capacity for self-realization and control over their own destiny was an illusion. According to him, human beings are not free but determined by nature and they can only *adapt themselves to it*. For this reason he also rejected democracy in favor of a social system in which might makes right.

## 10.4 *Functionalism and pragmatism: The response of James and Dewey to Spencer*

It will be clear that the social Darwinian outgrowth of Spencer's evolutionary view wrecks the liberal democratic values of the American dream. Thus, while James initially saw Spencer's formula as a fruitful hypothesis for developing a psychology "with which one could get to work," he had strong reservations about its central concept of adaptation. The concept of adaptation implies only one-way traffic. In Spencer's view the influence flows from the environment to consciousness, but consciousness itself can only mirror and adjust itself to the external world. It leaves no room for an active consciousness, which looks at the world in terms of its own aims and goals. Yet, James argued, the active goal-directed intentionality of consciousness is an essential part of what all people can observe within themselves. What they observe is a consciousness that is "up to something." Hence, James posited a formula in which the direction of influence between consciousness and the world is *interactive*. It flows in two directions, from the world to consciousness and vice versa.

John Dewey (1859–1952), the cofounder of functionalism and pragmatism, agreed with James. He said that Spencer's "world" (i.e., the world we react or adapt to) is not the world of natural phenomena at all. Rather, it is the world we ourselves have made and miss-made. "World" is the effect of industrialization by human beings, an industrialization that occurred in the first place as a realization of human goals. The world we live in and adapt to is a manmade world. The relation of human beings to the world is "*experimental*." "World" is an interaction between goal and possibility. The adaptation process itself is an interactive process in which each party, the world and human beings, adapts to the other. Human beings experiment or interact with the world in order to realize their goals, and they can only tell whether they have been successful by the consequences of their actions in the environment (Dewey, 1920).

This is how James and Dewey harmonized the evolutionary process with the American dream. Their solution is essentially the solution of pragmatism and it formed the basis for the American formula in psychology. Dewey stated that psychology should not focus on consciousness but on the interaction of the *organism* (!) and the environment. The test of the validity of psychology lies in whether its results contribute to our understanding of how to improve society. Thus, both James and Dewey reaffirmed their belief in the American dream, or in *progress*, i.e., in the belief that human beings have the capacity to perfect themselves. They both felt that research in psychology should find ways of speeding up human progress.

## References

Angell, J.R. (1907). The Province of Functional Psychology, *Psychological Review*, 14, 61–91.

De Tocqueville. (1845). *Democracy in America*. New York: Henry G. Langley.

Dewey, J. (1920). *Reconstruction in Philosophy*. New York: Random House.

James, W. (1950). *The Principles of Psychology*. USA: Dover Publications.

Spencer, H. (1897). *The Principle of Psychology*. New York: Appleton.

# SOME ISSUES TO STIMULATE DIALOGUE

1. Implicit in the functional psychology of James and Dewey was the emphasis of evolutionism that reality is dynamic rather than unchanging and implicit in evolutionism is the idea of progress. From this viewpoint not only is reality constantly changing, but it is also inevitably improving. As we know from our historical survey neither of these notions were new, but James and Dewy needed this utopian philosophy to be able to visualize the possibility of realizing of the American dream. That is why they found the philosophy of Spencer so attractive. However, they could not buy into Spencer's idea that individual human beings had to adapt themselves to this inevitable march of progress or risk the fate of being left behind. On the contrary, they believed that individuals are the indispensable agents of progress. In their view the minds of human beings were essential to direct the path of change toward progress.

2. Social Darwinism has been said to be implicit in Spencer's world-and-life view. Is social Darwinism a thing of the past, or do you see evidence of this doctrine in today's society? Some people argue that the Christian view of society is that God only helps those who help themselves. To me this sounds like the view of social Darwinism. What do you think? Compare and contrast the social Darwinist view of society with a Christian view of society.

3. With the rise of functionalism a methodological shift occurs in psychology. This shift is not fully completed until the rise of behaviorism, but it is already prefigured in functionalism. Essentially it is a shift from psychology as a science to psychology as a technology. New formula psychology sought to map out the content, i.e., the elements and the structure of the mind. Functionalism focused on the use of the mind for behavior as the adaptation to an environment. It was not so much interested in knowing what consciousness was as in studying the role it plays in the business of everyday living. Mind is well on the way toward becoming a tool for changing society. And psychology becomes a study of how best to use that tool. With behaviorism psychology simply becomes a means for changing human behavior. Its aim is to make people behave in a certain way. Psychology has become a behavioral technology.

# 11. FROM FUNCTIONALISM TO BEHAVIORISM: HOW PSYCHOLOGY LOST ITS MIND

## 11.1 *Functionalism and objectivism: The American formula for psychology*

The resounding question in American psychology of the late nineteenth and early twentieth century was not what *is* consciousness, but what does it *do* and what is its *function*? Why are we conscious at all? Is consciousness Darwinianly adaptive? What is consciousness *good for*? What is its *function for behavior*?

James decried European psychology because it viewed consciousness disconnected from behavior. According to James, psychology must study the *relation* between consciousness and behavior. Consciousness must make a difference in what we *do*. Influenced by his mentor Wundt, James had a voluntaristic view of consciousness, a view that equated consciousness and will. In his view the function of consciousness for behavior is *choosing*. Consciousness is our intention to act. It *results* in behavior (James, 1950). By contrast, Munsterberg, the successor of James, had a *motor* theory of consciousness. He reversed James. According to him consciousness is the byproduct of the organism's intention to act or of behavior. In itself consciousness does not cause behavior. It is an *epiphenomenon* (Kuklick, 1977; Hale, 1980). Likewise, Dewey held that consciousness is a *component* of behavior, i.e., a component of our overall adaptation to the environment. Behavior or adaptation is *ongoing*. Consciousness is *intermittent*. It occurs only when we are faced with novelty in our environment (Dewey, 1920).

Regardless of how these American psychologists viewed the relation between consciousness and behavior or adaptation, they were all functionalists. Functionalists viewed consciousness as *functional* in three ways: a) Consciousness has a distinct biological function selected by Darwinian evolution. Its task is to adapt the organism to novel circumstances. b) Consciousness is itself the result of the physiological function of the organism. It is a function of behavior. The behavior of organisms as adaptation to novelty in their environment *produces* consciousness. c)

Finally, consciousness is functional when it makes a positive difference in practice.

The other characteristic of functionalism, and later behaviorism, was its methodological objectivism. What is happening in the move from consciousness to behavior is the formation of a new research methodology. Methodologically there is a gradual shift from introspecting the *content* of consciousness (Titchener), to investigating the *process* of consciousness (how it works), to observing the *product* of consciousness (what it accomplishes). To understand the import of this methodological shift, we must return to Galton, although others in the psychology of adaptation said the same thing. Galton was the first to demonstrate that we can observe and research the mind or consciousness in a way that differs totally from the new formula approach.

The new formula psychology held that the mind is an inner box filled with psychic content that we can introspect. Galton argued that we can also investigate what the mind *can produce*, for example via a person's performance or score on an I.Q. test. Who cares how the mind works, Galton stated. What we want to know is *how well* it works; that is, we want to know the *results* of the working of the mind. What we want to know is the *function* of the mind; we want to investigate *what good it does*. Psychology should not be interested in the structure or the content of the mind but in what it does, in its activities and its effects, in its function for everyday life (Galton, 1883).

Cattell (1860–1944), a student of Galton, extended this argument further. The use of tests gave rise to methodological objectivism in American psychology. As Cattell argued, Titchener, who was the representative of the N.F. in the U.S.A., used the "subjective" method of introspection. But by means of tests, psychology also has an objective method of access to human consciousness. In the N.F. psychology, the experimenter has only indirect knowledge of consciousness in that he must rely on and can only take note of the observation of the experimental subject of his consciousness. Moreover, by introspecting the subject has to perform a double task, he must think and must simultaneously observe his thinking, i.e., think about thinking.

In the natural sciences, the experimenter observes his "subject" directly. There the "subject" is only required to perform, i.e., it must exhibit changes in its state. The same holds true for the objective method in psychology, according to Cattell. Therefore, this method is natural scientific, whereas the new formula approach is not. Via tests psychology has obtained the instruments for becoming an objective science. Cattell added one more critique. Introspective new formula psychology can never guarantee the reliability of its data, because the experimenter cannot observe what the subject observes. Therefore, he cannot replicate and therefore he cannot verify his results. By contrast, test results are publicly observable, controllable, replicable, and therefore verifiable.

In conclusion, Cattell and others felt that by using tests psychology could become methodologically united with the physical sciences because by using tests it was using the same method as the physical sciences. It could therefore lay claim to being a natural science. Because new formula psychology could not make the same claim it soon became extinct as a method of research in American psychology (Cattell, 1890; Eisenga & van Rappard, 1987).

An era of objectivism began in American psychology, further augmented by the rise of comparative psychology. Animal researchers argued that psychology should cease to use introspection as its experimental method; in comparative psychology we cannot ask animals to tell us what goes on in their minds. In such situations we are constrained to draw our conclusions objectively, on the basis of behavior. This finally led Herbert Jennings, the teacher of the behaviorist Watson to propose that we research and describe the subject matter of psychology purely on the basis of what people and animals do (Jennings, 1906). This formulation, however, essentially means the elimination of consciousness.

## 11.2 *Doubt about the existence of consciousness*

So the question shifted again from "What is consciousness good for?" to "Does it exist?" Neo-realists in philosophy at that time substituted a relational theory of consciousness for the traditional copy theory. They stated that as an inner representation of the outside world, consciousness does not exist. But consciousness as *our relation to* the outside world does. For them this meant at the same time that relational consciousness is publicly observable. Hence an objective psychology of consciousness is possible. Mind is *evident* from behavior. Likewise Dewey held that consciousness comes to expression in behavior and is a function of behavior. That is, whether a person has a good mind or not is demonstrated in the way that person responds to her environment (Dewey, 1920).

## 11.3 *From functionalism to behaviorism*

The American formula for psychology was a mixture of common sense psychology, evolutionary theory, and an emphasis on prediction and control. It had a preference for functional and objective methods of research.

It was dynamic and functional rather than structural in its approach. It asked "why" and "what for" rather than "what." What was the effect of James' American formula for psychology? Because of its desire to be of service to everyday life and because of its drive to be objective, the American formula opened up new areas of research in intelligence, in development, in social psychology, in educational psychology, and in animal psychology. But it also had another effect. It led to the elimination of consciousness as the subject matter for psychology. From 1900–1940 or roughly from James to Skinner, there was a clear anti-mentalistic trend visible in psychology everywhere. This development is what Sigmund Koch has referred to as the *"repression of consciousness"* (Koch, 1959). Before we deal with behaviorism, I will briefly summarize the steps in this process from Titchener to Watson.

Titchener, one of the founders of new formula psychology defined psychology as the study of consciousness via replicable introspection. By contrast, James the father of the American formula in psychology argued that psychology must not focus (only) on consciousness, but (also) on the relation between consciousness and behavior. The Chicago School of Functional Psychology, or functionalism, represented by James, Angell, and Carr took another step toward anti-mentalism. They stated that psychology must investigate the function or role of consciousness in behavior. Galton and Cattell contributed to this development by showing that the use of tests can make psychology more functional and objective. In addition, comparative psychology argued that psychology must use the observation of performance or behavior as the empirical basis for pronouncements on mental processes. Only in this way can we have a psychology that can be applied to both human and animal studies. Dewey moved the process along by stating that what we mean by consciousness, or "mind," is the mental operations involved in our behavior. Finally, Watson argued that we can avoid this entire discussion by saying that psychology simply is the study of human and animal behavior. Watson suggested that psychology forget such terms like "mind" and "consciousness" altogether. If we continue to use these terms, he said, then psychology will perennially get caught in unfruitful theoretical hassles and it will never get to its primary task, which is the prediction and control of behavior. Watson's views represent anti-mentalism without compromise. Watson also said that if we can operate a radio without knowledge of its inner workings, we should be able to do the same with people (Watson, 1913).

## References

Cattell, J. M. (1890). Mental Tests and Measurement, *Mind*, 15, 373–380.

Dewey, J. (1920). *Reconstruction in Philosophy*. New York: Random House.

Eisenga, L.K.A. & van Rappard, J.F.H. (1987). *Hoofdstromen en Mensbeelden in de Psychologie*. Amsterdam: Boom Meppel.

Galton, F. (1883). *Inquiries into the Human Faculty and its Development*. London: J. M. Dent.

Hale, M. (1980). *Human Science and Social Order*. Philadelphia: Temple University Press.

James, W. (1950). *The Principles of Psychology*. USA: Dover Publications.

Jennings, H. S. (1906). *Behavior of the Lower Organisms*. New York: Columbia University Press.

Koch, S. (1959). *Psychology: A study of a Science*. New York: McGraw-Hill.

Kuklick, B. (1977). *The Rise of American Philosophy*. New Haven CT: Yale University Press.

Watson, J.B. (1913). Psychology as the Behaviorist views it, *Psychological Review*, 20, 158–177.

# SOME ISSUES TO STIMULATE DIALOGUE

1. There are several essential differences between James and Watson. First of all, James was a dualist. He held on to the importance of both consciousness and behavior in human life. By contrast Watson adhered to an outspoken materialistic monism. Second, James believed that psychology should use multiple research methods. Watson was a strict adherent to the scientific method. Can you think of any other differences? What were the implications of these differences for the further development of psychology?

2. There is something very laudable in the aim of objectivism in the history of psychology. By means of a rigorous application of the scientific method it tried to safeguard psychologists from seeing what is not there. The tragic irony of objectivism, some would argue, was that with its emphasis on a rigorous methodology the actual subject matter of psychology is distorted. What do you think?

# 12. THE MINDLESS PSYCHOLOGY OF BEHAVIORISM

## 12.1 *Behaviorism: Emphasis on the psychology of learning*

This chapter is all about how psychology lost its mind and got it back again. It begins with a description of the school of behaviorism. The central focus of behaviorism as a school or movement was on the psychology of learning. "Learning" in this context refers to how animals, people, or, as it is usually put, "*organisms*" adapt to changes (or "stimuli") in the environment. What are stimuli? A stimulus is not a constant level of physical energy but the difference between two or more levels of physical energy. This difference in levels of energy is why we see contours and respond to novelty. We easily adapt to constant levels of physical energy. It is the adaptation to changes in the environment that require the effort of learning. Learning is finding responses that allow us to adapt to the changes in our environment.

Note that learning can also be conceptualized differently. For example, it can be pictured as storing bits of knowledge in our minds, as memorizing and retaining and recalling what we experience, or as processing information. Learning has been defined by Vygotsky as *closing the zone of proximal development*, by which he means the gap between what you know by yourself and what you know with the help of a teacher (Vygotsky, 1962). But none of these definitions have the meaning per se of "*adjusting*," or adaptation. The view of learning in behaviorism is entirely influenced by the evolutionistic concept of adaptation. Behavioristic learning is an adaptive, adjustive kind of learning. Actually behaviorism is more a theory of teaching than of learning, more a technology than a psychology. It is not a theory of how people or animals behave, but a theory of how one can *make* people or animals behave. It is a theory of how to train or condition people or animals.

Behaviorism knows three theories of learning: classical conditioning, operant conditioning, and purposive behaviorism. We will deal with each in succession.

## 12.2 *Classical conditioning (associative shifting, respondent learning)*

First I should mention something about the terms. We know classical conditioning as the psychology of learning based on Pavlov's paradigm. *Associative shifting* is a description of the same by Thorndike to indicate that in classical conditioning behavior *shifts* from being associated with, or being a response to an *unconditioned stimulus* to being associated with, or being a response to a *conditioned stimulus*. *Respondent learning* is a designation by Skinner of classical conditioning to distinguish it from his operant conditioning theory of learning. Skinner's theory of learning does not deal with responses but with *operants*.

### 12.2.1 *Pavlov*

The guts of classical conditioning can be found in the well-known dog experiments of Pavlov (1849–1936). Pavlov was a Russian. His teacher Sechenov was a positivist who wanted to rid psychology of all subjectivism and turn it into a positive science. Sechenov was also a peripheralist, as was Watson about whom later. Sechenov wrote: "The initial cause of behavior always lies, *not* in thought, but in external sensory stimulation" (Sechenov, 1863, p. 321).

Following his teacher, Pavlov's attitude was uncompromisingly objectivistic and materialistic. He rejected the reference in psychological explanations to the inner mind, referring only to the influence of external stimuli and their summation. He discovered classical conditioning. He systematically investigated aspects of conditioned reflexes such as *generalization, discrimination, extinction, spontaneous recovery*, and *conditioned inhibition* (Pavlov, 1957). I will assume that the reader is familiar with these terms.

### 12.2.2 *Watson*

Watson (1878–1958) is the father of classical behaviorism. He wrote a paper that has become a classic, *Psychology as the Behaviorist Views It*. This was his manifesto. In it he wrote the following:

> Psychology as the behaviorist views it is a purely objective experimental branch of natural science. Its theoretical goal is the prediction and control of behavior. Introspection forms no essential part of its methods, nor is the scientific value of its data dependent on the readiness with which they lend themselves to interpretation in terms of consciousness. The behaviorist, in his efforts to get a unitary scheme of animal response, recognizes no dividing line between man and brute. The behavior of man, with all of its refinement and complexity, forms only a part of the behaviorist's total scheme of investigation. (1913, p. 158)

The starting point of Watson's psychology was the fact that "organisms, man and animal alike, do adjust themselves to their environment. . . ." According to Watson, there is a direct relation between behavior (response) and (stimuli in) the environment. For this reason if the response is known, the stimuli can be predicted, and if the stimuli are known the response can be predicted. This fact, according to Watson, gives us control over behavior. His research program of description, prediction, and control is pure positivism. This was Watson's program, but he was vague on how to implement it. The working out of the program was left to others.

For Watson there are no mental processes playing a causal role in determining behavior. There are only chains of behavior. His position was an extremely radical peripheralism in which there is no soul or cortex needed in explaining behavior. The brain is only a relay station connecting stimulus and response. Watson was an extreme environmentalist, as is evident from the following quote:

> Give me a dozen healthy infants, well-formed, and my own specified world to bring them up in and I'll guarantee to take anyone at random and train him to become any type of specialist I might select—doctor, lawyer, merchant-chief, and, yes, even beggar-man and thief, regardless of his talents, penchants, tendencies, abilities, vocations, and race of his ancestors. (1930, p. 104)

## 12.3 *The influence of logical positivism on behaviorism*

The rise of behaviorism was greatly influenced by logical positivism. This philosophical theory is an epistemology, or a theory of knowledge, and a philosophy of science that seeks to *explicate and formalize* the scientific method.

Positivism, the philosophy of science preceding logical positivism, held that science consists of description, prediction, and control. In this view the scientific method dictates that one first observe and find the facts, then that one verify the facts and formulate them into scientific statements or theories. By means of this process Positivists believed one could control reality. According to them a statement is scientific when it tested in observations. A theory is true only if it is supported by data. This is the most traditional view of science. We are all familiar with it.

*Logical* positivism clarified this view further by explicitly distinguishing between *theoretical* statements and *observation* statements. In this view of science scientific statements are first of all *protocol sentences*, which consist of *observation statements* about the data of experience and no more. An example of a protocol sentence would be: This raven that I can see here is black. However, if science were to restrict itself to protocol sentences only (as positivism had done) then it would restrict itself only to what *is*. It would be purely descriptive and not have any *explanatory* power. Thus, say the logical positivists, science also needs to have *theoretical* statements, such as: All ravens everywhere are black. Or this raven here is black *because* all ravens everywhere and without exception are black. (Even though the Haida Indians claim to have seen a white raven recently.) Theoretical statements are not observation statements. They are beliefs, expectations, and thoughts about what is true. We *expect*, or *it is our opinion* that all ravens are black, but there may be a white raven somewhere that we have not seen. In science we should keep theoretical statements separate from observation statements. We can only connect the two via *operational definitions*. A theoretical statement is only based in fact insofar as we can spell out the operations one would have to perform to make it so. In our case we would have to observe all ravens to determine whether in fact they are all black. This of course is an impossible ideal. But we can approximate it by experimental observation, using replicable experiments and statistical measures that allow us to extrapolate from random samples to populations. A theory is only scientific insofar as it is confirmed by observations. Nevertheless, for reasons noted above we can never be absolutely sure about the truth of scientific explanations (Bridgman, 1927).

Behaviorism as psychology fits this notion of truth and science perfectly, because it refuses to accept anything that is not observable nor will it accept any theoretical statement that cannot be operationally connected to observations as part of its theories of learning. That is to say, behaviorism bases all of its pronouncements on experimental results.

This marriage between logical positivism and behaviorism resulted in several learning theories that were influential in psychology in the 1930s and 1940s. Notable among them were Guthrie's one trial learning and especially Hull's mechanistic behaviorism.

### 12.4 *Guthrie's one trial learning*

Guthrie (1886–1959) based his view of learning on one simple learning principle: that learning arises because the organism always tends to do what was last done in the same situation. This means that no learning ever takes place if the situation stays the same. But, of course, situations never are exactly the same. Take, for example, the skill to be learned in order to score in a basketball game. If everything were the same each time, one trial at learning to score would be enough. But everything is not alike. Different games are played in different places, with different obstacles, etc. Therefore, the player must learn numerous habits related to scoring in a basketball game before she can eventually develop an expertise in playing basketball (Guthrie, 1952).

## 12.5 *Hull's mechanistic behaviorism*

Mechanistic in his conception of learning, Hull (1884–1952) worked long and hard on building a learning machine. He wanted to develop quantitative laws of behavior and their deductive systematization. He saw the study of behavior as a natural science. His psychology followed a hypothetical-deductive or geometric model, complete with postulates, corollaries, theorems, and proofs. He searched for a "calculus" of behavior. His system is not S→R psychology, but essentially an elaboration of Woodworth's S-O-R diagram, in which a stimulus (S) produces changes in the organism (O) that eventuate in a response (R). What this means is that behavior is based on drive reduction. It is the reinforcing or drive reducing nature of stimuli that makes people behave in certain ways.

Hull's psychology was reductionistic. He sought to reduce purposive behavior to mechanical laws, and psychology to physics. He stated, "The complex forms of purposive behavior will be found to derive from . . . the basic entities of theoretical physics, such as electrons and protons" (Hull, 1937).

Together with Thorndike, Pavlov, Guthrie, and Skinner, Hull based his theories on animal experimentation. They all believed, guided by Ockham's razor, i.e., the principle of parsimony, that there is very little difference between animal and human learning. This is implied in the theory of evolution. Comparative psychology and its major proponent, Lloyd Morgan, had earlier argued that the minds of animals were as marvelous as those of human beings. Guided by the same principle of parsimony, Morgan anthropomorphized animal behavior, saying in effect that animals are as smart as human beings (Morgan, 1904). In reaction to this, the behaviorists reduced human mental functions to those of lower animals, saying in effect that human beings are just as dumb as or no smarter than animals.

## 12.6 *Operant conditioning*

The essential differences between classical conditioning and operant conditioning are several. First, for classical conditioning behavior is *elicited* (by a stimulus), for operant conditioning it is *emitted* (by the organism). Second, for operant conditioning learning is not connecting responses to stimuli, but shaping behavior by increasing the probability of some behaviors over others. Third, the extent to which behaviors are emitted is determined by the extent to which a given set of behaviors is rewarded. According to operant conditioning, behavior is *instrumental.* It is used by the organism as an instrument for getting rewards.

### 12.6.1 *Thorndike's connectionism, trial and error learning, instrumental learning*

Thorndike (1874–1949) was a forerunner of operant conditioning, and he laid the groundwork for it. He reduced learning to its simplest form by constructing a puzzle box, placing a half-starved cat in it, and placing food outside the box near the box. The cat had to learn that she had to step on a treadle to open the box to get the food. Thorndike noted that the cat would display or emit many random movements, but via trial and error she would eventually trip the latch and get out. After many trials and errors, the cat would open the box immediately upon being placed in it. By that time the cat had made the right connections. But before that time the cat took initially a long time to get out and progressively less time. By plotting these times on a curve, Thorndike objectively showed the rate of learning.

Thorndike held that the process of error elimination or success learning is governed by two laws, a) *the law of effect* and b) *the law of exercise or repetition.* Thorndike defined the law of effect as follows:

> Of several responses made to the same situation, those which are accompanied or followed closely by satisfaction to the animal will, other things being equal, be more firmly connected with the situation, so that when it recurs, they will be more likely to recur. (1911, p. 244)

The law of exercise or repetition he defined this way:

> Any response to a situation will, all other things being equal, be more strongly connected with the situation in proportion to the number of times it has been connected with that situation, and to the average vigor and duration of the connections. (1911, p. 244)

Thorndike called himself a connectionist (recall associationism) because he believed that learning is making connections between the situation and behavior. He also called his theory "trial and error" (actually trial and success) learning. His theory of learning was one of instrumental learning because we learn in order to obtain a reward, or we use our learning as an instrument for obtaining effect.

### 12.6.2 *Skinner's operant conditioning*

Skinner (1904–1990) stands in the tradition of Thorndike's instrumental learning. He also emphasized that behavior is not so much a response to stimuli as governed by effect, or reward, or *reinforcement*. His theory can be described briefly as follows. Imagine that organisms are big bags of operants or possible ways of operating on the environment. Organisms naturally emit these operants at random. Learning takes place when some operants are reinforced, whereas others are not. The result is that the organisms will emit the reinforced operants more frequently. In this way, by means of *differential reinforcement*, one can shape the behavior of animals and people.

Like Watson, Skinner was a radical behaviorist. Skinner's radical behaviorism more than any other form of behaviorism was an attempt to exorcise mentalism from psychology. Skinner cites two reasons for his anti-mentalism: First, mental concepts do not add anything to the explanation. Behavior can be explained without them. So, why include these "*intervening variables,*" as they were called, between the influence of the environment and behavior? Secondly, mental concepts complicate the explanation since one is required to show their link to both the environmental influences, or stimuli, and to behavior. If one includes mental or intervening variables in one's explanation one must answer the question how one gets from the environment to the intervening variables to behavior. Furthermore if there is more than one intervening variable, one must show the causal links in between these variables as well. For these reasons and motivated by Ockham's razor, Skinner preferred explanations that did not make use of mental concepts (Skinner, 1953).

### 12.7 *Sign learning or latent learning*

One of the major problems facing both classical and operant conditioning theories of learning was the obvious evidence of *sign learning* and *latent learning* because this evidence went directly counter to the anti-mentalism of behaviorism. Apparently, learning can take place without the organism doing any kind of behavior and in the absence of reinforcement. Moreover, it was demonstrated that behavior can be learned at one time in one situation and be emitted at another time in another situation. In short, there is evidence that what organisms learn are signs rather than behaviors and that this process occurs without anyone being able to observe it. The learning is covert; it occurs inside organisms hidden from view. None of these are supposed to happen according to behaviorism.

### 12.7.1 *Tolman's purposive behaviorism (learning vs. performance)*

Tolman (1886–1959) was the first behaviorist to bring this to our attention. He demonstrated via maze learning experiments with kittens that these kittens learned a *"cognitive map"* of the maze in the absence of both behavior and reinforcement. He ferried kittens through the maze so they did not do anything, and he did not reward them. Yet, their later maze running behavior clearly showed that they had learned something without performing it and without reinforcement. Tolman set the stage for reintroducing cognition into behaviorism, so that today we can talk about *cognitive* behaviorism (Tolman, 1932).

### 12.7.2 *Bandura's social learning (acquisition vs. shaping)*

One other behaviorist who was responsible for reintroducing the mind into behaviorism was Bandura (1925– ). He allowed that operant conditioning can show how behaviors are *shaped* but not how they are *acquired*. How, he asked, do we get the operants, which we naturally emit at random? His answer was: Via observation; purely by watching other people model them. Furthermore, apparently we are able to retain these modeled behaviors and complex constellations of behavior somewhere because we can view certain behaviors being performed at one time in one situation, and perform them later in the absence of the model in a different situation. Thus, Bandura postulated *cognitive mediating symbolizing, coding,* and *memory processes* between the viewing of the model and the performance of the learned behavior. In other words, in attempting to explain learning or acquiring complex behaviors we cannot do without the use of cognitive processes. In the words of Sigmund Koch, behaviorism had repressed cognition in favor of behavior. But more and more, as time goes on we note that there is a return of the repressed, until the conditioning paradigm is replaced by a cognitive science paradigm (Bandura, 1977).

### References

Bandura, A. (1977). *Social Learning Theory.* Englewood Cliffs, N.J: Prentice-Hall.

Bridgman, P. (1927). *The Logic of Modern Physics.* New York: MacMillan.

Guthrie, E. R. (1952). *The Psychology of Learning.* New York: Harper & Row.

Hull, C. L. (1937). Mind, Mechanism, and Adaptive Behavior, *Psychological Review,* 44, 1–32.

Morgan, C. L. (1904). *An Introduction to Comparative Psychology.* New York: Scribner's.

Pavlov, I. P. (1957). *Experimental Psychology and Other Essays.* New York:

Philosophical Library.

Sechenov, I. M. (1863/1965). Reflexes of the Brain, in R. Hernstein and E. Boring (eds.) *A Source Book in the History of Psychology.* Cambridge: Harvard University Press.

Skinner, B. F. (1953). *Science and Human Behavior.* New York: MacMillan.

Thorndike, E. L. (1911). *Animal Intelligence.* New York: Hafner.

Tolman, E. (1932). *Purposive Behavior.* New York: Century.

Vygotsky, L. S. (1962). *Thought and Language.* Cambridge: M.I.T. Press.

Watson, J.B. (1913). Psychology as the Behaviorist Views It, *Psychological Review,* 20, 158–177.

Watson, J.B. (1930). *Behaviorism.* New York: Norton.

## SOME ISSUES TO STIMULATE DIALOGUE

1. Write a paper on the various meanings of the term "stimulus" in psychology. Do the same for the term "behavior."

2. List the as many of the number of definitions of "learning" you know. Discuss the different theories in psychology from which these meanings derive.

3. Discuss the following bald assertion about behaviorism: Behaviorism is not a school of psychology because it is not interested in what goes on inside people, i.e., they are not interested in studying the mind or consciousness. It is not even a theory on how people and animals behave. Rather, it is a theory on how one can *make* people and animals behave. At best it is a theory of teaching, or training, or manipulation. For all of its methodological rigor it is not a science at all but just a technology.

4. Describe the philosophical influences of British empiricism, French sensationalism, and positivism on behaviorism.

5. Many psychologists – myself included – tend to be critical of behaviorism because of its persistent reductionism. But I am also convinced that psychologists of whatever theoretical stripe, who study human life intensely are bound to come up with some insights about human beings. So what can we learn from behaviorism? Specifically, what is the kernel of truth in classical and operant conditioning? How do you account for their phenomenal success in educational settings?

# 13. The Rise of Cognitive Psychology♦

During World War II, Skinner was hired to train pigeons to guide missiles for the U.S. Army. Six months later, his research grant was cancelled. An electronic system had been discovered that could do a better job. Computer technology or its beginning had replaced behavioral technology. This event is telling for what happened in psychology after the war. The behavioristic view was replaced by a view inspired by *information theory*, *cybernetics*, and *computer technology*.

This *"repression of behaviorism"* (Koch, 1959) occurred gradually. The students of the founders of behaviorism were already less interested in methodology than their teachers were. Students of Hull, for instance, became preoccupied with personality theory, psychotherapy, and psychoanalysis, all *"mentalistic"* matters. Dollard and Miller's attempt to express psychoanalysis in behavioristic terms is one example. In short, the generation of behaviorists who came after the founders liberalized behaviorism. But even though it occurred gradually, a very definite *"cognitive shift"* became discernible in psychology after the war.

### 13.1 *The cognitive shift in psychology*
Cognitive psychology really took off after the appearance of the following publications during the late 1950s, J. Bruner et al., *A Study of Thinking*, 1956; N. Chomsky, *Syntactic Structures*, 1957; A. Newell, J.C. Shaw, and H.A. Simon, *Logic Theorist*, 1956; G. Miller, *The Magical Number Seven, plus or minus two*, 1956; and somewhat later, G.A. Miller, E. Galanter, and K.H. Pribram, *Plans and the Structure of Behavior*, 1960. Every one of these publications focused on the research of complex, internal processes. They represent a cognitive reorientation, a shift from a focus on behavior to a focus on cognition. I will briefly discuss the central issues of each of these publications.

---

♦NOTE: For much of this chapter I am indebted to: Eisenga, L.K.A. and J.F.H. van Rappard *Hoofdstromen en Mensbeelden in de Psychologie*. Amsterdam: Boom Meppel, 1987.

### 13.1.1 *Bruner:* A Study of Thinking

Bruner represents the "New Look" movement in perception theory, which holds that perception is influenced by the perceiver's personality and by social factors. More importantly for our topic, it holds that perception is *an active mental* process that occurs between the sensation of a person and the response of that person. Bruner studied the process of concept learning or concept formation in a new way. He did not view it as the association of elements, but as the process of learning *decision rules* or *definitions*. It is an active process in which the subject creates a *strategy* for forming concepts.

### 13.1.2 *Chomsky:* Syntactic Structure

Chomsky invented a *transformational grammar*, which implies that language is a creative process. According to behaviorism, every sentence that we speak we must have heard and learned first. However, this view of learning a language proved to be most unsatisfactory. Miller (1960) estimates that to learn English on that basis one must have heard $10^3$ sentences, and this would take several centuries.

Chomsky stated that language is newly created every moment that it is used or spoken. According to him, people have an inborn system of grammatical rules through which they generate sentences. Chomsky was a nativist. He based his views on Descartes' notion of "inborn ideas." Over against the behaviorists' peripheralism he argued that language acquisition and use is an internal process.

In any language, he stated, there are two kinds of sentences, a) simple, directly generated, basic sentences and b) sentences that are produced via a "transformation" of basic sentences. Later Chomsky distinguished between "surface" and "depth" structures in language usage. "*Surface structure*" means that signs in the depth structure of language determine all the sentences we utter. To speak we must transform these signs in the depth structure. Every sentence we utter is a transformation of *a depth structure.*

In 1957 Skinner published his *Verbal Behavior*, in which he argued that language is simply verbal behavior. According to this view, sentences are generalizations and repetitions of earlier S→R connections. The import of this view is that language is not creative. Language just happens as a result of external influences.

In an article in *Language* (1959) Chomsky published a lengthy review of Skinner's *Verbal Behavior*. This review has been called ". . . the single most influential psychological paper published since Watson's behaviorist manifesto of 1913" (Leahey, 1987, p. 412). In this paper Chomsky virtually demolished Skinner's arguments and with them the influence of behaviorism on American psychology.

Psychologists interpreted Chomsky's linguistic theory as a theory of mental processes. To them it was a cognitive alternative to behaviorism, because it deals with the internal structures of operations on the basis of which new operations are possible.

### 13.1.3 *Newell, Shaw, and Simon:* Logic Theorist

In 1956 Newell, Shaw, and Simon wrote a computer program called "*Logic Theorist*" (L.T.) that was capable of demonstrating logical proofs. Later (in 1972) they developed a more efficient program called the "*British Museum Algorithm*" (B.M.A.). The L.T. program is an example of "*Artificial Intelligence*" (A.I.). Artificial intelligence research is research that writes computer programs that are capable of doing tasks that are assumed to require intelligence. Soon thereafter, A.I. researchers joined hands with cognitive psychologists. Later, linguists, cultural anthropologists, and philosophers were added to this group. Together these researchers formed a new interdisciplinary science called "*Cognitive Science.*" What drove them together was the inadequacy of the behavioristic S→R model as an instrument for analyzing and describing cognitive processes. The behaviorist model could describe simple, peripheral functions, but not the higher, more complex functions.

Initially, A.I. researchers restricted themselves to developing computer programs that were the most efficient in logically solving problems. In writing their programs they did not try to simulate human cognition. In 1958, however, they developed a program that did simulate human intelligence. This program was a further extension of the *Logic Theorist* and they called it the "*General Problem Solver*" (G.P.S.). This program was interesting for psychologists because, while it was objective like the S→R model, it was a far more sophisticated theory of problem solving than the behavioristic theory. G.P.S. viewed problem solving as a central process. For this reason it was seen as an adequate alternative to behaviorism (Newell et al., 1972).

### 13.1.4 *Miller:* The Magical Number Seven (plus or minus two)

In 1949, Shanon and Weaver formulated their "*information theory,*" also called "*communication theory,*" because it is a mathematical theory of how information is transmitted from a sender via a channel to a receiver. According to this theory, a sender must "encode" a message to be able to send it via a channel, at the end of which a receiver must *"decode"* the message to be able to understand it. Understanding a message, according to this theory, is basically the process of guessing what it is, i.e., making a series of yes-no decisions about it and these can be mathematically described in base one as 1–0. *"Information"* in this theory is defined as the number of possible alternatives a message contains, or the number of times a receiver must guess before she "gets" it. The more complex the message (i.e., the more stimuli it contains) the more information it contains, i.e., the greater number of guesses or 1–0 decisions it requires.

Using this theory in an experiment, G. Miller (1956) gave his subjects the task of assigning a numerical value to tones of different "height" (high=10, low=0). The important discovery he made was that his subjects could faultlessly complete the task of judging tone height, provided that he presented his subjects with no more than 7 tones (give or take 2) at a time. Any more than that, and their judgments would become unreliable. Thus, Miller concluded that our *"decision span" is limited to 7 decisions, + or – 2.* (Our memory span is also limited to seven digits. Think of telephone numbers.)

If this were all the capacity our human mind had, then our ability to judge complex stimulus situations would be very limited indeed. Fortunately for us, Miller also discovered the cognitive ability of judgment (and memory), which he called *"chunking."* Apparently, when we re-code complex messages into chunks, we, in effect, collect the individual stimuli into chunks by holding off making a judgment on them. We gather them into groups, as it were, and then we first make decisions on these groups or chunks. Only afterwards do we tackle the individual stimuli of the chunks themselves. It was at this time that Miller discovered that the magical number 7 also holds for the chunks, i.e., he found that a subject also could not process more than 7 chunks at a time. Nevertheless, it will be clear that chunking greatly increases our decision span and therefore our ability to process complex stimulus information.

In summary, via this process of re-coding and chunking, according to Miller, we can now begin to research the higher, inner psychological processes, such as thinking, that the new formula and behaviorism had left un-researched. We must view the mind, he held, as an information processing activity, thus as an active, organizational process and not as a matter of associated elements.

### 13.1.5 *Miller et al.:* Plans and the Structure of Behavior

Miller and his associates also concentrated their research on a perennial problem of American psychology, i.e., the problem of finding a "bridge" from cognition to behavior. They stated that ". . . unless we can convert cognitive images into deeds, we are like people who collect maps without ever going on a trip." They thought to have found this bridge in the notion of the "*feedback loop.*"

This notion is the central construct of a theory called *Cybernetics* that was developed by Norbert Wiener at the Massachusetts Institute of Technology during World War II to keep artillery guns on target. Keeping on target is an obvious goal of artillery guns. By feeding back information about over- or undershooting to the gun mechanism, the gun can adjust its aim continually so that it stays on target. A simple thermostat is another example of the usefulness of a feedback loop. By feeding back information about the temperature in the house (too high, too low) to the furnace, it can control the temperature in the house to keep the house at a steady room temperature. Yet another example is the way our bodies maintain an inner steady state called "*homeostasis.*" In all these cases, we use (feedback) information about the consequences of a goal or a plan in order to execute our goal or plan most efficiently.

This idea of the feedback loop helped Miller and his associates to develop their T.O.T.E. model of behavior. This model of a behavioral sequence (Test→Operation→Test→Exit) holds that we typically start with a plan of operating on the environment, the environment feeds back information about the adequacy of our plan and we thereupon adjust our plan and finally meet with success. In this way it can be understood how human action is guided by images the organism has of its environment. This led Miller and his associates to assert that the basic structure of human behavior is not S→R, but that the basic unit of analysis for studying behavior is the feedback loop. This, finally, would make *both* the stimulus and the response integral components of a feedback loop (Miller et al., 1960).

### 13.1.6 *Conclusion*

Since the appearance of these publications a definite cognitive shift has occurred in psychology. What behaviorism had banned from psychology returns with a vengeance: concept formation, linguistic "behavior," problem solving, memory, "inner" processes, etc. The shift moves from peripheralism to centralism. Present day psychology *is* cognitive psychology. Koch has called it "the return of the repressed" (1964) and in a sense he is right. European psychology had always been cognitive, and the cognitive shift in contemporary psychology was for a large part due to the influence of Piaget's cognitive development theories. In the United States, the shift to a focus on classical problems of attention and cognition was also due to the work of computer scientists.

Anthropologically the human-being-as-computer model has replaced the human-being-as-machine model. (Compare the various analogies or models of humankind in the history of psychology, such as, angel, clock, tinker toy, hydraulic system, telephone circuit, organism, text, computer program, and lately under the influence of postmodernism, story.) It was computer language that made it possible for psychologists to conceptualize complex cognitive processes.

## 13.2 *The central problem of computer-based cognition: No windows to the world*

### 13.2.1 *Ulric Neisser:* Cognitive Psychology

However, a cognitive psychology based on the model of a computer program is not without its own problems either. In 1967 Ulric Neisser (1928–2012) published *Cognitive Psychology*, in which cognitive psychology is for the first time described as a separate psychological approach. In this book Neisser stated that from the point of view of cognition the person who experiences the world *creates* the world of experience. This implies that even the peripheral psychological processes like perception and sensation are not merely the passive receptors of information. Rather the whole psychological process of experiencing the world is a *constructive,* active process.

From a cognitive point of view the "outside" world may or may not exist, but we can have no direct access to it. We obtain our knowledge of it via a complicated cognitive system that interprets and reinterprets incoming data. Therefore we can have only *mediate* knowledge of the world, i.e., knowledge by means of something else.

In fact, cognitive activity does not even need the outside world. It can carry on quite well in the absence of and independent of stimuli. You will recall that, from an empiricistic point of view, our direct access to the outside world is absolutely essential, since there is from that vantage point nothing in the mind that was not at some point outside of it. The mind at birth is a *tabula rasa.* This is why Hume's assertion that causality does not exist represented such a crisis for the empiricists. For if causality does not exist, then the world cannot cause anything to exist in the mind either. Likewise, the behaviorists held that responses exist only by the grace of stimuli. Both points of view operate with a machine model of man, and for such a mechanism the direct causal connection between human beings and the world is absolutely essential.

From a cognitive point of view, however, the independent existence of an outside world is not essential. This shows how radical the shift from peripheralism to centralism was. Neisser shows how inadequate the human-being-as-machine analogy really is. Take, for example, the model of human-being-as-a-telephone-circuit (S→receptors→interneurons→e ffectors/R). Machines like telephone circuits do not *pay attention* to the incoming information. However, from the point of view of cognition, human beings not only *pay attention* but they also *select, process,* and *interpret* the incoming information. Machines do not do that; therefore, the mechanistic model is a faulty view of humankind.

Instead, Neisser wants to choose the computer program as a model for what goes on in human beings cognitively. A computer program is a set of instructions to a computer to actively manipulate the information with which it is confronted. With the help of a program, computers do what a human being does, i.e., process incoming information. Therefore, says Neisser, the computer program is a more adequate model for human cognition (Neisser, 1967).

### 13.2.2 *Subsequent critique: The reduction of knowledge to a formula*

However, computer programs have one major drawback, and so does a view of human cognition that is based on computer programs. *They have no windows to outside reality.* If we base our view of human cognition on the analogy of a computer program, then we run into two major problems: 1) we reduce human knowledge to a formula, and 2) we cut it off from reality.

Neisser stated that people behave on the basis of the images of the physical world they have. They base their actions on "*worldviews*" or on their mental models of the world. He defines cognitive knowledge as "knowledge of the world via cognitive models." However, these models imply an enormous amount of (non-cognitive) experiential tacit knowledge that we have of the world. Human cognitive knowledge is like an iceberg; it consists of 10 percent explicit, cognitive knowledge that is essentially a shorthand formula for the other 90 percent of unspoken, tacit knowledge.

Computers can only deal with explicit knowledge, i.e., with knowledge that has been spelled out in detail. At its best, computer knowledge refers to the 10 percent without the 90 percent. If, therefore, we view (even cognitive) human knowledge as analogous to a computer program, then we reduce it to only 10 percent of what it is. We reduce it to a formula, to a representation.

### 13.2.3 *Additional critique: Cutting off knowledge from reality*

Furthermore, we say that computers work with models, i.e., with representations. If so, then there must be an object to which these representations refer, because you cannot have a representation without something to which it refers. What is this object? It is not reality. Computer programs cannot refer to real objects. The objects that computer programs refer to are models or representations of reality. And what do these representations refer to? The answer is, to yet other representations or models, which in turn are models or representations of . . . *ad infinitum.* Computer programs cannot refer outside themselves to the real world. They can only make models of models, or programs about programs. Representations in computers are *re-representations*. Computers have no windows to the real world.

Computer-based cognitive psychology has the same problem. It is the problem of "*cognitivism*" (which roughly holds that cognition *precedes* reality). Cognitivism is an idealism (only ideas exist) or even a form of "solipsism" (I can only know myself, not the outside world, nor anyone in it). Jerry Fodor, who is the guru of cognitivism, has stated that the only research strategy that fits with cognitivist psychology is methodological solipsism. This means that we must explain human behavior strictly in terms of what goes on inside people, or in their cognitive system. Methodologically, the external world and other people may play no role.

What this means may be made clear by an example. Common sense says, it rains "*outside*" (i.e., not in my head), therefore I'll look for my umbrella (i.e., behavior). However, cognitivism says, No, I look for my umbrella because I *believe*, I *suspect*, or I am *convinced* that it is raining outside. My behavior, it says, is caused by my representations (i.e., by mental formulae), and these, per definition, have no relation to the outside world (Van der Veer, 1985).

Way back in history, Leibniz described reality in terms of self-contained units of consciousness, and he called them "monads." Of these monads he said that they have no windows. Likewise, computers, or the computer-based cognitive human beings have no windows to reality.

### 13.3 *Ulric Neisser:* Cognition and Reality

In 1976 Neisser wrote another book, *Cognition and Reality*, that in many ways is a repudiation of the position he took in his book of 1967. In his new book, he states that the problem with viewing human cognitive processes as computer programs is that it makes them too *"single minded."* Like behaviorism, computer-based psychology is in danger of becoming trivial because it has no *"ecological validity."* It does not talk about real people in real life situations any more than new formula psychology, psychoanalysis, or behaviorism did. It does not *"look at"* but only *"processes"* information from the outside world. It stresses the *"method"* rather than the *"object"* of psychology. *What* is processed is never discussed.

Computer-based cognitive psychology, Neisser now says, places far too much emphasis on cognition and makes cognition far too constructive. In real life, perception is already active, attentive, and constructive long before cognition comes into play. Prior to that, the senses are actively busy with discovering meaningful structures in the environment. Cognition merely tabulates, codifies, orders, and formulates. The combined force of all these processes together, and not just cognition, changes the behavior of a person, behaviors which in turn change the environment. In real life, says Neisser, the

> behavior of people is interactive with the environment and in this process both human behavior and the environment are mutually changed.

In this latest book Neisser states that the computer image of human cognition is artificial and too single-minded. The publication of this book unleashed a debate between the proponents of a *"representational theory of mind"* (Fodor) and the proponents of *"natural intelligence,"* who tend to be *"ecological"* psychologists like Neisser. The key issue in this debate is the place of cognition in real life (Neisser, 1976).

This issue is not only important for psychologists, but also for computer scientists and that for the following reasons. If human cognition is essentially modeled after a computer program, then the latter is the ideal for the former. This implies that human cognition is inferior to the operations of the computer. It also implies that it is the task of computer scientists to teach people how to think, since every time that computers change, human beings will have to change their thinking as well. If, however, computer scientists were to view it as their task to computer-simulate the human mind, with all its limitations, then human cognition would become the model for computer science. From that perspective computer scientists could ask people to think out loud in order to discover their cognitive strategies, with the aim of incorporating these strategies into their computer programs. This approach would not only make their programs more efficient, but also more lifelike. Today, the trend in computer science seems to be in that direction.

# References

Chomsky, N. (1957). *Syntactic Structures*. The Hague, The Netherlands: Mouton.

Chomsky, N. Review of B. F. Skinner's *Verbal Behavior, Language*, 35, 26–58.

Barzun, J. (1967). Misbehavioral Science, in F.W. Matson & A. Montagu, *The Human Dialogue*. New York: Free Press, 105.

Eisenga, L.K.A. & van Rappard, J.F.H. (1987). *Hoofdstromen en Mensbeelden in de Psychologie*. Amsterdam: Boom Meppel.

Koch, S. (1959). *Psychology: A study of a Science*. New York: McGraw-Hill.

Koch, S. (1964). Psychology and the Emerging Conceptions of Knowledge as Unitary, in T.W. Wann (Ed.) *Behaviorism and Phenomenology*. Ohio: University of Chicago Press.

Leahy, T. H. (1987). *A History of Psychology*. (4th. ed.) Upper Saddle River, N.J: Prentice Hall.

Miller, G. A. The Magical Number Seven, plus or minus two, *Psychological Review*, 63, 81–97.

Miller, G.A., Galanter, E. and Pribram, K.H. (1960). *Plans and the Structure of Behavior*. New York: Holt & Co.

Neisser, U. (1967). *Cognitive Psychology*. New York: Appleton-Century-Crofts.

Neisser, U. (1976). *Cognition and Reality, Principles and Implications of Cognitive Psychology*. San Francisco: Freeman.

Newell, A. and Simon, H.A. (1972). *Human Problem Solving*. Englewood Cliffs: Prentice-Hall.

Skinner, B. F. (1957). *Verbal Behavior*. Englewood Cliffs, N.J.: Prentice-Hall.

Veer, R. van der (1985). *Cultuur en Cognitie*. Groningen, The Netherlands: Wolters-Noordhoff.

## Some Issues to Stimulate Dialogue

1. With the rise of cognitive psychology, the paradigm once again has shifted from psychology as the study of how (we can make) people adapt to their environment to the study of how people *cope* with their environment. Psychology now becomes the investigation of *processing* information. What cognition *does* is now more important than what information *is*. Cognition is the processing of information; it is the handling of complexity. Central terms in cognitive psychology are "strategizing," "organization," "decision making," and "chunking." The mind as the central processing agency is back and is now viewed as constructive of reality rather than reactive to reality. Information (processing) theory is really a theory about strategic ways of making decisions.

2. Of course, this new paradigm brings with it its own problems. Our knowledge of the world via cognition is at best mediate knowledge. In fact, cognition does not need a world to operate. It can and does create its own *virtual reality*. And so the question becomes how this fabricated picture that we have in our heads corresponds to the real life we live. This is the problem of the *ecological validity* of cognition. Does this sound familiar to you? Where in the history of psychology have we heard this before?

3. While the cognitive psychology paradigm was an improvement over the behavioristic view, it is equally reductionistic. Cognitive psychology can only work with models, with formula, and with cognitive representations of reality that according to Neisser can only represent about 10 percent of actual reality.

4. In fact, I think that one of the marks of living in the twenty-first century is that not only our thinking but our whole life is being pressed to conform itself to the machine model of the computer. More than any other age we today are in a daily love-hate relationship with computing machines. To us the words of Jacques Barzun apply appropriately: "*Greater love of a machine cannot be conceived than that man should think his own mind inferior to the thing he has made*" (Matson, 1967, p. 105).

5. Information (processing) theory is based on the cybernetics of Norbert Wiener. The basic concept of cybernetics is the feedback loop. This notion is essentially a shorthand formulation of John Dewey's instrumentalist or experimentalist view of our relation to the environment. This view holds that human beings propose certain changes in their environment, the implementation of which will give them information about the feasibility of their proposals. The truth of a given assertion is determined by the consequences it engenders. Someone should write a paper in which they work this idea out in more detail.

# 14. The Historical Development of Humanistic Psychology

## 14.1 *Introduction*

Humanistic psychology is a movement within psychology that emphasizes what it perceives to be the central human characteristics of human beings. These are: spontaneity, internal locus of control, uniqueness, wholeness, personality, and the capacity for self-actualization, or growth. Humanistic psychology views persons as creative self-transcending beings who are not controlled by outside influences or unconscious drives but by their own values and choices alone. Prominent proponents of the movement are Buhler, Fromm, Frankl, May, Murray, Allport, Maslow, and Rogers. The American branch of this Humanistic movement championed by Maslow and Rogers is usually distinguished from the movement as a whole by calling it *the school* of *humanistic psychology*. It is this school of psychology that is the specific focus of this last chapter.

The adherents to this movement are united in their opposition to the mechanistic, deterministic view of human life held to by positivism in philosophy and by behaviorism in psychology.

## 14.2 *History and development*

The school of humanistic psychology is an American product that has incorporated many of the typically European phenomenological and existentialistic themes. But in doing so, it has remained firmly rooted in the American individualistic and evolutionistic tradition.

The origin of this school in psychology dates back to 1954, when Maslow (1908–1970) described its adherents as people "who are interested in the scientific study of creativity, love, higher values, autonomy, growth, self-actualization, need gratification, etc." (Misiak, 1973, p. 127). In 1961 the first issue of the *Journal of Humanistic Psychology* was published. One year later the *American Association for Humanistic Psychology* was established.

### 14.3 *Philosophical roots: Phenomenological existentialism and pragmatism*

The reader will already have noticed that this school of therapy stands in the metaphysical rationalism-romanticism tradition. But beyond that it is most formatively influenced by phenomenological existentialism. This influence goes back to Franz Brentano's notion of *intentionality* and to Husserl's *philosophical phenomenology*. Humanistic psychology borrows from Brentano and Husserl the notion that the human subject (which it calls "the organism") is active in the sense that it organizes the world that surrounds it. The organism responds only to an environment that it itself has constructed or "perceived" (Rogers, 1961). But the human organism also finds it purpose and direction in this perceived "phenomenal (i.e., experienced) field." This environment of experience is said to have its own meaning, and in organizing it the organism must open itself up to the meaning of that experience. Moreover, it must seek to enhance that part of this experience that constitutes the self. Thus, a number of basic notions of humanistic psychology such as "self," "experience," "percep-tion," and "phenomenal field" derive from the phenomenological-exis-tentialistic tradition.

Humanistic psychology is also rooted in the pragmatism of Dewey (1920), who served as a conduit for the influence of evolutionism on this therapeutic movement. Humanistic psychology owes a great deal to Dewey's pragmatism. Notions such as "becoming," "growth," "actualiza-tion," and "organism" are all derived from this philosophical root.

However, on one significant point humanistic psychology parts ways with Dewey. Dewey held that the innovative activity of the human subject can shape the ongoing process of growth and can redirect it to its own human ends. Humanistic psychologists deny this. On the contrary, in their view, the growth process itself has formative power and it natu-rally shapes human subjects rather than the reverse, provided that human subjects open themselves up to it (Van Belle, 1980).

### 14.4 *Essential characteristics*

Humanistic psychology is often called the "third force" in psychology because it pits itself against the deterministic picture of persons evident in both psychoanalysis and in behaviorism, schools of psychology that preceded it in time. Humanistic psychology rejects the pessimistic view of psychoanalysis, which holds that one's actions are wholly driven by the libidinal energy of the unconscious, irrational id. It also rejects the behav-ioristic view that human behavior is wholly determined by environmental forces. It rejects the internal determinism of psychoanalysis as well as the external determinism of behaviorism because both reduce human beings to something lower than what is human. Over against the position of traditional behaviorism that human beings are nothing but animals, it posits the view that human beings are *human*. Over against the view that behavior is nothing but a response to a stimulus, it states that human behavior is purposive. Over against the view that culture is nothing but a sublimated covert attempt at gratifying dark, sexual urges, it emphasizes the view that culture is the expression of humanity's higher aspirations. Over against the elementarism of Wundt and Watson alike, it argues that a person is a totality. Over against the determinism of mainline psychology, it stresses human freedom, creativity, spontaneity, and playfulness. Over against a preoccupation with needs and drives that drags people down to the level of animals, it talks about goals that draw people up to the height of the gods. Over against mechanism, which depicts human behavior as randomly governed by perilous chance, it steadfastly maintains the orderly organized character of human acts. Over against a depth psychology, it proposes a psychology of heights. In short, it states that human beings are always more than the reduced picture traditional psychology has given them. Humanistic psychology is a "more than" psychology rather than a "nothing but" psychology. It is a celebration of human potentiality.

### 14.5 *Basic themes*

Probably the most basic theme of this school is growth. Humanistic psychology is primarily a growth psychology rather than a depth psychology or a stimulus-response psychology. A second theme stresses the importance of such notions as "person," "autonomy," "self," "experience," and "(inter) subjectivity." These themes state that human beings are unique, that every human being alive is first and foremost universally, wholly, and totally unlike any other creature and completely unlike any other human being. This further implies that there is no commonality of experience. A reality that holds for everyone does not exist. There are as many realities as there are persons. For this reason also it behooves every human being to respect the otherness of the other('s) unique experience. Third, humanistic psychology holds that every human being, without exception, is a person. This means that every human being is the initiator, the director, and the evaluator of his or her own development. Personal growth, actualization, and enhancement are in no way externally controlled but occur entirely internal to the human person. Fourth, humanistic psychology points to the importance of the fact that people are aware of themselves as persons. This self-awareness makes that part of a person's experience that constitutes his or her own being the most important element in their entire experiential field. Finally, every person meets with others in his or her experience, who like him or her are also persons, i.e., masters of their own destiny. For this reason these others can never be counted, measured, or manipulated as objects because they are subjects. There is no such thing as objectivity among people. Human fellowship is always an *intersubjectivity*. Taking all these themes together, it is the view of humanistic psychology that each person is a unique principle of self-actualization and self-transcendence. This formulation characterizes this school of psychology both in its depth and its breadth.

### References

Dewey, J. (1920/1963). *Reconstruction in Philosophy.* Boston: Beacon Press.

Maslow, A.H. (1968). *Toward a Psychology of Being.* New York: Van Nostrand.

Misiak, H. (1973) *Phenomenological, Existential, and Humanistic Psychologies: A historical survey.* New York: Grune & Stratton.

Rogers, C. R. (1961). *On Becoming a Person.* Boston: Houghton Mifflin.

Van Belle, H.A. (1980). *Basic Intent and Therapeutic Approach of Carl R. Rogers.* Toronto: Wedge.

Van Belle, H.A. (2005). Philosophical Roots of Person-Centered Therapy in the History of Western Thought, in *The Person-Centered Journal*, Volume 12, Number 1/2, 50–60.

# Some Issues to Stimulate Dialogue

1. As with so many other schools of psychology humanistic psychology has deep roots in the thought world of Western civilization. Working backwards in history the main tenets of this school of psychology betray the influence of anti-positivism, of romanticism, and of metaphysical rationalism. But it also shows an affinity to the views of Pascal, Scotus, and Augustine. In an article published in the one of the journals of this movement (*Philosophical Roots of Person-Centered Therapy in the Thought world of Western Civilization*) I attempt to demonstrate that the roots of this movement reach as far back as ancient Greece.

2. Rogers argued somewhere that a reality that holds for all does not exist. He believed that there are as many realities as there are persons. I can appreciate his desire to do justice to the individuality with which every person experiences the world. However, if this were the end of the matter, it would lead to a wholesale particularization of human experience. I would like to leave open the possibility that there may be millions of people who essentially experience the world in the same way because they are all members of a given culture. Perhaps it is this way: that we differ from one another in what we have in common, but that we also have a sense of what it is that we have in common – otherwise dialogue would be impossible, or so it seems to me.

# INDEX

# SHORT BIOGRAPHY of Harry A. Van Belle, PhD

Dr. Harry A. Van Belle received a B.A. degree in 1965 from Calvin College in Grand Rapids, Michigan USA, the doctorandus degree in 1971 and the Ph.D. in Clinical Psychology in 1980 from The Free University of Amsterdam, The Netherlands.

From 1971–1977 he was the supervisor of the Psychology Department in the Brockville Psychiatric Hospital in Brockville, Ontario, Canada. From 1977–1982 he was the first Director-Therapist of the Cascade Christian Counseling Centre in Surrey, British Columbia, Canada, a therapy center that he founded.

From 1982–1992 he taught psychology at Redeemer University College in Ancaster, Ontario, Canada and from 1992–2000 he taught psychology at The Kings University College in Edmonton, Alberta, Canada.

He has been a practicing therapist, a workshop leader, and a popular lecturer for more than 40 years.

In 2000 he took early retirement to spend more time traveling, writing, and practicing therapy. He has written extensively about topics related to psychology, family life, psychological development, and psychotherapy, as well as on topics dealing with the relation between religion and psychology (see www.allofliferedeemed.co.uk/ → *Van Belle*).

He is married and has three children and four grandchildren.

Dr. Van Belle can be reached at harryvanbelle@hotmail.com, or by phone: 780-440-4661.

CPSIA information can be obtained at www.ICGtesting.com
Printed in the USA
LVOW11s0753170614

390369LV00003B/3/P

9 780932 914996